THE ULTIMATE

DIABETIC COOKBOOK

FOR BEGINNERS

1800 Days of Delicious, Low-Carb & Low-Sugar Recipes with a 30-Day Meal Plan to Help Manage Type 2 Diabetes and Prediabetes

Diabetic Cookbook

LUCY J. PERZ

◇ CONTENTS ◇

Vegetables, Fruit And Side Dishes Recipes 28

Potatoes, Pasta, And Whole Grains Recipes 35

Slow Cooker Favorites Recipes 43

Poultry Recipes 51

Soups, Stews, And Chilis Recipes 59

Fish & Seafood Recipes 68

Meat Recipes

Vegetarian Recipes

Salads Recipes

Special Treats Recipes 100

Shopping List 110

Appendix A: Measurement Conversions...............111

Appendix B: Recipes Index 113

◇ INTRODUCTION ◇

Hello, I'm Lucy J. Perz, and I'm thrilled to introduce you to my Diabetic Diet Cookbook. As someone who has personally navigated the challenges of diabetes, I understand the importance of not only managing blood sugar but also savoring delicious, nutritious meals. With a background in nutrition and a passion for cooking, I've poured my heart and expertise into creating this cookbook to help individuals like you take control of their health.

Having spent years experimenting with recipes and fine-tuning my culinary skills, I've crafted this cookbook with a clear purpose in mind: to make diabetes-friendly eating both enjoyable and attainable. Whether you're newly diagnosed or have been living with diabetes for years, this cookbook is designed to empower you with the knowledge and tools you need to create flavorful, balanced meals that promote overall well-being.

Inside, you'll find a treasure trove of recipes, each accompanied by step-by-step instructions, comprehensive shopping lists, estimated cooking times, and practical tips to simplify your time in the kitchen. From hearty breakfast options to satisfying dinners and delectable desserts, my goal is to prove that diabetes management doesn't mean sacrificing flavor or variety.

Join me on this culinary journey, where we'll transform everyday ingredients into extraordinary meals that support your health goals. Together, we'll learn how to make the most of fresh, wholesome ingredients while managing our blood sugar levels with confidence and creativity. Welcome to a world of delicious, diabetes-friendly cuisine—I can't wait to embark on this flavorful adventure with you!

Understanding Diabetes

Diabetes is a chronic medical condition characterized by elevated levels of glucose (sugar) in the blood. This occurs when the body's ability to regulate blood sugar is impaired, typically due to either insufficient production of insulin (Type 1 diabetes) or the body's inability to effectively use insulin (Type 2 diabetes). Insulin, produced by the pancreas, is a hormone that helps transport glucose from the bloodstream into cells to be used for energy. When this process malfunctions, it leads to high blood sugar levels, which can result in a range of health complications if left unmanaged. These complications may include heart disease, kidney problems, nerve damage, vision impairment, and more. Managing diabetes often involves lifestyle changes, such as diet and exercise, along with medication or insulin therapy, to help control blood sugar levels and reduce the risk of complications.

Causes of diabetes, people at risk, treatment options

ASPECT	CAUSES	SUSCEPTIBILITY FACTORS	TREATMENT
TYPE 1 DIABETES	Autoimmune destruction of insulin-producing beta cells in the pancreas.	Genetic predisposition.	Insulin therapy, often via injections or insulin pump. Monitoring blood sugar levels and lifestyle management.
TYPE 2 DIABETES	Insulin resistance, where the body's cells don't respond effectively to insulin, and inadequate insulin production. Often linked to obesity and lifestyle factors.	Genetic predisposition, obesity, physical inactivity, poor diet, and age.	Lifestyle changes (healthy diet and regular exercise), oral medications, insulin therapy (in advanced cases).
GESTATIONAL DIABETES	Hormonal changes during pregnancy lead to insulin resistance.	Family history, obesity, and age.	Lifestyle modifications, blood sugar monitoring, and sometimes medication during pregnancy. Usually resolves after childbirth, but requires postpartum monitoring.

Portion Control: Pay attention to portion sizes to help manage carbohydrate intake. Use measuring cups or a food scale when necessary to ensure you're not overeating, which can lead to spikes in blood sugar levels.

Choose Whole Grains: Whole grains like brown rice, quinoa, and whole wheat pasta are rich in fiber and have a lower glycemic index compared to refined grains. This means they cause a slower and more gradual rise in blood sugar levels.

Limit Sugars: Minimize the use of added sugars in recipes. Use natural sweeteners like stevia, erythritol, or monk fruit sparingly. You can also experiment with spices like cinnamon or vanilla extract for added sweetness without sugar.

Load Up on Veggies: Non-starchy vegetables like leafy greens, broccoli, cauliflower, and bell peppers are excellent choices. They are low in carbohydrates and high in fiber, which helps regulate blood sugar and promotes fullness.

Lean Proteins: Choose lean protein sources like skinless poultry, fish, tofu, and legumes. Protein can help stabilize blood sugar levels and keep you feeling full for longer.

Healthy Fats: Include heart-healthy fats like olive oil, avocados, and nuts in your cooking. These fats can improve insulin sensitivity and add flavor to dishes, but use them in moderation due to their calorie density.

Cooking Methods: Opt for healthier cooking methods like grilling, baking, steaming, or sautéing with minimal oil instead of frying. These methods reduce the need for added fats and excess calories.

Stay Hydrated: Drink plenty of water throughout the day to help control blood sugar levels and support overall health. Adequate hydration is crucial for maintaining proper bodily functions.

Regular Eating Schedule: Stick to a consistent eating schedule with balanced meals and snacks. This helps regulate blood sugar levels and prevents extreme fluctuations that can occur with irregular eating patterns.

Reasons for a Diabetes Diet Cookbook

MANAGING BLOOD SUGAR

Diabetes cookbooks are specifically designed to provide recipes and meal plans that help control blood sugar levels. They emphasize the use of ingredients with a lower glycemic index and appropriate portion sizes, which can be crucial for diabetes management.

NUTRITIONAL GUIDANCE

These cookbooks often come with detailed nutritional information for each recipe, making it easier for individuals to make informed choices about their meals. This information helps people understand the impact of different foods on their blood sugar.

VARIETY AND FLAVOR

Diabetes-friendly cookbooks offer a wide range of delicious and satisfying recipes. This variety can prevent dietary monotony, making it more likely for individuals to stick to a diabetes-friendly eating plan long-term.

EDUCATION

Many diabetes cookbooks include educational content about the condition, explaining the role of diet in diabetes management, how carbohydrates affect blood sugar, and other essential information. This education empowers individuals to make healthier food choices.

MEAL PLANNING MADE EASIER

Diabetes cookbooks often provide sample meal plans and tips on how to balance meals and snacks. This simplifies the meal planning process and helps individuals create well-rounded, diabetes-friendly menus.

ACCOMMODATING PREFERENCES

These cookbooks cater to different dietary preferences and restrictions, including vegetarian, vegan, gluten-free, and more. This ensures that individuals can find recipes that suit their tastes and dietary needs.

FAMILY-FRIENDLY

Diabetes cookbooks can be used by the entire family, promoting healthy eating habits for everyone. This is particularly important when a family member has diabetes, as it encourages a supportive and inclusive approach to mealtime.

WEIGHT MANAGEMENT

Many individuals with diabetes also need to manage their weight to improve their overall health. Diabetes cookbooks often offer recipes that support weight loss or maintenance while controlling blood sugar.

PRACTICAL COOKING TIPS

These cookbooks often include practical cooking tips and techniques to help individuals prepare diabetes-friendly meals more easily and efficiently.

◇ 30 Day Meal Plan ◇

DAY	BREAKFAST	LUNCH	DINNER
1	Double-duty Banana Pancakes 15	Garlicky Braised Kale 29	Sausage-topped White Pizza 52
2	Crunchy French Toast 15	Garlic-herb Pattypan Squash 29	Cumin-crusted Chicken Thighs With Cauliflower Couscous 52
3	Calico Scrambled Eggs 15	Smoky Cauliflower 29	Turkey Pinto Bean Salad With Southern Molasses Dressing 52
4	Toasted Corn Salsa 15	Pan-roasted Broccoli 29	Bacon & Swiss Chicken Sandwiches 52
5	Full Garden Frittata 16	Tomato-onion Green Beans 30	Apple-glazed Chicken Thighs 53
6	Steel-cut Oatmeal With Blueberries And Almonds 16	Skillet-roasted Veggies 30	Strawberry Minutest Chicken 53
7	Cheesy Mushroom Omelet 16	Greek-style Garlic-lemon Potatoes 30	Spring Chicken & Pea Salad 53
8	Southwest Breakfast Pockets 16	Golden Zucchini 31	Chicken Baked In Foil With Tomatoes And Zucchini 54
9	Sweet Onion Frittata With Ham 17	Sautéed Swiss Chard With Garlic 31	Chicken Cucumber Boats 54
10	Fresh Tomato Salsa 17	Pesto Pasta & Potatoes 31	Poached Chicken Breasts With Warm Tomato-ginger Vinaigrette 54
11	Ginger-kale Smoothies 17	Roasted Winter Squash With Tahini And Feta 31	In-a-pinch Chicken & Spinach 55
12	Omega-3 Granola 17	Two-tone Potato Wedges 32	Chicken With Fire-roasted Tomatoes 55
13	English Muffin Egg Sandwich 18	Crunchy Pear And Cilantro Relish 32	Feta Chicken Burgers 55
14	Sausage Potato Skillet Casserole 18	Sauteed Radishes With Green Beans 32	Turkey & Fruit Salad 55
15	Herbed Deviled Eggs 18	Roasted Broccoli 32	Seared Chicken With Spicy Chipotle Cream Sauce 55

DAY	BREAKFAST	LUNCH	DINNER
16	Guacamole 18	Hot Skillet Pineapple 32	Lime Chicken With Salsa Verde Sour Cream 56
17	Breakfast Grilled Swiss Cheese And Rye 19	Slow-cooked Whole Carrots 33	Turkey Lo Mein 56
18	Asparagus-mushroom Frittata 19	Sautéed Green Beans With Garlic And Herbs 33	Turkey Burgers 56
19	Coriander Shrimp Skewers With Lemon-tarragon Dipping Sauce 19	Squash Melt 33	Sausage & Pepper Pizza 57
20	Good Morning Power Parfait 20	Green Pea And Red Pepper Toss 33	Almond-crusted Chicken Breasts 57
21	Open-faced Poached Egg Sandwiches 20	Grilled Veggies With Mustard Vinaigrette 34	Italian Spaghetti With Chicken & Roasted Vegetables 57
22	Raisin French Toast With Apricot Spread 20	Buttery Dijon Asparagus 34	Wild Rice Salad 58
23	Blackberry Smoothies 20	Herbed Potato Packet 34	Cool & Crunchy Chicken Salad 58
24	Mixed Fruit With Lemon-basil Dressing 21	Roasted Smashed Potatoes 34	Easy Roast Turkey Breast 58
25	Fried Eggs With Garlicky Swiss Chard And Bell Pepper 21	Rigatoni With Turkey Ragu 36	Grilled Swordfish With Eggplant, Tomato, And Chickpea Salad 69
26	Chicken, Mango & Blue Cheese Tortillas 23	Lemony Beans And Potatoes 36	Pesto Grilled Salmon 69
27	Artichoke Hummus 24	Baked Brown Rice With Shiitakes And Edamame 36	Cilantro Shrimp & Rice 70
28	Tuna Salad Stuffed Eggs 24	Warm Farro With Mushrooms And Thyme 37	Lemon-peppered Shrimp 70
29	Tomato Cilantro Salsa 26	Rosemary Rice With Fresh Spinach Greens 37	Lime-cilantro Tilapia 70
30	Curried Chicken Meatball Wraps 27	Cuban Black Beans 37	Salmon & Spud Salad 70

BREAKFAST RECIPES

◇ Breakfast Recipes ◇

Double-duty Banana Pancakes

Servings: 8 | Cooking Time:6 Minutes

Ingredients:
- 2 ripe medium bananas, thinly sliced
- 1 cup buckwheat pancake mix
- 3/4 cup plus 2 tablespoons fat-free milk
- 4 tablespoons light pancake syrup

Directions:
1. Mash one half of the banana slices and place in a medium bowl with the pancake mix and the milk. Stir until just blended.
2. Place a large nonstick skillet over medium heat until hot. (To test, sprinkle with a few drops of water. If the water drops "dance" or jump in the pan, it's hot enough.) Coat the skillet with nonstick cooking spray, add two scant 1/4 cup measures of batter, and cook the pancakes until puffed and dry around the edges, about 1 minute.
3. Flip the pancakes and cook until golden on the bottom. Place on a plate and cover to keep warm.
4. Recoat the skillet with nonstick cooking spray, add three scant 1/4 cup measures of batter, and cook as directed. Repeat with the remaining batter.
5. Place 2 pancakes on each of 4 dinner plates, top with equal amounts of banana slices, and drizzle evenly with the syrup. If you like, place the dinner plates in a warm oven and add the pancakes as they are cooked.

Nutrition Info:
- 100 cal., 0g fat (0g sag. fat), 0mg chol, 140mg sod., 23g carb (9g sugars, 2g fiber), 3g pro.

Crunchy French Toast

Servings:4 | Cooking Time: 20 Minutes

Ingredients:
- 6 large eggs
- 1/3 cup fat-free milk
- 2 teaspoons vanilla extract
- 1/8 teaspoon salt
- 1 cup frosted cornflakes, crushed
- 1/2 cup old-fashioned oats
- 1/4 cup sliced almonds
- 8 slices whole wheat bread
- Maple syrup, optional

Directions:
1. In a shallow bowl, whisk eggs, milk, vanilla and salt until blended. In another shallow bowl, toss cornflakes with oats and almonds.
2. Heat a griddle coated with cooking spray over medium heat. Dip both sides of bread in egg mixture, then in cereal mixture, patting to help coating adhere. Place on griddle; toast 3-4 minutes on each side or until golden brown. If desired, serve with syrup.

Nutrition Info:
- 335 cal., 11g fat (2g sat. fat), 196mg chol., 436mg sod., 43g carb. (8g sugars, 5g fiber), 17g pro.

Calico Scrambled Eggs

Servings:4 | Cooking Time: 15 Minutes

Ingredients:
- 8 large eggs
- 1/4 cup 2% milk
- 1/8 to 1/4 teaspoon dill weed
- 1/8 to 1/4 teaspoon salt
- 1/8 to 1/4 teaspoon pepper
- 1 tablespoon butter
- 1/2 cup chopped green pepper
- 1/4 cup chopped onion
- 1/2 cup chopped fresh tomato

Directions:
1. In a bowl, whisk the first five ingredients until blended. In a 12-in. nonstick skillet, heat butter over medium-high heat. Add green pepper and onion; cook and stir until tender. Remove from pan.
2. In same pan, pour in egg mixture; cook and stir over medium heat until eggs begin to thicken. Add tomato and pepper mixture; cook until heated through and no liquid egg remains, stirring gently.

Nutrition Info:
- 188 cal., 13g fat (5g sat. fat), 381mg chol., 248mg sod., 4g carb. (3g sugars, 1g fiber), 14g pro.

Toasted Corn Salsa

Servings:2 | Cooking Time: 1 Hour

Ingredients:
- 4½ teaspoons extra-virgin olive oil
- 2 ears corn, kernels cut from cobs
- 1 red bell pepper, stemmed, seeded, and chopped fine
- ½ jalapeño chile, stemmed, seeded, and minced
- 1 scallion, sliced thin
- 2 garlic cloves, minced
- 2 tablespoons lime juice, plus extra for seasoning
- 2 tablespoons minced fresh cilantro
- ½ teaspoon ground cumin
- ¼ teaspoon salt
- ⅛ teaspoon pepper

Directions:
1. Heat 1½ teaspoons oil in 12-inch nonstick skillet over medium-high heat until shimmering. Add corn and cook, stirring occasionally, until golden brown, 6 to 8 minutes.
2. Transfer corn to medium serving bowl and stir in remaining 1 tablespoon oil, bell pepper, jalapeño, scallion, garlic, lime juice, cilantro, cumin, salt, and pepper. Cover and refrigerate until flavors meld, at least 1 hour or up to 2

days. Season with extra lime juice to taste before serving.

Nutrition Info:
• 50 cal., 3g fat (0g sag. fat), 0mg chol, 75mg sod., 6g carb (2g sugars, 1g fiber), 1g pro.

Full Garden Frittata

Servings:2 | Cooking Time: 10 Minutes

Ingredients:
• 4 large eggs
• 1/3 cup 2% milk
• 1/4 teaspoon salt, divided
• 1/8 teaspoon coarsely ground pepper
• 2 teaspoons olive oil
• 1/2 medium zucchini, chopped
• 1/2 cup chopped baby portobello mushrooms
• 1/4 cup chopped onion
• 1 garlic clove, minced
• 2 tablespoons minced fresh basil
• 1 teaspoon minced fresh oregano
• 1 teaspoon minced fresh parsley

Directions:
1. Preheat oven to 375°. In a bowl, whisk eggs, milk, 1/8 teaspoon salt and pepper. In an 8-in. ovenproof skillet, heat oil over medium-high heat. Add zucchini, mushrooms and onion; cook and stir until tender. Add garlic, herbs and the remaining salt; cook 1 minute longer. Pour in egg mixture.
2. Bake, uncovered, 10-15 minutes or until eggs are set. Cut into four wedges. If desired, serve with toppings.

Nutrition Info:
• 227 cal., 15g fat (4g sat. fat), 375mg chol., 463mg sod., 7g carb. (5g sugars, 1g fiber), 15g pro.

Steel-cut Oatmeal With Blueberries And Almonds

Servings:4 | Cooking Time: 12 Hours

Ingredients:
• 3 cups water
• 1 cup steel-cut oats
• ¼ teaspoon salt
• ½ cup 1 percent low-fat milk
• 1 tablespoon packed brown sugar
• ¼ teaspoon ground cinnamon
• Pinch ground nutmeg
• 2½ ounces (½ cup) blueberries
• ⅓ cup whole almonds, toasted and chopped coarse

Directions:
1. Bring water to boil in large saucepan over high heat. Off heat, stir in oats and salt, cover, and let sit for at least 12 hours or up to 24 hours.
2. Stir milk, sugar, cinnamon, and nutmeg into oats and bring to boil over medium-high heat. Reduce heat to medium and cook, stirring occasionally, until oats are softened but still retain some chew and mixture thickens and resembles warm pudding, 4 to 6 minutes.
3. Remove saucepan from heat and let sit for 5 minutes.

Stir to recombine and serve, sprinkling individual portions with blueberries and almonds.

Nutrition Info:
• 270 cal., 8g fat (1g sag. fat), 0mg chol, 170mg sod., 42g carb (8g sugars, 6g fiber), 9g pro.

Cheesy Mushroom Omelet

Servings: 2 | Cooking Time:6 Minutes

Ingredients:
• 6 ounces sliced mushrooms
• 1/8 teaspoon black pepper
• 1/3 cup finely chopped green onion (green and white parts)
• 1 cup egg substitute
• 2 tablespoons crumbled bleu cheese (about 1/4 cup) or 1/4 cup shredded, reduced-fat, sharp cheddar cheese

Directions:
1. Place a small skillet over medium-high heat until hot. Coat with nonstick cooking spray and add mushrooms and pepper. Coat the mushrooms with nonstick cooking spray and cook 4 minutes or until soft, stirring frequently.
2. Add the onions and cook 1 minute longer. Set the pan aside.
3. Place another small skillet over medium heat until hot. Coat with nonstick cooking spray and add the egg substitute. Cook 1 minute without stirring. Using a rubber spatula, lift up the edges to allow the uncooked portion to run under. Cook 1–2 minutes longer or until eggs are almost set and beginning to puff up slightly.
4. Spoon the mushroom mixture on one half of the omelet, sprinkle the cheese evenly over the mushrooms, and gently fold over. Cut in half to serve.

Nutrition Info:
• 110 cal., 2g fat (1g sag. fat), 5mg chol, 340mg sod., 6g carb (3g sugars, 1g fiber), 16g pro.

Southwest Breakfast Pockets

Servings:2 | Cooking Time: 20 Minutes

Ingredients:
• 2 large eggs
• 2 large egg whites
• 1 teaspoon olive oil
• 1 small onion, chopped
• 1 garlic clove, minced
• 1/2 cup canned pinto beans, rinsed and drained
• 4 whole wheat pita pocket halves, warmed
• 1/4 cup salsa
• Sliced avocado, optional

Directions:
1. Whisk together eggs and egg whites. In a large nonstick skillet, heat oil over medium heat; saute onion until tender, 3-4 minutes. Add garlic; cook and stir 1 minute. Add eggs and beans; cook and stir until eggs are thickened and no liquid egg remains.
2. Spoon into pitas. Serve with salsa and, if desired, avoca-

do.

Nutrition Info:
- 339 cal., 9g fat (2g sat. fat), 186mg chol., 580mg sod., 47g carb. (4g sugars, 7g fiber), 19g pro.

Sweet Onion Frittata With Ham

Servings: 4 | Cooking Time:8 Minutes

Ingredients:
- 4 ounces extra-lean, low-sodium ham slices, chopped
- 1 cup thinly sliced Vidalia onion
- 1 1/2 cups egg substitute
- 1/3 cup shredded, reduced-fat, sharp cheddar cheese

Directions:
1. Place a medium nonstick skillet over medium-high heat until hot. Coat the skillet with nonstick cooking spray, add ham, and cook until beginning to lightly brown, about 2–3 minutes, stirring frequently. Remove from skillet and set aside on separate plate.
2. Reduce the heat to medium, coat the skillet with nonstick cooking spray, add onions, and cook 4 minutes or until beginning to turn golden, stirring frequently.
3. Reduce the heat to medium low, add ham to the onions, and cook 1 minute (this allows the flavors to blend and the skillet to cool slightly before the eggs are added). Pour egg substitute evenly over all, cover, and cook 8 minutes or until puffy and set.
4. Remove the skillet from the heat, sprinkle cheese evenly over all, cover, and let stand 3 minutes to melt the cheese and develop flavors.

Nutrition Info:
- 110 cal., 2g fat (1g sag. fat), 20mg chol, 460mg sod., 6g carb (4g sugars, 0g fiber), 17g pro.

Fresh Tomato Salsa

Servings:2 | Cooking Time:30 Minutes

Ingredients:
- 1 pound ripe tomatoes, cored and cut into ½-inch pieces
- 1 jalapeño chile, stemmed, seeded, and minced
- ⅓ cup finely chopped red onion
- 1 small garlic clove, minced
- 3 tablespoons minced fresh cilantro
- 1 tablespoon lime juice, plus extra for seasoning
- ¼ teaspoon salt

Directions:
1. Place tomatoes in large colander and let drain for 30 minutes. As tomatoes drain, layer jalapeño, onion, garlic, and cilantro on top. Shake colander to drain off excess juice, then transfer to serving bowl. Stir in lime juice and salt. (Salsa can be refrigerated for up to 3 days.) Season with extra lime juice to taste before serving.

Nutrition Info:
- 15 cal., 0g fat (0g sag. fat), 0mg chol, 75mg sod., 3g carb (2g sugars, 1g fiber), 1g pro.

Ginger-kale Smoothies

Servings:2 | Cooking Time: 15 Minutes

Ingredients:
- 1 1/4 cups orange juice
- 1 teaspoon lemon juice
- 2 cups torn fresh kale
- 1 medium apple, peeled and coarsely chopped
- 1 tablespoon minced fresh gingerroot
- 4 ice cubes
- 1/8 teaspoon ground cinnamon
- 1/8 teaspoon ground turmeric or 1/4-inch piece fresh turmeric, peeled and finely chopped
- Dash cayenne pepper

Directions:
1. Place all ingredients in a blender; cover and process until blended. Serve the smoothie immediately.

Nutrition Info:
- 121 cal., 0 fat (0 sat. fat), 0 chol., 22mg sod., 29g carb. (21g sugars, 2g fiber), 1g pro.

Omega-3 Granola

Servings:6 | Cooking Time:20 Minutes

Ingredients:
- ⅓ cup slivered almonds
- ⅓ cup walnuts, chopped
- 3 cups (9 ounces) old-fashioned rolled oats
- 3 tablespoons canola oil
- ¼ cup raw sunflower seeds
- 2 tablespoons sesame seeds
- ½ cup honey
- 2 tablespoons ground flaxseeds
- ¼ teaspoon salt
- ½ cup raisins

Directions:
1. Adjust oven rack to middle position and heat oven to 325 degrees. Line rimmed baking sheet with parchment paper and lightly spray with canola oil spray. Toast almonds and walnuts in 12-inch skillet over medium heat, stirring often, until fragrant and beginning to darken, about 3 minutes. Stir in oats and oil and continue to toast until oats begin to turn golden, about 2 minutes. Stir in sunflower seeds and sesame seeds and continue to toast until mixture turns golden, about 2 minutes.
2. Off heat, stir in honey, flaxseeds, and salt until well coated. Spread granola evenly over prepared sheet. Bake, stirring every few minutes, until granola is light golden brown, about 15 minutes.
3. Stir in raisins. With lightly greased stiff metal spatula, push granola onto one-half of baking sheet and press gently into ½-inch-thick slab. Let granola cool to room temperature, about 30 minutes. Loosen dried granola with spatula, break into small clusters, and serve. (Granola can be stored at room temperature in airtight container for up to 2 weeks.)

Nutrition Info:
- 240 cal., 11g fat (1g sag. fat), 0mg chol, 55mg sod., 32g

carb (16g sugars, 4g fiber), 5g pro.

English Muffin Egg Sandwich

Servings:8 | Cooking Time: 25 Minutes

Ingredients:
- 1/2 pound sliced fresh mushrooms
- 1 small sweet red pepper, chopped
- 1 small sweet onion, chopped
- 1/2 teaspoon garlic salt
- 1/4 teaspoon pepper
- 1/4 teaspoon crushed red pepper flakes, optional
- 7 large eggs, lightly beaten
- 8 whole wheat English muffins, split and toasted
- 4 ounces reduced-fat cream cheese

Directions:
1. Place a large nonstick skillet coated with cooking spray over medium-high heat. Add mushrooms, red pepper, onion and seasonings; cook and stir 5-7 minutes or until mushrooms are tender. Remove from pan.
2. Wipe skillet clean and coat with cooking spray; place over medium heat. Add eggs; cook and stir just until eggs are thickened and no liquid egg remains. Add vegetables; heat through, stirring mixture gently.
3. Spread muffin bottoms with cream cheese; top with egg mixture. Replace the tops.

Nutrition Info:
- 244 cal., 9g fat (4g sat. fat), 173mg chol., 425mg sod., 30g carb. (7g sugars, 5g fiber), 14g pro.

Sausage Potato Skillet Casserole

Servings: 4 | Cooking Time:17 Minutes

Ingredients:
- 5 ounces reduced-fat, smoked turkey sausage, kielbasa style
- 2 cups chopped onion
- 4 cups frozen hash brown potatoes with peppers and onions
- 1/3 cup shredded, reduced-fat, sharp cheddar cheese

Directions:
1. Cut the sausage in fourths lengthwise. Cut each piece of sausage in 1/4-inch pieces.
2. Place a large nonstick skillet over medium-high heat until hot. Coat the skillet with nonstick cooking spray, add sausage, and cook 3 minutes or until the sausage begins to brown, stirring frequently. Set the sausage aside on a separate plate.
3. Recoat the skillet with nonstick cooking spray, add the onions, and cook 5 minutes or until the onions begin to brown, stirring frequently.
4. Reduce the heat to medium, add the frozen potatoes and sausage, and cook 9 minutes or until the potatoes are lightly browned, stirring occasionally.
5. Remove the skillet from the heat, top with cheese, cover, and let stand 5 minutes to melt the cheese and develop flavors.

Nutrition Info:
- 190 cal., 5g fat (2g sag. fat), 25mg chol., 450mg sod., 26g carb (5g sugars, 4g fiber), 9g pro.

Herbed Deviled Eggs

Servings:6 | Cooking Time:25minutes

Ingredients:
- 6 large eggs
- ¼ cup cottage cheese
- 2 tablespoons mayonnaise
- 1 tablespoon minced fresh parsley, chives, or cilantro
- ½ teaspoon white wine vinegar
- ½ teaspoon Dijon mustard
- ⅛ teaspoon ground turmeric
- ⅛ teaspoon ground coriander
- ⅛ teaspoon salt
- ⅛ teaspoon pepper

Directions:
1. Bring 1 inch water to rolling boil in medium saucepan over high heat. Place eggs in steamer basket. Transfer basket to saucepan. Cover, reduce heat to medium-low, and cook eggs for 13 minutes.
2. When eggs are almost finished cooking, combine 2 cups ice cubes and 2 cups cold water in medium bowl. Using tongs or spoon, transfer eggs to ice bath. Let sit for 15 minutes, then peel.
3. Halve eggs lengthwise. Transfer 3 yolks to fine-mesh strainer set over medium bowl (reserve remaining yolks for another use or discard). Arrange whites on large serving platter. Using spatula, press yolks and cottage cheese through fine-mesh strainer into bowl. Stir in mayonnaise, parsley, 1 tablespoon warm water, vinegar, mustard, turmeric, coriander, salt, and pepper until well combined and smooth. (Egg whites and yolk filling can be refrigerated, separately, for up to 2 days.)
4. Fit pastry bag with large open-star tip. Fill bag with yolk mixture, twisting top of pastry bag to help push mixture toward tip of bag. Pipe yolk mixture into egg white halves, mounding filling about ½ inch above flat surface of whites. Serve at room temperature.

Nutrition Info:
- 110 cal., 8g fat (2g sag. fat), 190mg chol, 190mg sod., 1g carb (1g sugars, 0g fiber), 7g pro.

Guacamole

Servings:2 | Cooking Time:28minutes

Ingredients:
- 2 tablespoons finely chopped onion
- 1 serrano chile, stemmed, seeded, and minced
- 1 teaspoon kosher salt
- ¼ teaspoon grated lime zest plus 1½–2 tablespoons juice
- 3 ripe avocados, halved, pitted, and cut into ½-inch pieces
- 1 plum tomato, cored, seeded, and minced
- 2 tablespoons chopped fresh cilantro

Directions:
1. Place onion, serrano, salt, and lime zest on cutting board

and chop until very finely minced. Transfer onion mixture to medium serving bowl and stir in 1½ tablespoons lime juice. Add avocados and, using sturdy whisk, mash and stir mixture until well combined with some ¼- to ½-inch chunks of avocado remaining. Stir in tomato and cilantro. (Guacamole can be refrigerated for up to 1 day by pressing plastic wrap directly against its surface.) Season with up to additional 1½ teaspoons lime juice to taste before serving.

Nutrition Info:
• 120 cal., 11g fat (1g sag. fat), 0mg chol, 160mg sod., 7g carb (1g sugars, 5g fiber), 2g pro.

Breakfast Grilled Swiss Cheese And Rye

Servings: 2 | Cooking Time:7 Minutes

Ingredients:
• 2 slices rye bread
• 4 teaspoons reduced-fat margarine (35% vegetable oil)
• 2 large eggs
• 1 1/2 ounces sliced, reduced-fat Swiss cheese, torn in small pieces

Directions:
1. Spread one side of each bread slice with 1 teaspoon margarine and set aside.
2. Place a medium skillet over medium heat until hot. Coat with nonstick cooking spray and add the egg substitute. Cook 1 minute without stirring. Using a rubber spatula, lift up the edges to allow the uncooked portion to run under. Cook 1–2 minutes longer or until eggs are almost set and beginning to puff up slightly. Flip and cook 30 seconds.
3. Remove the skillet from the heat and spoon half of the eggs on the unbuttered sides of two of the bread slices. Arrange equal amounts of the cheese evenly over each piece.
4. Return the skillet to medium heat until hot. Coat the skillet with nonstick cooking spray. Add the two sandwiches and cook 3 minutes. If the cheese doesn't melt when frying the sandwich bottom, put it under the broiler until brown. Using a serrated knife, cut each sandwich in half.

Nutrition Info:
• 250 cal., 13g fat (4g sag. fat), 200mg chol, 360mg sod., 17g carb (2g sugars, 2g fiber), 16g pro.

Asparagus-mushroom Frittata

Servings:8 | Cooking Time: 20 Minutes

Ingredients:
• 8 large eggs
• 1/2 cup whole-milk ricotta cheese
• 2 tablespoons lemon juice
• 1/2 teaspoon salt
• 1/4 teaspoon pepper
• 1 tablespoon olive oil
• 1 package (8 ounces) frozen asparagus spears, thawed
• 1 large onion, halved and thinly sliced
• 1/2 cup finely chopped sweet red or green pepper
• 1/4 cup sliced baby portobello mushrooms

Directions:

1. Preheat oven to 350°. In a bowl, whisk eggs, ricotta cheese, lemon juice, salt and pepper. In a 10-in. ovenproof skillet, heat oil over medium heat. Add the asparagus, onion, red pepper and mushrooms; cook and stir 6-8 minutes or until onion and pepper are tender.
2. Remove from heat; remove asparagus from skillet. Reserve eight spears; cut remaining asparagus into 2-in. pieces. Return cut asparagus to skillet; stir in egg mixture. Arrange the reserved asparagus spears over eggs to resemble spokes of a wheel.
3. Bake, uncovered, 20-25 minutes or until eggs are completely set. Let stand 5 minutes. Cut into 8 wedges.

Nutrition Info:
• 135 cal., 8g fat (3g sat. fat), 192mg chol., 239mg sod., 7g carb. (2g sugars, 1g fiber), 9g pro.

Coriander Shrimp Skewers With Lemon-tarragon Dipping Sauce

Servings:8 | Cooking Time:30 Minutes

Ingredients:
• DIPPING SAUCE
• ⅓ cup 2 percent Greek yogurt
• 2 tablespoons mayonnaise
• 1 tablespoon minced fresh tarragon, dill, or basil
• ½ teaspoon grated lemon zest plus 1 teaspoon juice
• 1 garlic clove, minced
• Pepper
• SHRIMP
• 1 pound large shrimp (26 to 30 per pound), peeled and deveined
• 2 tablespoons extra-virgin olive oil
• ¾ teaspoon ground coriander
• ¼ teaspoon pepper
• Pinch cayenne pepper
• 8 wooden skewers

Directions:
1. FOR THE DIPPING SAUCE Whisk all ingredients together in bowl until smooth and season with pepper to taste. Cover and refrigerate until flavors meld, at least 30 minutes or up to 2 days.
2. FOR THE SHRIMP Adjust oven rack 3 inches from broiler element and heat broiler. (If necessary, set overturned rimmed baking sheet on oven rack to get closer to broiler element.) Pat shrimp dry with paper towels, then toss with oil, coriander, pepper, and cayenne in bowl. Thread 3 or 4 shrimp onto each skewer.
3. Set wire rack in aluminum foil–lined rimmed baking sheet and lightly spray with canola oil spray. Lay skewers on prepared rack and cover skewer ends with foil. Broil until shrimp are opaque throughout, 3 to 5 minutes. Transfer skewers to serving platter and serve with sauce.

Nutrition Info:
• 90 cal., 7g fat (1g sag. fat), 55mg chol, 90mg sod., 1g carb (0g sugars, 0g fiber), 7g pro.

Good Morning Power Parfait

Servings: 4 | Cooking Time: 5 Minutes

Ingredients:
• 1 ripe medium banana
• 2 cups fat-free, artificially sweetened, vanilla-flavored yogurt (divided use)
• 1 teaspoon ground cinnamon
• 1 cup whole strawberries, sliced
• 1/2 cup grape-nut-style cereal, preferably with raisins and almonds

Directions:
1. Add the banana, 1 cup yogurt, and 1 teaspoon cinnamon, if desired, to a blender and blend until smooth. Pour into 4 wine or parfait glasses.
2. Top each parfait with 1/4 cup sliced strawberries, 1/4 cup yogurt, and 2 tablespoons cereal.

Nutrition Info:
• 140 cal., 0g fat (0g sag. fat), 0mg chol, 125mg sod., 32g carb (14g sugars, 3g fiber), 5g pro.

Open-faced Poached Egg Sandwiches

Servings:4 | Cooking Time:8minutes

Ingredients:
• 2 ounces goat cheese, crumbled and softened (½ cup)
• ½ teaspoon lemon juice
• ⅛ teaspoon pepper
• 2 whole-wheat English muffins, split in half, toasted, and still warm
• 1 small tomato, cored, seeded, and sliced thin (about 8 slices)
• 2 teaspoons extra-virgin olive oil
• 1 shallot, minced
• 1 garlic clove, minced
• 4 ounces (4 cups) baby spinach
• ⅛ teaspoon salt
• 2 tablespoons distilled vinegar
• 4 large eggs

Directions:
1. Adjust oven rack to middle position and heat oven to 300 degrees. Stir goat cheese, lemon juice, and pepper together in bowl until smooth. Spread goat cheese mixture evenly over warm English muffin halves and top with tomato slices. Arrange English muffins on rimmed baking sheet and keep warm in oven while preparing spinach and eggs.
2. Heat oil in 12-inch nonstick skillet over medium heat until shimmering. Add shallot and cook until softened, about 2 minutes. Stir in garlic and cook until fragrant, about 30 seconds. Stir in spinach and salt and cook until wilted, about 1 minute. Using tongs, squeeze out any excess moisture from spinach, then divide evenly among English muffins.
3. Wipe skillet clean with paper towels, then fill it nearly to rim with water. Add vinegar and bring to boil over high heat. Meanwhile, crack eggs into two teacups (2 eggs in each). Reduce water to simmer. Gently tip cups so eggs slide into skillet simultaneously. Remove skillet from heat, cover, and poach eggs for 4 minutes (add 30 seconds for firm yolks).
4. Using slotted spoon, gently lift eggs from water and let drain before laying them on top of spinach. Serve immediately.

Nutrition Info:
• 210 cal., 11g fat (4g sag. fat), 195mg chol, 350mg sod., 17g carb (4g sugars, 3g fiber), 13g pro.

Raisin French Toast With Apricot Spread

Servings: 4 | Cooking Time:6 Minutes Per Batch

Ingredients:
• 8 slices whole-wheat cinnamon raisin bread
• 3 tablespoons no-trans-fat margarine (35% vegetable oil)
• 1/4 cup apricot or any flavor all-fruit spread
• 1 cup egg substitute (divided use)

Directions:
1. Arrange 4 bread slices on the bottom of a 13 × 9-inch baking pan. Pour 1/2 cup egg substitute evenly over all and turn several times to coat. Let stand 2 minutes to absorb egg slightly.
2. Meanwhile, using a fork, stir the margarine and fruit spread together in a small bowl until well blended.
3. Place a large nonstick skillet over medium heat until hot. Liberally coat the skillet with nonstick cooking spray, add 4 bread slices (leaving any remaining egg mixture in the baking pan), and cook 3 minutes.
4. Turn and cook 3 minutes longer or until the bread is golden brown. For darker toast, turn the slices again and cook 1 minute more. Set aside on a serving platter and cover to keep warm.
5. While the first batch is cooking, place the remaining bread slices in the baking pan and pour the remaining egg substitute evenly over all. Turn several times to coat. Cook as directed.
6. Serve each piece of toast topped with 1 tablespoon of the margarine mixture.

Nutrition Info:
• 260 cal., 6g fat (1g sag. fat), 0mg chol, 390mg sod., 37g carb (17g sugars, 4g fiber), 12g pro.

Blackberry Smoothies

Servings:4 | Cooking Time: 10 Minutes

Ingredients:
• 1 cup orange juice
• 1 cup (8 ounces) plain yogurt
• 2 to 3 tablespoons honey
• 1 1/2 cups fresh or frozen blackberries
• 1/2 cup frozen unsweetened mixed berries
• Additional blackberries and yogurt, optional

Directions:
1.In a blender, combine the first five ingredients; cover and process for about 15 seconds or until smooth. Pour into chilled glasses; serve immediately. If desired top with additional blackberries and yogurt.

Nutrition Info:
- 130 cal., 2g fat (1g sat. fat), 8mg chol., 29mg sod., 26g carb. (21g sugars, 3g fiber), 3g pro.

Mixed Fruit With Lemon-basil Dressing

Servings:8 | Cooking Time: 15 Minutes

Ingredients:
- 2 tablespoons lemon juice
- 1/2 teaspoon sugar
- 1/4 teaspoon salt
- 1/4 teaspoon ground mustard
- 1/8 teaspoon onion powder
- Dash pepper
- 6 tablespoons olive oil
- 4 1/2 teaspoons minced fresh basil
- 1 cup cubed fresh pineapple
- 1 cup sliced fresh strawberries
- 1 cup sliced peeled kiwifruit
- 1 cup cubed seedless watermelon
- 1 cup fresh blueberries
- 1 cup fresh raspberries

Directions:
1.In a blender, combine the lemon juice, sugar, salt, mustard, onion powder and pepper; cover and process for 5 seconds. While processing, gradually add oil in a steady stream. Stir in basil.

2.In a large bowl, combine the fruit. Drizzle with dressing and toss to coat. Refrigerate until serving.

Nutrition Info:
- 145 cal., 11g fat (1g sat. fat), 0 chol., 76mg sod., 14g carb. (9g sugars, 3g fiber), 1g pro.

Fried Eggs With Garlicky Swiss Chard And Bell Pepper

Servings:4 | Cooking Time:11minutes

Ingredients:
- 2 tablespoons extra-virgin olive oil
- 5 garlic cloves, minced
- 2 pounds Swiss chard, stemmed, 1 cup stems chopped fine, leaves sliced into ½-inch-wide strips
- 1 small red bell pepper, stemmed, seeded, and cut into ¼-inch pieces
- Pinch salt
- ⅛ teaspoon red pepper flakes
- 4 large eggs
- Lemon wedges

Directions:
1.Heat 1 tablespoon oil and garlic in 12-inch nonstick skillet over medium-low heat, stirring occasionally, until garlic is light golden, 3 to 5 minutes. Increase heat to high, add chard stems, then chard leaves, 1 handful at a time, and cook until wilted, about 2 minutes. Stir in bell pepper, salt, and pepper flakes and cook, stirring often, until chard is tender and peppers are softened, about 3 minutes. Transfer to colander set in bowl and let drain while preparing eggs;

discard liquid. Wipe skillet clean with paper towels.

2.Crack 2 eggs into small bowl. Repeat with remaining 2 eggs in second bowl. Heat remaining 1 tablespoon oil in now-empty skillet over medium-high heat until shimmering; quickly swirl to coat skillet. Working quickly, pour one bowl of eggs in one side of skillet and second bowl of eggs in other side. Cover and cook for 1 minute.

3.Remove skillet from heat and let sit, covered, 15 to 45 seconds for runny yolks (white around edge of yolk will be barely opaque), 45 to 60 seconds for soft but set yolks, and about 2 minutes for medium-set yolks.

4.Divide chard mixture between individual plates and top with eggs. Serve immediately with lemon wedges.

Nutrition Info:
190 cal., 12g fat (2g sag. fat), 185mg chol, 550mg sod., 11g carb (3g sugars, 4g fiber), 10g pro.

APPETIZERS AND SNACKS RECIPES

Zesty Lemony Shrimp

Servings: 8 | Cooking Time:7–10 Minutes

Ingredients:
- 12 ounces peeled raw medium shrimp, fresh, or frozen and thawed
- 2 tablespoons Worcestershire sauce
- 1 teaspoon lemon zest
- 3 tablespoons lemon juice
- 2 tablespoons no-trans-fat margarine (35% vegetable oil)
- 1 tablespoon finely chopped fresh parsley (optional)

Directions:
1. Place a large nonstick skillet over medium heat until hot. Add the shrimp, Worcestershire sauce, lemon zest, and lemon juice to the skillet. Cook 5 minutes or until shrimp is opaque in center, stirring frequently.
2. Using a slotted spoon, remove the shrimp and set aside in serving bowl. Increase the heat to medium high, add the margarine, bring to a boil, and continue to boil 2 minutes or until the liquid measures 1/4 cup, stirring constantly.
3. Pour the sauce over the shrimp and sprinkle with 1 tablespoon finely chopped parsley, if desired. Serve with wooden toothpicks.

Nutrition Info:
- 50 cal., 0g fat (0g sag. fat), 70mg chol, 95mg sod., 1g carb (1g sugars, 0g fiber), 9g pro.

Baby Carrots And Spicy Cream Dip

Servings: 4 | Cooking Time: 5 Minutes

Ingredients:
- 1/3 cup fat-free sour cream
- 3 tablespoons reduced-fat tub-style cream cheese
- 3/4 teaspoon hot pepper sauce
- 1/8 teaspoon salt
- 48 baby carrots

Directions:
1. Stir the sour cream, cream cheese, pepper sauce, and salt together until well blended.
2. Let stand at least 10 minutes to develop flavors and mellow slightly. Serve with carrots.

Nutrition Info:
- 90 cal., 2g fat (1g sag. fat), 10mg chol, 240mg sod., 16g carb (7g sugars, 3g fiber), 3g pro.

Chicken, Mango & Blue Cheese Tortillas

Servings:16 | Cooking Time: 30 Minutes

Ingredients:
- 1 boneless skinless chicken breast (8 ounces)
- 1 teaspoon blackened seasoning
- 3/4 cup (6 ounces) plain yogurt
- 1 1/2 teaspoons grated lime peel
- 2 tablespoons lime juice
- 1/4 teaspoon salt
- 1/8 teaspoon pepper
- 1 cup finely chopped peeled mango
- 1/3 cup finely chopped red onion
- 4 flour tortillas (8 inches)
- 1/2 cup crumbled blue cheese
- 2 tablespoons minced fresh cilantro

Directions:
1. Lightly oil grill rack with cooking oil. Sprinkle the chicken with blackened seasoning; grill, covered, over medium heat 6-8 minutes on each side or until a thermometer reads 165°.
2. In a bowl, mix yogurt, lime peel, lime juice, salt and pepper. Cool chicken slightly; finely chop and transfer to a small bowl. Stir in mango and onion.
3. Grill tortillas, uncovered, over medium heat 2-3 minutes, until puffed. Turn; top with chicken mixture and blue cheese. Grill, covered, 2-3 minutes, until bottoms are lightly browned. Drizzle with yogurt mixture; sprinkle with cilantro. Cut each into four wedges.

Nutrition Info:
- 85 cal., 3g fat (1g sat. fat), 12mg chol., 165mg sod., 10g carb. (2g sugars, 1g fiber), 5g pro.

Avocado Endive Boats

Servings:2 | Cooking Time: 45 Minutes

Ingredients:
- 1 jar (12 ounces) roasted sweet red peppers, drained and finely chopped
- 1 cup finely chopped fennel bulb
- 1/4 cup sliced ripe olives, finely chopped
- 2 tablespoons olive oil
- 1 tablespoon minced fresh cilantro
- 1/2 teaspoon salt, divided
- 1/2 teaspoon pepper, divided
- 2 medium ripe avocados, peeled and pitted
- 3 tablespoons lime juice
- 2 tablespoons diced jalapeno pepper
- 1 green onion, finely chopped
- 1 garlic clove, minced
- 1/2 teaspoon ground cumin
- 1/4 teaspoon hot pepper sauce
- 2 plum tomatoes, choppped
- 30 endive leaves
- Chopped fennel fronds

Directions:
1. In a small bowl, combine first five ingredients; stir in 1/4 teaspoon each salt and pepper.
2. In another bowl, mash avocados with a fork. Stir in next six ingredients and the remaining salt and pepper. Stir in tomatoes.

3. Spoon about 1 tablespoon avocado mixture onto each endive leaf; top each with about 1 tablespoon pepper mixture. Sprinkle with fennel fronds.

Nutrition Info:
• 43 cal., 3g fat (0 sat. fat), 0 chol., 109mg sod., 4g carb. (1g sugars, 3g fiber), 1g pro.

Roasted Red Pepper Tapenade
Servings:2 | Cooking Time: 15 Minutes

Ingredients:
• 3 garlic cloves, peeled
• 2 cups roasted sweet red peppers, drained
• 1/2 cup blanched almonds
• 1/3 cup tomato paste
• 2 tablespoons olive oil
• 1/4 teaspoon salt
• 1/4 teaspoon pepper
• Minced fresh basil
• Toasted French bread baguette slices or water crackers

Directions:
1. In a small saucepan, bring 2 cups water to a boil. Add garlic; cook, uncovered, 6-8 minutes or just until tender. Drain and pat dry. Place red peppers, almonds, tomato paste, oil, garlic, salt and pepper in a small food processor; process until blended. Transfer to a small bowl. Refrigerate at least 4 hours to allow flavors to blend.
2. Sprinkle with basil. Serve with baguette slices.

Nutrition Info:
• 58 cal., 4g fat (0 sat. fat), 0 chol., 152mg sod., 3g carb. (2g sugars, 1g fiber), 1g pro.

Garlicky Herbed Shrimp
Servings:3 | Cooking Time: 25 Minutes

Ingredients:
• 2 pounds uncooked jumbo shrimp, peeled and deveined
• 5 garlic cloves, minced
• 2 green onions, chopped
• 1/2 teaspoon garlic powder
• 1/2 teaspoon ground mustard
• 1/4 teaspoon seasoned salt
• 1/4 teaspoon crushed red pepper flakes
• 1/8 teaspoon pepper
• 1/2 cup butter, divided
• 1/4 cup lemon juice
• 2 tablespoons minced fresh parsley
• 1 tablespoon minced fresh tarragon

Directions:
1. In a large bowl, combine the first eight ingredients; toss to combine. In a large skillet, heat 1/4 cup butter over medium-high heat. Add half of the shrimp mixture; cook and stir for 4-5 minutes or until shrimp turns pink. Transfer to a clean bowl.
2. Repeat with remaining butter and shrimp mixture. Return cooked shrimp to pan. Stir in lemon juice; heat through. Stir in herbs.

Nutrition Info:
• 46 cal., 3g fat (2g sat. fat), 37mg chol., 61mg sod., 1g carb. (0 sugars, 0 fiber), 4g pro.

Artichoke Hummus
Servings:2 | Cooking Time: 15 Minutes

Ingredients:
• 1 can (15 ounces) chickpeas, rinsed and drained
• 1 jar (7 1/2 ounces) marinated quartered artichoke hearts, drained
• 1/4 cup tahini
• 1 tablespoon capers, drained
• 2 tablespoons lemon juice
• 4 garlic cloves, minced
• 2 teaspoons grated lemon peel
• 1 teaspoon ground cumin
• 1/2 teaspoon garlic powder
• 1/8 teaspoon salt
• Dash crushed red pepper flakes, optional
• Dash pepper
• 2 fresh rosemary sprigs, chopped
• Assorted fresh vegetables or baked pita chips

Directions:
1. Place the first 12 ingredients in a food processor; cover and process until smooth. Transfer to a small bowl; stir in rosemary. Serve with vegetables.

Nutrition Info:
• 75 cal., 5g fat (1g sat. fat), 0 chol., 116mg sod., 6g carb. (1g sugars, 2g fiber), 2g pro.

Tuna Salad Stuffed Eggs
Servings: 4 | Cooking Time:10 Minutes

Ingredients:
• 4 large eggs
• 1 (2.6-ounce) packet tuna (or 5-ounce can of tuna packed in water, rinsed and well drained)
• 2 tablespoons reduced-fat mayonnaise
• 1 1/2–2 tablespoons sweet pickle relish

Directions:
1. Place eggs in a medium saucepan and cover with cold water. Bring to a boil over high heat, then reduce the heat and simmer 10 minutes.
2. Meanwhile, stir the tuna, mayonnaise, and relish together in a small bowl.
3. When the eggs are cooked, remove them from the water and let stand one minute before peeling under cold running water. Cut eggs in half, lengthwise, and discard 4 egg yolk halves and place the other 2 egg yolk halves in the tuna mixture and stir with a rubber spatula until well blended. Spoon equal amounts of the tuna mixture in each of the egg halves.
4. Serve immediately, or cover with plastic wrap and refrigerate up to 24 hours.

Nutrition Info:
• 90 cal., 4g fat (1g sag. fat), 105mg chol, 240mg sod., 3g

carb (2g sugars, 0g fiber), 9g pro.

Meatballs In Cherry Sauce

Servings:3 | Cooking Time: 15 Minutes

Ingredients:
- 1 cup seasoned bread crumbs
- 1 small onion, chopped
- 1 large egg, lightly beaten
- 3 garlic cloves, minced
- 1 teaspoon salt
- 1/2 teaspoon pepper
- 1 pound lean ground beef (90% lean)
- 1 pound ground pork
- SAUCE
- 1 can (21 ounces) cherry pie filling
- 1/3 cup sherry or chicken broth
- 1/3 cup cider vinegar
- 1/4 cup steak sauce
- 2 tablespoons brown sugar
- 2 tablespoons reduced-sodium soy sauce
- 1 teaspoon honey

Directions:
1. Preheat oven to 400°. In a large bowl, combine the first six ingredients. Add the beef and pork; mix lightly but thoroughly. Shape into 1-in. balls. Place on a greased rack in a shallow baking pan. Bake for11-13 minutes or until cooked through. Drain on paper towels.
2. In a saucepan, combine the sauce ingredients. Bring to a boil over medium heat, stirring constantly. Reduce heat; simmer, uncovered, 2-3 minutes or until thickened. Add meatballs; heat through.

Nutrition Info:
- 76 cal., 3g fat (1g sat. fat), 19mg chol., 169mg sod., 7g carb. (5g sugars, 0 fiber), 5g pro.

Pickled Shrimp With Basil

Servings:20 | Cooking Time: 15 Minutes

Ingredients:
- 1/2 cup red wine vinegar
- 1/2 cup olive oil
- 2 teaspoons seafood seasoning
- 2 teaspoons stone-ground mustard
- 1 garlic clove, minced
- 2 pounds peeled and deveined cooked shrimp (31-40 per pound)
- 1 medium lemon, thinly sliced
- 1 medium lime, thinly sliced
- 1/2 medium red onion, thinly sliced
- 1/4 cup thinly sliced fresh basil
- 2 tablespoons capers, drained
- 1/4 cup minced fresh basil
- 1/2 teaspoon kosher salt
- 1/4 teaspoon coarsely ground pepper

Directions:
1. In a large bowl, whisk the first five ingredients. Add shrimp, lemon, lime, onion, sliced basil and capers; toss gently to coat. Refrigerate, covered, up to 8 hours, stirring occasionally.
2. Just before serving, stir minced basil, salt and pepper into the shrimp mixture. Serve with a slotted spoon.

Nutrition Info:
- 64 cal., 2g fat (0 sat. fat), 69mg chol., 111mg sod., 1g carb. (0 sugars, 0 fiber), 9g pro.

Homemade Guacamole

Servings:2 | Cooking Time: 10 Minutes

Ingredients:
- 3 medium ripe avocados, peeled and cubed
- 1 garlic clove, minced
- 1/4 to 1/2 teaspoon salt
- 2 medium tomatoes, seeded and chopped, optional
- 1 small onion, finely chopped
- 1/4 cup mayonnaise, optional
- 1 to 2 tablespoons lime juice
- 1 tablespoon minced fresh cilantro

Directions:
1. Mash avocados with garlic and salt. Stir in remaining ingredients.

Nutrition Info:
- 111 calories, 10g fat (1g saturated fat), 0mg cholesterol, 43mg sodium, 6g carbohydrate (1g sugars, 5g fiber), 1g protein.

Balsamic-goat Cheese Grilled Plums

Servings:8 | Cooking Time: 25 Minutes

Ingredients:
- 1 cup balsamic vinegar
- 2 teaspoons grated lemon peel
- 4 medium firm plums, halved and pitted
- 1/2 cup crumbled goat cheese

Directions:
1. For glaze, in a small saucepan, combine vinegar and lemon peel; bring to a boil. Cook 10-12 minutes or until mixture is thickened and reduced to about 1/3 cup (do not overcook).
2. Grill plums, covered, over medium heat 2-3 minutes on each side or until tender. Drizzle with glaze; top with goat cheese.

Nutrition Info:
- 58 cal., 2g fat (1g sat. fat), 9mg chol., 41mg sod., 9g carb. (8g sugars, 1g fiber), 2g pro.

Minutesi Feta Pizzas

Servings:4 | Cooking Time: 20 Minutes

Ingredients:
- 2 whole wheat English muffins, split and toasted
- 2 tablespoons reduced-fat cream cheese
- 4 teaspoons prepared pesto
- 1/2 cup thinly sliced red onion
- 1/4 cup crumbled feta cheese

Directions:

1. Preheat oven to 425°. Place muffins on a baking sheet.
2. Mix cream cheese and pesto; spread over muffins. Top with onion and feta cheese. Bake until lightly browned, 6-8 minutes.

Nutrition Info:
- 136 cal., 6g fat (3g sat. fat), 11mg chol., 294mg sod., 16g carb. (4g sugars, 3g fiber), 6g pro.

Bleu Cheese'd Pears

Servings: 4 | Cooking Time: 5 Minutes

Ingredients:
- 2 ounces fat-free cream cheese
- 3 1/2 tablespoons crumbled bleu cheese
- 2 medium firm pears, halved, cored, and sliced into 20 slices

Directions:
1. In a small bowl, microwave the cheeses on HIGH for 10 seconds to soften. Use a rubber spatula to blend well.
2. Top each pear slice with 3/4 teaspoon cheese.
3. To prevent the pear slices from discoloring, toss them with a tablespoon of orange, pineapple, or lemon juice. Shake off the excess liquid before topping them with cheese.

Nutrition Info:
- 90 cal., 2g fat (1g sag. fat), 10mg chol, 190mg sod., 14g carb (9g sugars, 3g fiber), 4g pro.

Tomato Cilantro Salsa

Servings: 4 | Cooking Time: 10 Minutes

Ingredients:
- 3 medium tomatoes, seeded and finely chopped
- 1/4 cup chopped cilantro
- 2 medium jalapeño peppers, stems removed, halved, seeded, and minced
- 3–4 tablespoons lime juice
- 1/8 teaspoon salt
- 3 ounces baked low-fat tortilla chips

Directions:
1. Combine all ingredients except chips in a small bowl. Serve with chips.
2. For peak flavor, serve this within 1 hour of preparing it.

Nutrition Info:
- 110 cal., 1g fat (0g sag. fat), 0mg chol, 230mg sod., 25g carb (4g sugars, 3g fiber), 4g pro.

Baked Pot Stickers With Dipping Sauce

Servings:4 | Cooking Time: 15 Minutes

Ingredients:
- 2 cups finely chopped cooked chicken breast
- 1 can (8 ounces) water chestnuts, drained and chopped
- 4 green onions, thinly sliced
- 1/4 cup shredded carrots
- 1/4 cup reduced-fat mayonnaise
- 1 large egg white
- 1 tablespoon reduced-sodium soy sauce
- 1 garlic clove, minced
- 1 teaspoon grated fresh gingerroot
- 48 wonton wrappers
- Cooking spray
- SAUCE
- 1/2 cup jalapeno pepper jelly
- 1/4 cup rice vinegar
- 2 tablespoons reduced-sodium soy sauce

Directions:
1. Preheat the oven to 425°. In a large bowl, combine the first nine ingredients. Place 2 teaspoons of filling in the center of a wonton wrapper. Cover the rest of wrappers with a damp paper towel until ready to use.
2. Moisten filled wrapper edges with water. Fold edge over filling and roll to form a log; twist ends to seal. Repeat with remaining wrappers and filling.
3. Place pot stickers on a baking sheet coated with cooking spray; spritz each with cooking spray. Bake 12-15 minutes or until edges are golden brown.
4. Meanwhile, place jelly in a small microwave-safe bowl; microwave, covered, on high until melted. Stir in vinegar and soy sauce. Serve sauce with pot stickers.

Nutrition Info:
- 52 cal., 1g fat (0 sat. fat), 6mg chol., 101mg sod., 8g carb. (2g sugars, 0 fiber), 3g pro.

Tomato-jalapeno Granita

Servings:6 | Cooking Time: 15 Minutes

Ingredients:
- 2 cups tomato juice
- 1/3 cup sugar
- 4 mint sprigs
- 1 jalapeno pepper, sliced
- 2 tablespoons lime juice
- Fresh mint leaves, optional

Directions:
1. In a small saucepan, bring the tomato juice, sugar, mint sprigs and jalapeno to a boil. Cook and stir until sugar is dissolved. Remove from the heat; cover and let stand 15 minutes.
2. Strain and discard solids. Stir in lime juice. Transfer to a 1-qt. dish; cool to room temperature. Freeze for 1 hour; stir with a fork.
3. Freeze 2-3 hours longer or until completely frozen, stirring every 30 minutes. Scrape granita with a fork just before serving; spoon into dessert dishes. If desired garnish with additional mint leaves.

Nutrition Info:
- 59 cal., 0 fat (0 sat. fat), 0 chol., 205mg sod., 15g carb. (13g sugars, 0 fiber), 1g pro.

Lime'd Blueberries

Servings: 6 | Cooking Time: 5 Minutes

Ingredients:
- 2 cups frozen unsweetened blueberries, partially thawed
- 1/4 cup frozen grape juice concentrate
- 1 1/2 tablespoons lime juice

Directions:
1. Place all ingredients in a medium bowl and toss gently.
2. Serve immediately for peak flavor and texture.

Nutrition Info:
- 50 cal., 0g fat (0g sag. fat), 0mg chol, 5mg sod., 13g carb (11g sugars, 1g fiber), 0g pro.

Curried Chicken Meatball Wraps

Servings:2 | Cooking Time: 20 Minutes

Ingredients:
- 1 large egg, lightly beaten
- 1 small onion, finely chopped
- 1/2 cup Rice Krispies
- 1/4 cup golden raisins
- 1/4 cup minced fresh cilantro
- 2 teaspoons curry powder
- 1/2 teaspoon salt
- 1 pound lean ground chicken
- SAUCE
- 1 cup (8 ounces) plain yogurt
- 1/4 cup minced fresh cilantro
- WRAPS
- 24 small Bibb or Boston lettuce leaves
- 1 medium carrot, shredded
- 1/2 cup golden raisins
- 1/2 cup chopped salted peanuts
- Additional minced fresh cilantro

Directions:
1. Preheat oven to 350°. In a large bowl, combine first seven ingredients. Add chicken; mix lightly but thoroughly. With wet hands, shape mixture into 24 balls (about 1 1/4-in.).
2. Place meatballs on a greased rack in a 15x10x1-in. baking pan. Bake 17-20 minutes or until cooked through.
3. In a small bowl, mix the sauce ingredients. To serve, place 1 teaspoon sauce and one meatball in each lettuce leaf; top with remaining ingredients.

Nutrition Info:
- 72 cal., 3g fat (1g sat. fat), 22mg chol., 89mg sod., 6g carb. (4g sugars, 1g fiber), 6g pro.

Basil Spread And Water Crackers

Servings: 4 | Cooking Time: 5 Minutes

Ingredients:
- 2 ounces reduced-fat garlic and herb cream cheese
- 1/2 cup finely chopped fresh basil
- 12 fat-free water crackers

Directions:
1. Stir the cream cheese and basil together in a small bowl until well blended.
2. Place 1 teaspoon spread on each cracker.

Nutrition Info:
- 70 cal., 2g fat (1g sag. fat), 0mg chol, 200mg sod., 9g carb (1g sugars, 0g fiber), 3g pro.

Gorgonzola Polenta Bites

Servings:16 | Cooking Time: 25 Minutes

Ingredients:
- 1/3 cup balsamic vinegar
- 1 tablespoon orange marmalade
- 1/2 cup panko (Japanese) bread crumbs
- 1 tube (18 ounces) polenta, cut into 16 slices
- 2 tablespoons olive oil
- 1/2 cup crumbled Gorgonzola cheese
- 3 tablespoons dried currants, optional

Directions:
1. In a small saucepan, combine vinegar and marmalade. Bring to a boil; cook 5-7 minutes or until liquid is reduced to 2 tablespoons.
2. Meanwhile, place bread crumbs in a shallow bowl. Press both sides of the polenta slices in bread crumbs. In a large skillet, heat oil over medium-high heat. Add polenta in batches; cook for 2-4 minutes on each side or until slices are golden brown.
3. Arrange polenta on a serving platter; spoon cheese over top. If desired, sprinkle with currants; drizzle with vinegar mixture. Serve bites warm or at room temperature.

Nutrition Info:
- 67 cal., 3g fat (1g sat. fat), 3mg chol., 161mg sod., 9g carb. (3g sugars, 0 fiber), 1g pro.

VEGETABLES, FRUIT AND SIDE DISHES RECIPES

◇ Vegetables, Fruit And Side Dishes Recipes ◇

Garlicky Braised Kale

Servings:8 | Cooking Time:19 Minutes

Ingredients:
- 6 tablespoons extra-virgin olive oil
- 1 large onion, chopped fine
- 10 garlic cloves, minced
- ¼ teaspoon red pepper flakes
- 2 cups unsalted chicken broth
- Salt and pepper
- 4 pounds kale, stemmed and cut into 3-inch pieces
- 1 tablespoon lemon juice, plus extra for seasoning

Directions:
1. Heat 3 tablespoons oil in Dutch oven over medium heat until shimmering. Add onion and cook until softened and lightly browned, 5 to 7 minutes. Stir in garlic and pepper flakes and cook until fragrant, about 1 minute. Stir in broth, 1 cup water, and ½ teaspoon salt and bring to simmer.
2. Add one-third of kale, cover, and cook, stirring occasionally, until wilted, 2 to 4 minutes. Repeat with remaining kale in 2 batches. Continue to cook, covered, until kale is tender, 13 to 15 minutes.
3. Remove lid and increase heat to medium-high. Cook, stirring occasionally, until most liquid has evaporated and greens begin to sizzle, 10 to 12 minutes. Off heat, stir in remaining 3 tablespoons oil and lemon juice. Season with pepper and extra lemon juice to taste. Serve.

Nutrition Info:
- 190 cal., 12g fat (1g sag. fat), 0mg chol, 240mg sod., 17g carb (5g sugars, 6g fiber), 8g pro.

Garlic-herb Pattypan Squash

Servings:4 | Cooking Time: 25 Minutes

Ingredients:
- 5 cups halved small pattypan squash (about 1 1/4 pounds)
- 1 tablespoon olive oil
- 2 garlic cloves, minced
- 1/2 teaspoon salt
- 1/4 teaspoon dried oregano
- 1/4 teaspoon dried thyme
- 1/4 teaspoon pepper
- 1 tablespoon minced fresh parsley

Directions:
1. Preheat oven to 425°. Place squash in a greased 15x10x1-in. baking pan. Mix oil, garlic, salt, oregano, thyme and pepper; drizzle over squash. Toss to coat. Roast 15-20 minutes or until tender, stirring occasionally. Sprinkle with parsley.

Nutrition Info:
- 58 cal., 3g fat (0 sat. fat), 0 chol., 296mg sod., 6g carb. (3g sugars, 2g fiber), 2g pro.

Smoky Cauliflower

Servings:8 | Cooking Time: 30 Minutes

Ingredients:
- 1 large head cauliflower, broken into 1-inch florets (about 9 cups)
- 2 tablespoons olive oil
- 1 teaspoon smoked paprika
- 3/4 teaspoon salt
- 2 garlic cloves, minced
- 2 tablespoons minced fresh parsley

Directions:
1. Place cauliflower florets in a large bowl. Combine the oil, paprika and salt. Drizzle over cauliflower; toss to coat. Transfer to a 15x10x1-in. baking pan. Bake, uncovered, at 450° for about 10 minutes.
2. Stir in garlic. Bake 10-15 minutes longer or until cauliflower is tender and lightly browned, stirring occasionally. Sprinkle with parsley.

Nutrition Info:
- 58 cal., 4g fat (0 sat. fat), 0 chol., 254mg sod., 6g carb. (3g sugars, 3g fiber), 2g pro.

Pan-roasted Broccoli

Servings:6 | Cooking Time:10minutes

Ingredients:
- ¼ teaspoon salt
- ⅛ teaspoon pepper
- 2 tablespoons extra-virgin olive oil
- 1¾ pounds broccoli, florets cut into 1½-inch pieces, stalks peeled and cut on bias into ¼-inch-thick slices

Directions:
1. Stir 3 tablespoons water, salt, and pepper together in small bowl until salt dissolves; set aside. Heat oil in 12-inch nonstick skillet over medium-high heat until just smoking. Add broccoli stalks in even layer and cook, without stirring, until browned on bottoms, about 2 minutes. Add florets to skillet and toss to combine. Cook, without stirring, until bottoms of florets just begin to brown, 1 to 2 minutes.
2. Add water mixture and cover skillet. Cook until broccoli is bright green but still crisp, about 2 minutes. Uncover and continue to cook until water has evaporated, broccoli stalks are tender, and florets are crisp-tender, about 2 minutes. Serve.

Nutrition Info:
- 70 cal., 5g fat (0g sag. fat), 0mg chol, 125mg sod., 5g carb (1g sugars, 2g fiber), 2g pro.

Grilled Portobello Mushrooms And Shallots With Rosemary-dijon Vinaigrette

Servings:6 | Cooking Time:30 Minutes

Ingredients:
- 6 tablespoons extra-virgin olive oil
- 1 small garlic clove, minced
- 2 teaspoons lemon juice
- 1 teaspoon Dijon mustard
- 1 teaspoon minced fresh rosemary
- Salt and pepper
- 8 shallots, peeled
- 6 portobello mushroom caps (4 to 5 inches in diameter), gills removed

Directions:
1. Whisk 2 tablespoons oil, garlic, lemon juice, mustard, rosemary, and ½ teaspoon salt together in small bowl. Season with pepper to taste; set aside for serving.
2. Thread shallots through roots and stem ends onto two 12-inch metal skewers. Using paring knife, cut ½-inch crosshatch pattern, ¼ inch deep, on tops of mushroom caps. Brush shallots and mushroom caps with remaining ¼ cup oil and season with pepper.
3. FOR A CHARCOAL GRILL Open bottom vent completely. Light large chimney starter half filled with charcoal briquettes (3 quarts). When top coals are partially covered with ash, pour evenly over grill. Set cooking grate in place, cover, and open lid vent completely. Heat grill until hot, about 5 minutes.
4. FOR A GAS GRILL Turn all burners to high, cover, and heat grill until hot, about 15 minutes. Turn all burners to medium.
5. Clean and oil cooking grate. Place shallots and mushrooms, gill side up, on grill. Cook (covered if using gas) until mushrooms have released their liquid and vegetables are charred on first side, about 8 minutes. Flip mushrooms and shallots and continue to cook (covered if using gas) until vegetables are tender and charred on second side, about 8 minutes. Transfer vegetables to serving platter. Remove skewers from shallots and discard any charred outer layers, if desired. Whisk vinaigrette to recombine and drizzle over vegetables. Serve.

Nutrition Info:
- 170 cal., 14g fat (2g sag. fat), 0mg chol, 230mg sod., 9g carb (5g sugars, 2g fiber), 3g pro.

Tomato-onion Green Beans

Servings:6 | Cooking Time: 30 Minutes

Ingredients:
- 2 tablespoons olive oil
- 1 large onion, finely chopped
- 1 pound fresh green beans, trimmed
- 3 tablespoons tomato paste
- 1/2 teaspoon salt
- 2 tablespoons minced fresh parsley

Directions:

1. In a large skillet, heat the oil over medium-high heat. Add chopped onion; cook until tender and lightly browned, stirring occasionally.
2. Meanwhile, place green beans in a large saucepan; add water to cover. Bring to a boil. Cook, covered, for 5-7 minutes or until crisp-tender. Drain; add to onion. Stir in tomato paste and salt; heat through. Sprinkle with parsley.

Nutrition Info:
- 81 cal., 5g fat (1g sat. fat), 0 chol., 208mg sod., 9g carb. (4g sugars, 3g fiber), 2g pro.

Skillet-roasted Veggies

Servings: 4 | Cooking Time:6 Minutes

Ingredients:
- 5 ounces asparagus spears, trimmed and cut into 2-inch pieces (1 cup total), patted dry
- 3 ounces sliced portobello mushrooms (1/2 of a 6-ounce package)
- 1/2 medium red bell pepper, cut in thin strips
- 1/4 teaspoon salt
- 1/8 teaspoon black pepper

Directions:
1. Place a large nonstick skillet over medium-high heat until hot. Coat the skillet with nonstick cooking spray and add the asparagus, mushrooms, and bell pepper. Coat the vegetables with nonstick cooking spray and sprinkle evenly with the salt and black pepper.
2. Cook 5–6 minutes, or until the vegetables begin to richly brown on the edges. Use two utensils to stir as you would when stir-frying.
3. Remove from the heat, cover tightly, and let stand 2 minutes to develop flavors.

Nutrition Info:
- 15 cal., 0g fat (0g sag. fat), 0mg chol, 150mg sod., 3g carb (1g sugars, 1g fiber), 1g pro.

Greek-style Garlic-lemon Potatoes

Servings:6 | Cooking Time:30 Minutes

Ingredients:
- 3 tablespoons extra-virgin olive oil
- 3 Yukon Gold potatoes (about 8 ounces each), peeled and cut lengthwise into 8 wedges
- 1½ tablespoons minced fresh oregano
- 3 garlic cloves, minced
- 2 teaspoons grated lemon zest plus 1½ tablespoons juice
- Salt and pepper
- 1½ tablespoons minced fresh parsley

Directions:
1. Heat 2 tablespoons oil in 12-inch nonstick skillet over medium-high heat until shimmering. Add potatoes cut side down in single layer and cook until golden brown on first side (skillet should sizzle but not smoke), about 6 minutes. Using tongs, flip potatoes onto second cut side and cook until golden brown, about 5 minutes. Reduce heat to medium-low, cover, and cook until potatoes are tender, 8 to 12

minutes.

2. Meanwhile, whisk remaining 1 tablespoon oil, oregano, garlic, lemon zest and juice, ½ teaspoon salt, and ½ teaspoon pepper together in small bowl. When potatoes are tender, gently stir in garlic mixture and cook, uncovered, until fragrant, about 2 minutes. Off heat, gently stir in parsley and season with pepper to taste. Serve.

Nutrition Info:
• 160 cal., 7g fat (1g sag. fat), 0mg chol, 200mg sod., 21g carb (0g sugars, 2g fiber), 3g pro.

Golden Zucchini

Servings:8 | Cooking Time: 10 Minutes

Ingredients:
• 3 cups shredded zucchini
• 2 large eggs
• 2 garlic cloves, minced
• 3/4 teaspoon salt
• 1/2 teaspoon pepper
• 1/4 teaspoon dried oregano
• 1/2 cup all-purpose flour
• 1/2 cup finely chopped sweet onion
• 1 tablespoon butter
• Marinara sauce, warmed, optional

Directions:
1. Place zucchini in a colander to drain; squeeze well to remove excess liquid. Pat dry.
2. In a large bowl, whisk eggs, garlic, salt, pepper and oregano until blended. Stir in flour just until moistened. Fold in zucchini and onion.
3. Lightly grease a griddle with butter; heat over medium heat. Drop the zucchini mixture by 1/4 cupfuls onto griddle; flatten to 1/2-in. thickness (3-in. diameter). Cook 4-5 minutes on each side or until golden brown. If desired, serve with marinara sauce.

Nutrition Info:
• 145 cal., 6g fat (3g sat. fat), 101mg chol., 510mg sod., 18g carb. (3g sugars, 2g fiber), 6g pro.

Sautéed Swiss Chard With Garlic

Servings:6 | Cooking Time:8 Minutes

Ingredients:
• 2 tablespoons extra-virgin olive oil
• 3 garlic cloves, sliced thin
• 1½ pounds Swiss chard, stems sliced ¼ inch thick on bias, leaves sliced into ½-inch-wide strips
• 2 teaspoons lemon juice
• Pepper

Directions:
1. Heat oil in 12-inch nonstick skillet over medium-high heat until just shimmering. Add garlic and cook, stirring constantly, until lightly browned, 30 to 60 seconds. Add chard stems and cook, stirring occasionally, until spotty brown and crisp-tender, about 6 minutes.
2. Add two-thirds of chard leaves and cook, tossing with

tongs, until just starting to wilt, 30 to 60 seconds. Add remaining chard leaves and continue to cook, stirring frequently, until leaves are tender, about 3 minutes. Off heat, stir in lemon juice and season with pepper to taste. Serve.

Nutrition Info:
• 60 cal., 5g fat (0g sag. fat), 0mg chol, 220mg sod., 5g carb (1g sugars, 2g fiber), 2g pro.

Pesto Pasta & Potatoes

Servings:12 | Cooking Time: 30 Minutes

Ingredients:
• 1 1/2 pounds small red potatoes, halved
• 12 ounces uncooked whole grain spiral pasta
• 3 cups cut fresh or frozen green beans
• 1 jar (6 1/2 ounces) prepared pesto
• 1 cup grated Parmigiano-Reggiano cheese

Directions:
1. Place potatoes in a large saucepan; add water to cover. Bring to a boil. Reduce heat; cook, uncovered, until tender, 8-10 minutes. Drain; transfer to a large bowl.
2. Meanwhile, cook pasta according to package directions, adding green beans during the last 5 minutes of cooking. Drain, reserving 3/4 cup pasta water, and add to potatoes. Toss with the pesto, cheese blend and enough pasta water to moisten.

Nutrition Info:
• 261 cal., 10g fat (3g sat. fat), 11mg chol., 233mg sod., 34g carb. (2g sugars, 5g fiber), 11g pro.

Roasted Winter Squash With Tahini And Feta

Servings:6 | Cooking Time:50 Minutes

Ingredients:
• 3 pounds butternut squash
• 3 tablespoons extra-virgin olive oil
• Salt and pepper
• 1 tablespoon tahini
• 1½ teaspoons lemon juice
• 1 ounce feta cheese, crumbled (¼ cup)
• ¼ cup shelled pistachios, toasted and chopped fine
• 2 tablespoons chopped fresh mint

Directions:
1. Adjust oven rack to lowest position and heat oven to 425 degrees. Using sharp vegetable peeler or chef's knife, remove squash skin and fibrous threads just below skin (squash should be completely orange with no white flesh). Halve squash lengthwise and scrape out seeds. Place squash cut side down on cutting board and slice crosswise into ½-inch-thick pieces.
2. Toss squash with 2 tablespoons oil, ½ teaspoon salt, and ½ teaspoon pepper and arrange in rimmed baking sheet in single layer. Roast squash until sides touching sheet toward back of oven are well browned, 25 to 30 minutes. Rotate sheet and continue to roast until sides touching sheet toward back of oven are well browned, 6 to 10 minutes.

3. Use metal spatula to flip each piece and continue to roast until squash is very tender and sides touching sheet are browned, 10 to 15 minutes.

4. Transfer squash to serving platter. Whisk tahini, lemon juice, remaining 1 tablespoon oil, and pinch salt together in bowl. Drizzle squash with tahini dressing and sprinkle with feta, pistachios, and mint. Serve.

Nutrition Info:
• 210 cal., 12g fat (2g sag. fat), 5mg chol, 250mg sod., 25g carb (5g sugars, 5g fiber), 4g pro.

Two-tone Potato Wedges

Servings:4 | Cooking Time: 40 Minutes

Ingredients:
• 2 medium potatoes
• 1 medium sweet potato
• 1 tablespoon olive oil
• 1/4 teaspoon salt
• 1/4 teaspoon pepper
• 1 tablespoon grated Parmesan cheese
• 2 garlic cloves, minced

Directions:
1. Cut each potato and sweet potato into eight wedges; place in a large resealable plastic bag. Add the oil, salt and pepper; seal bag and shake to coat. Arrange in a single layer in a 15x10x1-in. baking pan coated with cooking spray.

2. Bake, uncovered, at 425° for about 20 minutes. Turn potatoes; sprinkle with cheese and garlic. Bake 20-25 minutes longer or until golden brown.

Nutrition Info:
• 151 cal., 4g fat (1g sat. fat), 1mg chol., 176mg sod., 27g carb. (4g sugars, 3g fiber), 3g pro.

Crunchy Pear And Cilantro Relish

Servings: 4 | Cooking Time: 6 Minutes

Ingredients:
• 2 firm medium pears, peeled, cored, and finely chopped (about 1/4-inch cubes)
• 3/4 teaspoon lime zest
• 3 tablespoons lime juice
• 1 1/4 tablespoons sugar
• 3 tablespoons chopped cilantro or mint

Directions:
1. Place all ingredients in a bowl and toss well.
2. Serve immediately for peak flavor and texture.

Nutrition Info:
• 50 cal., 0g fat (0g sag. fat), 0mg chol, 0mg sod., 14g carb (9g sugars, 3g fiber), 0g pro.

Sauteed Radishes With Green Beans

Servings:4 | Cooking Time: 20 Minutes

Ingredients:
• 1 tablespoon butter
• 1/2 pound fresh green or wax beans, trimmed
• 1 cup thinly sliced radishes

• 1/2 teaspoon sugar
• 1/4 teaspoon salt
• 2 tablespoons pine nuts, toasted

Directions:
1. In a large skillet, heat butter over medium-high heat. Add the beans; cook and stir 3-4 minutes or until beans are crisp-tender.

2. Add radishes; cook 2-3 minutes longer or until vegetables are tender, stirring occasionally. Stir in sugar and salt; sprinkle with nuts.

Nutrition Info:
• 75 cal., 6g fat (2g sat. fat), 8mg chol., 177mg sod., 5g carb. (2g sugars, 2g fiber), 2g pro.

Roasted Broccoli

Servings:6 | Cooking Time: 11 Minutes

Ingredients:
• 1¾ pounds broccoli
• 3 tablespoons extra-virgin olive oil
• 3 garlic cloves, minced
• ½ teaspoon salt
• Pinch pepper
• Lemon wedges

Directions:
1. Adjust oven rack to lowest position, place rimmed baking sheet on rack, and heat oven to 500 degrees. Cut broccoli horizontally at juncture of crowns and stalks. Cut crowns into 4 wedges (if 3 to 4 inches in diameter) or 6 wedges (if 4 to 5 inches in diameter). Trim tough outer peel from stalks, then cut into ½-inch-thick planks that are 2 to 3 inches long.

2. Combine oil, garlic, salt, and pepper in large bowl. Add broccoli and toss to coat. Working quickly, lay broccoli in single layer, flat sides down, on preheated sheet. Roast until stalks are well browned and tender and florets are lightly browned, 9 to 11 minutes. Transfer to serving dish and serve with lemon wedges.

Nutrition Info:
• 90 cal., 7g fat (1g sag. fat), 0mg chol, 220mg sod., 6g carb (1g sugars, 2g fiber), 2g pro.

Hot Skillet Pineapple

Servings: 4 | Cooking Time:7 Minutes

Ingredients:
• 2 tablespoons no-trans-fat margarine (35% vegetable oil)
• 1 1/2 teaspoons packed dark brown sugar
• 1/2 teaspoon ground curry powder
• 8 slices pineapple packed in juice

Directions:
1. Place a large nonstick skillet over medium-high heat until hot. Add the margarine, sugar, and curry and bring to a boil. Stir to blend.

2. Arrange the pineapple slices in a single layer in the skillet. Cook 6 minutes until the pineapples are richly golden in color, turning frequently.

3. Arrange the pineapples on a serving platter and let stand 5 minutes to develop flavors and cool slightly. Serve hot or room temperature.

Nutrition Info:
• 70 cal., 2g fat (0g sag. fat), 0mg chol, 45mg sod., 13g carb (12g sugars, 1g fiber), 0g pro.

Slow-cooked Whole Carrots

Servings:6 | Cooking Time:45 Minutes

Ingredients:
• 1 tablespoon extra-virgin olive oil
• ½ teaspoon salt
• 1½ pounds carrots, peeled

Directions:
1. Cut parchment paper into 11-inch circle, then cut 1-inch hole in center, folding paper as needed.
2. Bring 3 cups water, oil, and salt to simmer in 12-inch skillet over high heat. Off heat, add carrots, top with parchment, cover skillet, and let sit for 20 minutes.
3. Uncover, leaving parchment in place, and bring to simmer over high heat. Reduce heat to medium-low and cook until most of water has evaporated and carrots are very tender, about 45 minutes.
4. Discard parchment, increase heat to medium-high, and cook, shaking skillet often, until carrots are lightly glazed and no water remains, 2 to 4 minutes. Serve.

Nutrition Info:
• 60 cal., 2g fat (0g sag. fat), 0mg chol, 100mg sod., 10g carb (5g sugars, 3g fiber), 1g pro.

Sautéed Green Beans With Garlic And Herbs

Servings:4 | Cooking Time:14 Minutes

Ingredients:
• 4 teaspoons extra-virgin olive oil
• 3 garlic cloves, minced
• 1 teaspoon minced fresh thyme
• 1 pound green beans, trimmed and cut into 2-inch lengths
• Salt and pepper
• 2 teaspoons lemon juice
• 1 tablespoon minced fresh parsley, basil, and/or mint

Directions:
1. Combine 1 tablespoon oil, garlic, and thyme in bowl. Heat remaining 1 teaspoon oil in 12-inch nonstick skillet over medium heat until just smoking. Add beans, ¼ teaspoon salt, and ⅛ teaspoon pepper and cook, stirring occasionally, until spotty brown, 4 to 6 minutes. Add ¼ cup water, cover, and cook until beans are bright green and still crisp, about 2 minutes.
2. Uncover, increase heat to high, and cook until water evaporates, 30 to 60 seconds. Add oil mixture and cook, stirring often, until beans are crisp-tender, lightly browned, and beginning to wrinkle, 1 to 3 minutes. Off heat, stir in lemon juice and parsley and season with pepper to taste. Serve.

Nutrition Info:
• 80 cal., 5g fat (0g sag. fat), 0mg chol, 150mg sod., 8g carb (3g sugars, 3g fiber), 2g pro.

Squash Melt

Servings: 4 | Cooking Time:8 Minutes

Ingredients:
• 2 medium yellow squash (about 12 ounces total), cut in 1/8-inch rounds
• 1 medium green bell pepper, chopped or 1 cup thinly sliced yellow onion
• 1/4–1/2 teaspoon dried oregano
• 1/4 teaspoon salt
• 1/4 cup shredded, reduced-fat, sharp cheddar cheese

Directions:
1. Place a medium nonstick skillet over medium-high heat until hot. Coat the skillet with nonstick cooking spray and add all the ingredients except the cheese.
2. Coat the vegetables with nonstick cooking spray and cook 6–7 minutes or until the vegetables are tender, stirring constantly. Use two utensils to stir as you would when stir-frying.
3. Remove the skillet from the heat and sprinkle the vegetables evenly with the cheese. Cover and let stand 2 minutes to melt the cheese.

Nutrition Info:
• 40 cal., 1g fat (0g sag. fat), 5mg chol, 190mg sod., 5g carb (3g sugars, 2g fiber), 3g pro.

Green Pea And Red Pepper Toss

Servings: 4 | Cooking Time:9 Minutes

Ingredients:
• 4 ounces sliced mushrooms (about 1 1/2 cups)
• 1 medium red bell pepper, thinly sliced, then cut in 2-inch pieces
• 1 cup frozen green peas, thawed
• 2 tablespoons no-trans-fat margarine (35% vegetable oil)
• 1/4 teaspoon salt
• 1/8 teaspoon black pepper

Directions:
1. Place a large nonstick skillet over medium-high heat until hot. Coat the skillet with nonstick cooking spray and add the mushrooms. Coat the mushrooms with nonstick cooking spray and cook 4 minutes, stirring frequently. Use two utensils to stir as you would when stir-frying.
2. Add the bell peppers and cook 2 minutes. Add the peas and cook for 1 minute.
3. Remove the skillet from the heat and stir in the remaining ingredients.

Nutrition Info:
• 70 cal., 3g fat (0g sag. fat), 0mg chol, 230mg sod., 8g carb (4g sugars, 3g fiber), 3g pro.

Grilled Veggies With Mustard Vinaigrette

Servings:10 | Cooking Time: 15 Minutes

Ingredients:
- 1/4 cup red wine vinegar
- 1 tablespoon Dijon mustard
- 1 tablespoon honey
- 1/2 teaspoon salt
- 1/8 teaspoon pepper
- 1/4 cup canola oil
- 1/4 cup olive oil
- VEGETABLES
- 2 large sweet onions
- 2 medium zucchini
- 2 yellow summer squash
- 2 large sweet red peppers, halved and seeded
- 1 bunch green onions, trimmed
- Cooking spray

Directions:
1. In a small bowl, whisk the first five ingredients. Gradually whisk in the oils until blended.
2. Peel and quarter each sweet onion, leaving root ends intact. Cut zucchini and yellow squash lengthwise into 1/2-in.-thick slices. Lightly spritz onions, zucchini, yellow squash and remaining vegetables with cooking spray, turning to coat all sides.
3. Grill sweet onions, covered, over medium heat 15-20 minutes until tender, turning occasionally. Grill zucchini, squash and peppers, covered, over medium heat 10-15 minutes or until crisp-tender and lightly charred, turning once. Grill the green onions, covered, 2-4 minutes or until lightly charred, turning once.
4. Cut vegetables into bite-size pieces; place in a large bowl. Add 1/2 cup vinaigrette and toss to coat. Serve with remaining vinaigrette.

Nutrition Info:
- 155 cal., 12g fat (1g sat. fat), 0 chol., 166mg sod., 13g carb. (8g sugars, 2g fiber), 2g pro.

Buttery Dijon Asparagus

Servings: 4 | Cooking Time:3 Minutes

Ingredients:
- 1 tablespoon no-trans-fat margarine (35% vegetable oil)
- 1 tablespoon Dijon mustard
- 1 tablespoon finely chopped fresh parsley
- 1/8 teaspoon salt
- 1 cup water
- 20 asparagus spears, trimmed (about 1 pound)

Directions:
1. Using a fork, stir the margarine, mustard, parsley, and salt together in a small bowl until well blended.
2. Place the water and asparagus in a large skillet and bring to a boil over high heat. Cover tightly and boil 2–3 minutes or until the asparagus is tender-crisp.
3. Drain the asparagus well and place it on a serving platter. Using the back of a spoon, spread the margarine mixture evenly on the asparagus.

Nutrition Info:
- 40 cal., 1g fat (0g sag. fat), 0mg chol, 190mg sod., 5g carb (2g sugars, 3g fiber), 3g pro.

Herbed Potato Packet

Servings:4 | Cooking Time: 25 Minutes

Ingredients:
- 1 pound baby red potatoes (about 16), halved
- 1/4 cup cranberry juice
- 2 tablespoons butter, cubed
- 1 teaspoon each minced fresh dill, oregano, rosemary and thyme
- 1/2 teaspoon salt
- 1/8 teaspoon pepper

Directions:
1. In a large bowl, combine all the ingredients; place on a piece of heavy-duty foil (about 18x12-in. rectangle). Fold foil around mixture, sealing tightly.
2. Grill, covered, over medium heat 25-30 minutes or until potatoes are tender. Open foil carefully to allow steam to escape.

Nutrition Info:
- 117 cal., 6g fat (4g sat. fat), 15mg chol., 351mg sod., 15g carb. (3g sugars, 1g fiber), 2g pro.

Roasted Smashed Potatoes

Servings:6 | Cooking Time:60 Minutes

Ingredients:
- 2 pounds small Red Bliss potatoes (about 18), scrubbed
- 1/4 cup extra-virgin olive oil
- 1 teaspoon chopped fresh thyme
- 1 teaspoon kosher salt
- 1/8 teaspoon pepper

Directions:
1. Adjust oven racks to top and bottom positions and heat oven to 500 degrees. Arrange potatoes on rimmed baking sheet, pour 3/4 cup water into baking sheet, and wrap tightly with aluminum foil. Cook on bottom rack until paring knife or skewer slips in and out of potatoes easily (poke through foil to test), 25 to 30 minutes. Remove foil and cool 10 minutes. If any water remains on baking sheet, blot dry with paper towel.
2. Drizzle 2 tablespoons oil over potatoes and roll to coat. Space potatoes evenly on baking sheet and place second baking sheet on top; press down firmly on baking sheet, flattening potatoes until 1/3 to 1/2 inch thick. Remove top sheet and sprinkle potatoes evenly with thyme, salt, and pepper. Drizzle evenly with remaining 2 tablespoons oil.
3. Roast potatoes on top rack for 15 minutes. Transfer potatoes to bottom rack and continue to roast until well browned, 20 to 30 minutes longer. Serve immediately.

Nutrition Info:
- 190 cal., 10g fat (1g sag. fat), 0mg chol, 210mg sod., 24g carb (2g sugars, 3g fiber), 3g pro.

POTATOES, PAS-TA, AND WHOLE GRAINS RECIPES

Rigatoni With Turkey Ragu

Servings:6 | Cooking Time:1hour

Ingredients:
- 1 onion, chopped coarse
- 1 carrot, chopped coarse
- 1 celery rib, chopped coarse
- 6 ounces cremini mushrooms, trimmed and quartered
- 1 ounce dried porcini mushrooms, rinsed and chopped coarse
- 1 (28-ounce) can no-salt-added whole peeled tomatoes
- 1 tablespoon extra-virgin olive oil
- Salt and pepper
- 2 garlic cloves, minced
- 1 tablespoon no-salt-added tomato paste
- 2 anchovy fillets, minced
- 1 pound ground turkey
- 1 cup 1 percent low-fat milk
- ½ cup dry red wine
- 12 ounces (3⅓ cups) 100 percent whole-wheat rigatoni

Directions:
1. Pulse onion, carrot, and celery in food processor until finely chopped, about 10 pulses; transfer to large bowl. Pulse cremini and porcini mushrooms in now-empty processor until finely chopped, about 5 pulses; transfer to bowl with onion mixture.
2. Pulse tomatoes with their juice in now-empty processor until mostly smooth, about 8 pulses. Transfer to separate bowl.
3. Heat oil in 12-inch skillet over medium heat until just shimmering. Add vegetable mixture, ¼ teaspoon salt, and ⅛ teaspoon pepper and cook until softened and lightly browned, 8 to 10 minutes. Stir in garlic and cook until fragrant, about 30 seconds. Stir in tomato paste and anchovies and cook for 1 minute.
4. Stir in turkey and cook, breaking up meat with wooden spoon, until no longer pink and mixture begins to look dry, about 4 minutes. Stir in milk and bring to simmer, scraping up any browned bits. Cook until milk is nearly evaporated, 8 to 10 minutes.
5. Stir in wine and simmer until nearly evaporated, about 10 minutes. Stir in processed tomato mixture and simmer until sauce has thickened, 15 to 20 minutes.
6. Meanwhile, bring 4 quarts water to boil in large pot. Add pasta and 1 teaspoon salt and cook, stirring often, until al dente. Reserve ½ cup of cooking water, then drain pasta and return it to pot. Add sauce and toss to combine. Adjust consistency with reserved cooking water as needed. Serve.

Nutrition Info:
- 380 cal., 6g fat (2g sag. fat), 35mg chol, 390mg sod., 49g carb (10g sugars, 9g fiber), 32g pro.

Lemony Beans And Potatoes

Servings: 4 | Cooking Time:8 Minutes

Ingredients:
- 8 ounces green beans, trimmed and broken into 2-inch pieces
- 6 ounces new potatoes, scrubbed and quartered
- 1 teaspoon lemon zest
- 1 1/2 tablespoons no-trans-fat margarine (35% vegetable oil)
- 1/4 teaspoon salt

Directions:
1. Steam the beans and potatoes 7 minutes or until the potatoes are just tender.
2. Place the vegetables in a decorative bowl, add the remaining ingredients, and toss gently. Serve immediately for peak flavor.

Nutrition Info:
- 70 cal., 2g fat (0g sag. fat), 0mg chol, 180mg sod., 12g carb (1g sugars, 2g fiber), 2g pro.

Baked Brown Rice With Shiitakes And Edamame

Servings:6 | Cooking Time: 60 Minutes

Ingredients:
- 1 cup long-grain brown rice, rinsed
- 1 tablespoon canola oil
- 4 ounces shiitake mushrooms, stemmed and sliced thin
- 4 scallions, white parts minced, green parts sliced thin on bias
- 2 teaspoons grated fresh ginger
- 2 cups low-sodium vegetable broth
- ½ teaspoon salt
- 1 cup frozen edamame, thawed
- 1 tablespoon unseasoned rice vinegar, plus extra for seasoning
- 1 teaspoon toasted sesame oil

Directions:
1. Adjust oven rack to middle position and heat oven to 375 degrees. Spread rice in 8-inch square baking dish.
2. Heat canola oil in medium saucepan over medium heat until shimmering. Add mushrooms, scallion whites, and ginger and cook, stirring occasionally, until softened, 5 to 7 minutes. Stir in broth and salt. Cover pot, increase heat to high, and bring to boil. Once boiling, stir to combine, then immediately pour mixture over rice. Cover dish tightly with aluminum foil and bake until rice is tender and liquid is absorbed, 50 to 60 minutes.
3. Remove dish from oven and uncover. Sprinkle edamame over rice, cover, and let sit for 5 minutes. Add scallion greens, vinegar, and sesame oil and fluff gently with fork to combine. Season with vinegar to taste. Serve.

Nutrition Info:
- 180 cal., 6g fat (1g sag. fat), 0mg chol, 240mg sod., 28g carb (2g sugars, 3g fiber), 5g pro.

Warm Farro With Mushrooms And Thyme
Servings:6 | Cooking Time: 30 Minutes

Ingredients:
- 1½ cups whole farro
- Salt and pepper
- 3 tablespoons extra-virgin olive oil
- 12 ounces cremini mushrooms, trimmed and chopped coarse
- 1 shallot, minced
- 1½ teaspoons minced fresh thyme or ½ teaspoon dried
- 3 tablespoons dry sherry
- 3 tablespoons minced fresh parsley
- 1½ teaspoons sherry vinegar, plus extra for seasoning

Directions:
1. Bring 4 quarts water to boil in large pot. Add farro and 1 teaspoon salt and cook until grains are tender with slight chew, 15 to 30 minutes. Drain farro, return to now-empty pot, and cover to keep warm.
2. Heat 2 tablespoons oil in 12-inch skillet over medium heat until shimmering. Add mushrooms, shallot, thyme, and ¼ teaspoon salt and cook, stirring occasionally, until moisture has evaporated and vegetables start to brown, 8 to 10 minutes. Stir in sherry, scraping up any browned bits, and cook until skillet is almost dry.
3. Add farro and remaining 1 tablespoon oil and cook until heated through, about 2 minutes. Off heat, stir in parsley and vinegar. Season with pepper and extra vinegar to taste and serve.

Nutrition Info:
- 250 cal., 9g fat (1g sag. fat), 0mg chol, 135mg sod., 39g carb (4g sugars, 4g fiber), 7g pro.

Rosemary Rice With Fresh Spinach Greens
Servings: 4 | Cooking Time:11 Minutes

Ingredients:
- 1 1/2 cups water
- 3/4 cup instant brown rice
- 1/8–1/4 teaspoon dried rosemary
- 1 cup packed spinach leaves, coarsely chopped
- 1 tablespoon no-trans-fat margarine (35% vegetable oil)
- 1/4 teaspoon salt

Directions:
1. Bring the water and rice to a boil in a medium saucepan. Add the rice and rosemary, reduce the heat, cover tightly, and simmer 10 minutes.
2. Remove the saucepan from the heat and stir in remaining ingredients. Toss gently, yet thoroughly, until the spinach has wilted.

Nutrition Info:
- 140 cal., 2g fat (0g sag. fat), 0mg chol, 190mg sod., 27g carb (0g sugars, 2g fiber), 3g pro.

Cuban Black Beans
Servings:8 | Cooking Time: 40 Minutes

Ingredients:
- Salt and pepper
- 1 pound dried black beans (2½ cups) picked over and rinsed
- 2 slices bacon, chopped fine
- 2 onions, chopped
- 1 red bell pepper, stemmed, seeded, and chopped
- 1 teaspoon ground cumin
- 6 garlic cloves, minced
- 2 teaspoons minced fresh oregano or ¾ teaspoon dried
- ¼ teaspoon red pepper flakes
- 3½ cups water
- 2 bay leaves
- ⅛ teaspoon baking soda
- ¼ cup minced fresh cilantro
- 1 tablespoon lime juice

Directions:
1. Dissolve 1½ tablespoons salt in 2 quarts cold water in large container. Add beans and soak at room temperature for at least 8 hours or up to 1 day. Drain and rinse well.
2. Adjust oven rack to lower-middle position and heat oven to 300 degrees. Cook bacon in Dutch oven over medium heat until crisp, 5 to 7 minutes. Stir in onions, bell pepper, cumin, and ½ teaspoon salt and cook until softened, 5 to 7 minutes. Stir in garlic, oregano, and red pepper flakes and cook until fragrant, about 30 seconds. Stir in water, scraping up any browned bits. Stir in beans, bay leaves, and baking soda and bring to simmer.
3. Cover, transfer pot to oven, and bake, stirring every 30 minutes, until beans are tender, about 1½ hours. Remove lid and continue to bake until liquid has thickened, 15 to 30 minutes, stirring halfway through cooking.
4. Discard bay leaves. Let beans sit for 10 minutes. Stir in cilantro and lime juice. Season with pepper to taste and serve.

Nutrition Info:
- 240 cal., 3g fat (1g sag. fat), 5mg chol, 240mg sod., 40g carb (8g sugars, 6g fiber), 13g pro.

Linguine With Meatless "meat" Sauce
Servings:6 | Cooking Time:19 Minutes

Ingredients:
- 5 ounces cremini mushrooms, trimmed
- 3 tablespoons extra-virgin olive oil
- Salt
- 1 small onion, chopped
- 3 garlic cloves, minced
- ½ teaspoon dried oregano
- ⅛ teaspoon red pepper flakes
- 2 tablespoons no-salt-added tomato paste
- 1 (14-ounce) can no-salt-added crushed tomatoes
- 1 cup low-sodium vegetable broth
- 1 cup no-salt-added canned chickpeas, rinsed
- 12 ounces 100 percent whole-wheat linguine

- 2 tablespoons chopped fresh basil
- 1 ounce Parmesan cheese, grated (½ cup)

Directions:

1. Pulse mushrooms in food processor until chopped into ⅛- to ¼-inch pieces, 7 to 10 pulses, scraping down sides of bowl as needed. (Do not clean workbowl.)

2. Heat 2 tablespoons oil in Dutch oven over medium-high heat until shimmering. Add mushrooms and ½ teaspoon salt and cook, stirring occasionally, until mushrooms are browned and fond has formed on bottom of pot, about 8 minutes.

3. While mushrooms cook, pulse onion in food processor until finely chopped, 7 to 10 pulses, scraping down sides of bowl as needed. (Do not clean workbowl.) Transfer onion to pot with mushrooms and cook, stirring occasionally, until onion is soft and translucent, about 5 minutes. Combine remaining 1 tablespoon oil, garlic, oregano, and pepper flakes in bowl.

4. Add tomato paste to pot and cook, stirring constantly, until mixture is rust-colored, 1 to 2 minutes. Reduce heat to medium and push vegetables to sides of pot. Add garlic mixture to center and cook, stirring constantly, until fragrant, about 30 seconds. Stir in tomatoes and broth; bring to simmer over high heat. Reduce heat to low and simmer sauce for 5 minutes, stirring occasionally.

5. While sauce simmers, pulse chickpeas in food processor until chopped into ¼-inch pieces, 5 to 7 pulses. Transfer chickpeas to fine-mesh strainer and rinse under cold running water until water runs clear; drain well. Add chickpeas to pot and simmer until sauce is slightly thickened, about 15 minutes.

6. Meanwhile, bring 4 quarts water to boil in large pot. Add pasta and 1 teaspoon salt and cook, stirring often, until al dente. Reserve ½ cup cooking water, then drain pasta and return it to pot. Add sauce and toss to combine. Adjust consistency with reserved cooking water as needed. Stir in 1 tablespoon basil. Sprinkle individual portions with Parmesan and remaining 1 tablespoon basil. Serve.

Nutrition Info:
- 350 cal., 10g fat (2g sag. fat), 5mg chol, 380mg sod., 49g carb (5g sugars, 9g fiber), 13g pro.

Farro Salad With Cucumber, Yogurt, And Mint

Servings:8 | Cooking Time: 30 Minutes

Ingredients:
- 1½ cups whole farro
- Salt and pepper
- 3 tablespoons extra-virgin olive oil
- 2 tablespoons lemon juice
- 2 tablespoons minced shallot
- 2 tablespoons plain 2 percent Greek yogurt
- 1 English cucumber, halved lengthwise, seeded, and cut into ¼-inch pieces
- 6 ounces cherry tomatoes, halved
- 1 cup baby arugula
- 3 tablespoons chopped fresh mint

Directions:

1. Bring 4 quarts water to boil in large pot. Add farro and 1 teaspoon salt and cook until grains are tender with slight chew, 15 to 30 minutes. Drain farro well. Transfer to parchment paper–lined rimmed baking sheet and spread into even layer. Let cool completely, about 15 minutes.

2. Whisk oil, lemon juice, shallot, yogurt, ¼ teaspoon salt, and ¼ teaspoon pepper together in large bowl. Add farro, cucumber, tomatoes, arugula, and mint and gently toss to combine. Season with pepper to taste. Serve.

Nutrition Info:
- 190 cal., 7g fat (1g sag. fat), 0mg chol, 100mg sod., 30g carb (3g sugars, 4g fiber), 5g pro.

Noodles With Mustard Greens And Shiitake-ginger Sauce

Servings:6 | Cooking Time:10 Minutes.

Ingredients:
- 8 ounces (⅛-inch-wide) brown rice noodles
- 2 tablespoons toasted sesame oil
- 1 tablespoon canola oil
- 8 ounces shiitake mushrooms, stemmed and sliced thin
- 2 cups water
- ¼ cup mirin
- 3 tablespoons rice vinegar
- 2 tablespoons low-sodium soy sauce
- 1 tablespoon grated fresh ginger
- 2 garlic cloves, minced
- ½ ounce dried shiitake mushrooms, rinsed and minced
- 1 teaspoon Asian chili-garlic sauce
- 1 pound mustard greens, stemmed and chopped into 1-inch pieces
- 4 ounces frozen shelled edamame
- 3 scallions, sliced thin
- 2 teaspoons sesame seeds, toasted
- Pepper

Directions:

1. Bring 3 quarts water to boil in large saucepan. Place noodles in large bowl and pour boiling water over noodles. Stir and let soak until noodles are soft and pliable but not fully tender, about 8 minutes, stirring once halfway through soaking. Drain noodles and rinse under cold running water until water runs clear. Drain noodles well, then toss with 2 teaspoons sesame oil. Portion noodles into 6 individual serving bowls; set aside.

2. Heat canola oil in Dutch oven over medium-high heat until shimmering. Add fresh mushrooms and cook, stirring occasionally, until softened and lightly browned, about 5 minutes. Stir in water, mirin, vinegar, soy sauce, ginger, garlic, dried mushrooms, chili-garlic sauce, and 1 teaspoon sesame oil. Bring to simmer and cook until liquid has reduced by half, 8 to 10 minutes.

3. Stir in mustard greens and edamame, return to simmer, and cook, stirring often, until greens are nearly tender, 5 to 7 minutes.

4. Divide mustard green–mushroom mixture and sauce among noodle bowls. Top with scallions and sesame seeds and drizzle with remaining 1 tablespoon sesame oil. Season with pepper to taste and serve.

Nutrition Info:
- 290 cal., 9g fat (1g sag. fat), 0mg chol, 250mg sod., 43g carb (7g sugars, 7g fiber), 9g pro.

Brown Rice With Tomatoes And Chickpeas
Servings:8 | Cooking Time:30 Minutes

Ingredients:
- 12 ounces grape tomatoes, quartered
- 5 scallions, sliced thin
- ¼ cup minced fresh cilantro
- 4 teaspoons extra-virgin olive oil
- 1 tablespoon lime juice
- Salt and pepper
- 2 red bell peppers, stemmed, seeded, and chopped fine
- 1 onion, chopped fine
- 1 cup long-grain brown rice, rinsed
- 4 garlic cloves, minced
- Pinch saffron threads, crumbled
- Pinch cayenne pepper
- 3¼ cups unsalted chicken broth
- 1 (15-ounce) can no-salt-added chickpeas, rinsed

Directions:
1. Combine tomatoes, scallions, cilantro, 2 teaspoons oil, lime juice, ⅛ teaspoon salt, and ⅛ teaspoon pepper in bowl; set aside for serving.
2. Heat remaining 2 teaspoons oil in 12-inch skillet over medium heat until shimmering. Add bell peppers, onion, and ¼ teaspoon salt and cook until softened and lightly browned, 8 to 10 minutes. Stir in rice, garlic, saffron, and cayenne and cook until fragrant, about 30 seconds.
3. Stir in broth, scraping up any browned bits, and bring to simmer. Reduce heat to medium-low, cover, and cook, stirring occasionally, for 25 minutes.
4. Stir in chickpeas and ⅛ teaspoon salt, cover, and cook until rice is tender and broth is almost completely absorbed, 25 to 30 minutes. Season with pepper to taste. Serve, topping individual portions with tomato mixture.

Nutrition Info:
- 180 cal., 3g fat (0g sag. fat), 0mg chol, 210mg sod., 30g carb (4g sugars, 4g fiber), 6g pro.

Bulgur Salad With Carrots And Almonds
Servings:8 | Cooking Time:1½ Hours

Ingredients:
- 1½ cups medium-grind bulgur, rinsed
- 1 cup water
- 6 tablespoons lemon juice (2 lemons)
- Salt and pepper
- ⅓ cup extra-virgin olive oil
- ½ teaspoon ground cumin
- ⅛ teaspoon cayenne pepper
- 4 carrots, peeled and shredded

- 3 scallions, sliced thin
- ½ cup sliced almonds, toasted
- ⅓ cup chopped fresh mint
- ⅓ cup chopped fresh cilantro

Directions:
1. Combine bulgur, water, ¼ cup lemon juice, and ¼ teaspoon salt in bowl. Cover and let sit at room temperature until grains are softened and liquid is fully absorbed, about 1½ hours.
2. Whisk remaining 2 tablespoons lemon juice, oil, cumin, cayenne, and ¼ teaspoon salt together in large bowl. Add bulgur, carrots, scallions, almonds, mint, and cilantro and gently toss to combine. Season with pepper to taste. Serve.

Nutrition Info:
- 230 cal., 13g fat (1g sag. fat), 0mg chol, 180mg sod., 26g carb (2g sugars, 6g fiber), 5g pro.

Couscous With Saffron, Raisins, And Toasted Almonds
Servings:6 | Cooking Time:12 Minutes

Ingredients:
- 1 cup whole-wheat couscous
- 2 tablespoons extra-virgin olive oil
- 1 onion, chopped fine
- Salt and pepper
- ⅛ teaspoon saffron threads, crumbled
- ⅛ teaspoon ground cinnamon
- ⅛ teaspoon cayenne pepper
- ¾ cup water
- ¾ cup unsalted chicken broth
- ½ cup raisins
- ¼ cup sliced almonds, toasted
- 1½ teaspoons lemon juice

Directions:
1. Toast couscous in medium saucepan over medium-high heat, stirring often, until a few grains begin to brown, about 3 minutes. Transfer couscous to large bowl and set aside.
2. Heat 1 tablespoon oil in now-empty saucepan over medium heat until shimmering. Add onion and ½ teaspoon salt and cook until softened, about 5 minutes. Stir in saffron, cinnamon, and cayenne and cook until fragrant, about 30 seconds. Stir in water, broth, and raisins and bring to boil.
3. Once boiling, immediately pour broth mixture over couscous, cover tightly with plastic wrap, and let sit until grains are tender, about 12 minutes.
4. Add remaining 1 tablespoon oil, almonds, and lemon juice and fluff gently with fork to combine. Season with pepper to taste and serve.

Nutrition Info:
- 230 cal., 7g fat (1g sag. fat), 0mg chol, 220mg sod., 36g carb (14g sugars, 5g fiber), 6g pro.

lentil Salad With Olives, Mint, And Feta

Servings:4 | Cooking Time:60 Minutes

Ingredients:
- Salt and pepper
- 1 cup lentilles du Puy, picked over and rinsed
- 5 garlic cloves, lightly crushed and peeled
- 1 bay leaf
- 5 tablespoons extra-virgin olive oil
- 3 tablespoons white wine vinegar
- ½ cup pitted kalamata olives, chopped coarse
- ½ cup chopped fresh mint
- 1 large shallot, minced
- 1 ounce feta cheese, crumbled (¼ cup)

Directions:
1. Dissolve 1 teaspoon salt in 4 cups warm water (about 110 degrees) in bowl. Add lentils and soak at room temperature for 1 hour. Drain well.
2. Adjust oven rack to middle position and heat oven to 325 degrees. Combine lentils, 4 cups water, garlic, bay leaf, and ½ teaspoon salt in medium ovensafe saucepan. Cover, transfer saucepan to oven, and cook until lentils are tender but remain intact, 40 to 60 minutes.
3. Drain lentils well; discard garlic and bay leaf. Whisk oil and vinegar together in large bowl. Add lentils, olives, mint, and shallot and gently toss to combine. Season with pepper to taste. Transfer to serving dish and sprinkle with feta. Serve.

Nutrition Info:
- 350 cal., 21g fat (3g sag. fat), 5mg chol, 200mg sod., 31g carb (2g sugars, 8g fiber), 12g pro.

Dal (spiced Red Lentils)

Servings:4 | Cooking Time: 25 Minutes

Ingredients:
- SPICE MIXTURE
- ½ teaspoon ground coriander
- ½ teaspoon ground cumin
- ¼ teaspoon ground cinnamon
- ¼ teaspoon ground turmeric
- ⅛ teaspoon ground cardamom
- ⅛ teaspoon red pepper flakes
- LENTILS
- 1 tablespoon canola oil
- 4 garlic cloves, minced
- 1½ teaspoons grated fresh ginger
- 1 onion, chopped fine
- Salt and pepper
- 3 cups water
- 1 cup red lentils, picked over and rinsed
- 12 ounces plum tomatoes, cored, seeded, and chopped
- ½ cup minced fresh cilantro
- 1 tablespoon unsalted butter

Directions:
1. FOR THE SPICE MIXTURE Combine all spices in smal bowl.

2. FOR THE LENTILS Cook spice mixture, oil, garlic, and ginger in large saucepan over medium heat, stirring occasionally, until fragrant, about 1 minute. Stir in onion and ¼ teaspoon salt and cook until softened, about 5 minutes.
3. Stir in water and lentils, bring to simmer, and cook until lentils are tender and resemble thick, coarse puree, 20 to 25 minutes. Off heat, stir in tomatoes, cilantro, butter, and ⅛ teaspoon salt. Season with pepper to taste and serve.

Nutrition Info:
- 260 cal., 8g fat (2g sag. fat), 10mg chol, 240mg sod., 36g carb (6g sugars, 9g fiber), 14g pro.

Fusilli With Skillet-roasted Cauliflower, Garlic, And Walnuts

Servings:6 | Cooking Time:20 Minutes

Ingredients:
- ¼ cup extra-virgin olive oil
- 1 head cauliflower (2 pounds), cored and cut into ½-inch florets
- Salt and pepper
- 3 garlic cloves, minced
- 1 teaspoon grated lemon zest plus 1–2 tablespoons juice
- ¼ teaspoon red pepper flakes
- 12 ounces (4½ cups) 100 percent whole-wheat fusilli
- 1 ounce Parmesan cheese, grated (½ cup)
- 2 tablespoons chopped fresh parsley
- ¼ cup walnuts, toasted and chopped coarse

Directions:
1. Combine 2 tablespoons oil and cauliflower florets in 12-inch nonstick skillet and sprinkle with ½ teaspoon salt and ¼ teaspoon pepper. Cover skillet and cook over medium-high heat until florets start to brown and edges just start to become translucent (do not lift lid), about 5 minutes. Remove lid and continue to cook, stirring every 2 minutes, until florets turn golden brown in many spots, about 12 minutes.
2. Push cauliflower to sides of skillet. Add 1 tablespoon oil, garlic, lemon zest, and pepper flakes to center and cook, stirring with rubber spatula, until fragrant, about 30 seconds. Stir garlic mixture into cauliflower and continue to cook, stirring occasionally, until cauliflower is tender but still firm, about 3 minutes.
3. Meanwhile, bring 4 quarts water to boil in large pot. Add pasta and 1 teaspoon salt and cook, stirring often, until al dente. Reserve 1 cup cooking water, then drain pasta and return it to pot.
4. Add cauliflower mixture, ¼ cup Parmesan, parsley, ½ cup reserved cooking water, 1 tablespoon lemon juice, and remaining 1 tablespoon oil to pasta and toss to combine. Season with extra lemon juice to taste and adjust consistency with reserved cooking water as needed. Sprinkle individual portions with walnuts and remaining ¼ cup Parmesan. Serve.

Nutrition Info:
- 360 cal., 16g fat (2g sag. fat), 5mg chol, 390mg sod., 44g carb (4g sugars, 10g fiber), 13g pro.

Couscous With Carrots, Chickpeas, And Herbs

Servings:8 | Cooking Time:12 Minutes

Ingredients:
- 1 cup whole-wheat couscous
- 2 tablespoons extra-virgin olive oil
- 2 carrots, peeled and chopped fine
- 1 onion, chopped fine
- Salt and pepper
- 2 garlic cloves, minced
- ½ teaspoon ground coriander
- ½ teaspoon ground ginger
- ¾ cup water
- ¾ cup unsalted chicken broth
- 1 (15-ounce) can no-salt-added chickpeas, rinsed
- ¼ cup minced fresh parsley, cilantro, and/or mint
- 1½ teaspoons lemon juice

Directions:
1. Toast couscous in medium saucepan over medium-high heat, stirring often, until a few grains begin to brown, about 3 minutes. Transfer couscous to large bowl and set aside.
2. Heat 1 tablespoon oil in now-empty saucepan over medium heat until shimmering. Add carrots, onion, and ½ teaspoon salt and cook until softened, 6 to 8 minutes. Stir in garlic, coriander, and ginger and cook until fragrant, about 30 seconds. Stir in water, broth, and chickpeas and bring to boil.
3. Once boiling, immediately pour broth mixture over couscous, cover tightly with plastic wrap, and let sit until grains are tender, about 12 minutes.
4. Add remaining 1 tablespoon oil, parsley, and lemon juice and fluff gently with fork to combine. Season with pepper to taste and serve.

Nutrition Info:
- 170 cal., 4g fat (0g sag. fat), 0mg chol, 180mg sod., 28g carb (3g sugars, 5g fiber), 6g pro.

Spiced Basmati Rice With Cauliflower And Pomegranate

Servings:6 | Cooking Time:30minutes

Ingredients:
- ½ head cauliflower (1 pound), cored and cut into ¾-inch florets
- 2 tablespoons extra-virgin olive oil
- Salt and pepper
- ¼ teaspoon ground cumin
- ½ onion, chopped coarse
- ¾ cup basmati rice, rinsed
- 2 garlic cloves, minced
- ¼ teaspoon ground cinnamon
- ¼ teaspoon ground turmeric
- 1¼ cups water
- ¼ cup pomegranate seeds
- 1 tablespoon chopped fresh cilantro
- 1 tablespoon chopped fresh mint

Directions:
1. Adjust oven rack to lowest position and heat oven to 475 degrees. Toss cauliflower with 1 tablespoon oil, ⅛ teaspoon salt, ¼ teaspoon pepper, and ⅛ teaspoon cumin. Arrange cauliflower in single layer on rimmed baking sheet and roast until just tender, 8 to 10 minutes; set aside.
2. Heat remaining 1 tablespoon oil in large saucepan over medium heat until shimmering. Add onion and ¼ teaspoon salt and cook until softened and lightly browned, 5 to 7 minutes. Add rice, garlic, cinnamon, turmeric, and remaining ⅛ teaspoon cumin and cook, stirring frequently, until grain edges begin to turn translucent, about 3 minutes.
3. Stir in water and bring to simmer. Reduce heat to low, cover, and simmer gently until rice is tender and water is absorbed, 16 to 18 minutes.
4. Off heat, lay clean dish towel underneath lid and let pilaf sit for 10 minutes. Add cauliflower to pilaf and fluff gently with fork to combine. Season with pepper to taste. Transfer to serving platter and sprinkle with pomegranate seeds, cilantro, and mint. Serve.

Nutrition Info:
- 150 cal., 5g fat (1g sag. fat), 0mg chol, 170mg sod., 23g carb (3g sugars, 3g fiber), 3g pro.

Couscous With Tomato, Scallion, And Lemon

Servings:6 | Cooking Time:12 Minutes

Ingredients:
- 1 cup whole-wheat couscous
- 2 tablespoons extra-virgin olive oil
- 1 onion, chopped fine
- Salt and pepper
- 2 garlic cloves, minced
- 1 teaspoon grated lemon zest plus 1½ teaspoons lemon juice
- ⅛ teaspoon cayenne pepper
- ¾ cup water
- ¾ cup unsalted chicken broth
- 1 tomato, cored, seeded, and chopped fine
- 1 scallion, sliced thin

Directions:
1. Toast couscous in medium saucepan over medium-high heat, stirring often, until a few grains begin to brown, about 3 minutes. Transfer couscous to large bowl and set aside.
2. Heat 1 tablespoon oil in now-empty saucepan over medium heat until shimmering. Add onion and ½ teaspoon salt and cook until softened, about 5 minutes. Stir in garlic, lemon zest, and cayenne and cook until fragrant, about 30 seconds. Stir in water and broth and bring to boil.
3. Once boiling, immediately pour broth mixture over couscous, cover tightly with plastic wrap, and let sit until grains are tender, about 12 minutes.
4. Add remaining 1 tablespoon oil, lemon juice, tomato, and scallion and fluff gently with fork to combine. Season with pepper to taste and serve.

Nutrition Info:

• 170 cal., 5g fat (0g sag. fat), 0mg chol, 210mg sod., 28g carb (3g sugars, 5g fiber), 6g pro.

Basmati Rice Pilaf With Herbs And Toasted Almonds

Servings:6 | Cooking Time:18 Minutes

Ingredients:
• 1 tablespoon extra-virgin olive oil
• 1 small onion, chopped fine
• Salt and pepper
• 1 cup basmati rice, rinsed
• 2 garlic cloves, minced
• ½ teaspoon ground turmeric
• ¼ teaspoon ground cinnamon
• 1½ cups water
• ¼ cup minced fresh parsley, chives, or basil
• ¼ cup sliced almonds, toasted

Directions:
1. Heat oil in large saucepan over medium heat until shimmering. Add onion and ½ teaspoon salt and cook until softened, about 5 minutes. Add rice, garlic, turmeric, and cinnamon and cook, stirring frequently, until grain edges begin to turn translucent, about 3 minutes.
2. Stir in water and bring to simmer. Reduce heat to low, cover, and simmer gently until rice is tender and water is absorbed, 16 to 18 minutes.
3. Off heat, lay clean dish towel underneath lid and let pilaf sit for 10 minutes. Add parsley and almonds to pilaf and fluff gently with fork to combine. Season with pepper to taste. Serve.

Nutrition Info:
• 150 cal., 4g fat (0g sag. fat), 0mg chol, 200mg sod., 25g carb (1g sugars, 2g fiber), 3g pro.

Pasta Alla Norma With Olives And Capers

Servings:6 | Cooking Time: 18 Minutes

Ingredients:
• 1½ pounds eggplant, cut into ½-inch pieces
• Kosher salt and pepper
• 3½ tablespoons extra-virgin olive oil
• 4 garlic cloves, minced
• 2 anchovy fillets, rinsed and minced
• ¼ teaspoon red pepper flakes
• 1 (28-ounce) can no-salt-added crushed tomatoes
• ½ cup pitted kalamata olives, chopped coarse
• 6 tablespoons minced fresh parsley
• 2 tablespoons capers, rinsed
• 12 ounces (3⅓ cups) 100 percent whole-wheat rigatoni
• 2 ounces ricotta salata, shredded (½ cup)

Directions:
1. Line large plate with double layer of coffee filters and lightly spray with vegetable oil spray. Toss eggplant with ½ teaspoon salt, then spread out over coffee filters. Microwave eggplant, uncovered, until dry to touch and slightly shriveled, about 10 minutes, tossing halfway through cooking.

Let cool slightly.
2. Transfer eggplant to large bowl, drizzle with 1 tablespoon oil, and gently toss to coat. Heat 1 tablespoon oil in 12-inch nonstick skillet over medium-high heat until shimmering. Add eggplant and cook, stirring occasionally, until well browned and fully tender, about 10 minutes; transfer to clean plate.
3. Let skillet cool slightly, about 3 minutes. Add 1 tablespoon oil, garlic, anchovies, and pepper flakes to now-empty skillet and cook over medium heat, stirring often, until garlic is lightly golden and fragrant, about 1 minute. Stir in tomatoes, increase heat to medium-high, and simmer, stirring occasionally, until slightly thickened, 8 to 10 minutes. Add eggplant and cook, stirring occasionally, until eggplant is heated through and flavors meld, 3 to 5 minutes. Stir in olives, parsley, capers, and remaining ½ tablespoon oil.
4. Meanwhile, bring 4 quarts water to boil in large pot. Add pasta and 2 teaspoons salt and cook, stirring often, until al dente. Reserve ½ cup cooking water, then drain pasta and return it to pot. Add sauce and toss to combine. Season with salt and pepper to taste and adjust consistency with reserved cooking water as needed. Serve with ricotta salata.

Nutrition Info:
• 370 cal., 13g fat (2g sag. fat), 10mg chol, 440mg sod., 50g carb (9g sugars, 12g fiber), 12g pro.

Black-eyed Peas With Walnuts And Pomegranate

Servings:4 | Cooking Time:1hours

Ingredients:
• 2 tablespoons extra-virgin olive oil
• 2 tablespoons lemon juice
• 2 tablespoons pomegranate molasses
• ¼ teaspoon ground coriander
• ¼ teaspoon ground cumin
• ⅛ teaspoon ground fennel seed
• Salt and pepper
• 2 (15-ounce) cans no-salt-added black-eyed peas, rinsed
• ½ cup pomegranate seeds
• ½ cup minced fresh parsley
• ⅓ cup walnuts, toasted and chopped
• 4 scallions, sliced thin

Directions:
1. Whisk oil, lemon juice, pomegranate molasses, coriander, cumin, fennel seed, ¼ teaspoon salt, and ⅛ teaspoon pepper together in large bowl until smooth. Add peas, pomegranate seeds, parsley, walnuts, and scallions and toss to combine. Season with ⅛ teaspoon salt and pepper to taste.

Nutrition Info:
• 260 cal., 14g fat (1g sag. fat), 0mg chol, 250mg sod., 29g carb (8g sugars, 7g fiber), 9g pro.

SLOW COOKER FAVORITES RECIPES

Lentil Pumpkin Soup

Servings:6 | Cooking Time: 7 Hours

Ingredients:
- 1 pound red potatoes (about 4 medium), cut into 1-inch pieces
- 1 can (15 ounces) solid-pack pumpkin
- 1 cup dried lentils, rinsed
- 1 medium onion, chopped
- 3 garlic cloves, minced
- 1/2 teaspoon ground ginger
- 1/2 teaspoon pepper
- 1/8 teaspoon salt
- 2 cans (14 1/2 ounces each) vegetable broth
- 1 1/2 cups water
- Minced fresh cilantro, optional

Directions:
1. In a 3- or 4-qt. slow cooker, combine first 10 ingredients. Cook, covered, on low 7-9 hours or until potatoes and lentils are tender. If desired, sprinkle servings with cilantro.

Nutrition Info:
- 210 cal., 1g fat (0 sat. fat), 0 chol., 463mg sod., 42g carb. (5g sugars, 7g fiber), 11g pro.

Butternut Squash With Whole Grains

Servings:12 | Cooking Time: 4 Hours

Ingredients:
- 1 medium butternut squash (about 3 pounds), cut into 1/2-inch cubes
- 1 cup uncooked whole grain brown and red rice blend
- 1 medium onion, chopped
- 1/2 cup water
- 3 garlic cloves, minced
- 2 teaspoons minced fresh thyme or 1/2 teaspoon dried thyme
- 1/2 teaspoon salt
- 1/4 teaspoon pepper
- 1 can (14 1/2 ounces) vegetable broth
- 1 package (6 ounces) fresh baby spinach

Directions:
1. In a 4-qt. slow cooker, combine the first eight ingredients. Stir in broth.
2. Cook, covered, on low 4-5 hours or until grains are tender. Stir in spinach before serving.

Nutrition Info:
- 97 cal., 1g fat (0 sat. fat), 0 chol., 252mg sod., 22g carb. (3g sugars, 4g fiber), 3g pro.

Carne Guisada

Servings:12 | Cooking Time: 7 Hours

Ingredients:
- 1 bottle (12 ounces) beer
- 1/4 cup all-purpose flour
- 2 tablespoons tomato paste
- 1 jalapeno pepper, seeded and chopped
- 4 teaspoons Worcestershire sauce
- 1 bay leaf
- 2 to 3 teaspoons crushed red pepper flakes
- 2 teaspoons chili powder
- 1 1/2 teaspoons ground cumin
- 1/2 teaspoon salt
- 1/2 teaspoon paprika
- 2 garlic cloves, minced
- 1/2 teaspoon red wine vinegar
- Dash liquid smoke, optional
- 1 boneless pork shoulder butt roast (3 pounds), cut into 2-inch pieces
- 2 large unpeeled red potatoes, chopped
- 1 medium onion, chopped
- Whole wheat tortillas or hot cooked brown rice, lime wedges and chopped fresh cilantro, optional

Directions:
1. In a 4- or 5-qt. slow cooker, mix first 13 ingredients and, if desired, the liquid smoke. Stir in pork, potatoes and onion. Cook mixture, covered, on low until pork is tender, 7-9 hours.
2. Discard bay leaf; skim fat from cooking juices. Shred pork slightly with two forks. Serve pork with the optional remaining ingredients as desired.

Nutrition Info:
- 261 cal., 12g fat (4g sat. fat), 67mg chol., 200mg sod., 16g carb. (3g sugars, 2g fiber), 21g pro.

Parsley Smashed Potatoes

Servings:8 | Cooking Time: 6 Hours

Ingredients:
- 16 small red potatoes (about 2 pounds)
- 1 celery rib, sliced
- 1 medium carrot, sliced
- 1/4 cup finely chopped onion
- 2 cups chicken broth
- 1 tablespoon minced fresh parsley
- 1 1/2 teaspoons salt, divided
- 1 teaspoon pepper, divided
- 1 garlic clove, minced
- 2 tablespoons butter, melted
- Additional minced fresh parsley

Directions:
1. Place potatoes, celery, carrot and onion in a 4-qt. slow

cooker. In a small bowl, mix broth, parsley, 1 teaspoon salt, 1/2 teaspoon pepper and garlic; pour over vegetables. Cook, covered, on low 6-8 hours or until potatoes are tender.

2. Transfer potatoes from slow cooker to a 15x10x1-in. pan; discard cooking liquid and vegetables or save for other use. Using bottom of a measuring cup, flatten potatoes slightly. Transfer to a large bowl; drizzle with butter. Sprinkle with remaining salt and pepper; toss to coat. Sprinkle with additional parsley.

Nutrition Info:
- 114 cal., 3g fat (2g sat. fat), 8mg chol., 190mg sod., 20g carb. (2g sugars, 2g fiber), 2g pro.

Spiced Carrots & Butternut Squash

Servings:6 | Cooking Time: 4 Hours

Ingredients:
- 5 large carrots, cut into 1/2-inch pieces (about 3 cups)
- 2 cups cubed peeled butternut squash (1-inch pieces)
- 1 tablespoon balsamic vinegar
- 1 tablespoon olive oil
- 1 tablespoon honey
- 1 teaspoon ground cinnamon
- 1/2 teaspoon salt
- 1/2 teaspoon ground cumin
- 1/4 teaspoon chili powder

Directions:
1. Place carrots and squash in a 3-qt. slow cooker. In a small bowl, mix remaining ingredients; drizzle over vegetables and toss to coat. Cook, covered, on low 4-5 hours or until vegetables are tender. Gently stir before serving.

Nutrition Info:
- 85 cal., 3g fat (0 sat. fat), 0 chol., 245mg sod., 16g carb. (8g sugars, 3g fiber), 1g pro.

Herbed Chicken With Warm Bulgur Salad And Yogurt Sauce

Servings:4 | Cooking Time:3 Hours

Ingredients:
- 1 cup medium-grind bulgur, rinsed
- 1 cup unsalted chicken broth
- Salt and pepper
- ¼ cup extra-virgin olive oil
- 4 teaspoons minced fresh oregano
- 1¼ teaspoons grated lemon zest plus 2 tablespoons juice
- 1 garlic clove, minced
- Salt and pepper
- ⅛ teaspoon ground cardamom
- 2 (12-ounce) bone-in split chicken breasts, skin removed, trimmed of all visible fat, and halved crosswise
- ½ cup 2 percent Greek yogurt
- ½ cup minced fresh parsley
- 3 tablespoons water
- 8 ounces cherry tomatoes, quartered
- 1 carrot, peeled and shredded
- ¼ cup chopped toasted pistachios

Directions:
1. Lightly coat oval slow cooker with vegetable oil spray. Combine bulgur, broth, and ⅛ teaspoon salt in prepared slow cooker. Microwave 1 tablespoon oil, 1 tablespoon oregano, 1 teaspoon lemon zest, garlic, ¼ teaspoon salt, ¼ teaspoon pepper, and cardamom in bowl until fragrant, about 30 seconds; let cool slightly. Rub chicken with oregano mixture, then arrange, skinned side up, in even layer in prepared slow cooker. Cover and cook until chicken registers 160 degrees, 2 to 3 hours on low.

2. Whisk yogurt, 1 tablespoon parsley, water, remaining 1 teaspoon oregano, remaining ¼ teaspoon lemon zest, and ⅛ teaspoon salt together in bowl. Season sauce with pepper to taste.

3. Transfer chicken to serving platter, brushing any bulgur that sticks to breasts back into slow cooker. Drain bulgur mixture, if necessary, and return to now-empty slow cooker. Add remaining 3 tablespoons oil, remaining 7 tablespoons parsley, lemon juice, tomatoes, carrot, and ⅛ teaspoon salt and fluff with fork to combine. Season with pepper to taste. Sprinkle bulgur salad with pistachios. Serve chicken with salad and yogurt sauce.

Nutrition Info:
- 500 cal., 23g fat (4g sag. fat), 100mg chol, 440mg sod., 36g carb (5g sugars, 7g fiber), 41g pro.

Latin-style Chicken With Tomatoes And Olives

Servings:4 | Cooking Time: 3 Hours

Ingredients:
- 1 onion, halved and sliced thin
- 4 garlic cloves, sliced thin
- 2 tablespoons extra-virgin olive oil
- 1 tablespoon no-salt-added tomato paste
- 2 teaspoons minced fresh oregano or ½ teaspoon dried
- ¼ teaspoon ground cumin
- 1 (14.5-ounce) can no-salt-added diced tomatoes, drained
- 2 (12-ounce) bone-in split chicken breasts, skin removed, trimmed of all visible fat, and halved crosswise
- Salt and pepper
- ⅓ cup pitted large brine-cured green olives, chopped coarse
- 2 tablespoons chopped fresh cilantro
- 1 tablespoon lime juice

Directions:
1. Microwave onion, garlic, oil, tomato paste, oregano, and cumin in bowl, stirring occasionally, until onion is softened, about 5 minutes; transfer to oval slow cooker. Stir in tomatoes. Sprinkle chicken with ¼ teaspoon salt and ⅛ teaspoon pepper and nestle into slow cooker. Cover and cook until chicken registers 160 degrees, 2 to 3 hours on low.

2. Transfer chicken to serving platter. Stir olives, cilantro, lime juice, and ¼ teaspoon salt into sauce and season with pepper to taste. Spoon sauce over chicken and serve.

Nutrition Info:
- 270 cal., 11g fat (2g sag. fat), 100mg chol, 410mg sod.,

9g carb (5g sugars, 2g fiber), 32g pro.

Braised Fennel With Orange-tarragon Dressing

Servings:4 | Cooking Time: 6 Hours

Ingredients:
- 2 garlic cloves, peeled and smashed
- 2 sprigs fresh thyme
- 1 teaspoon juniper berries
- 2 fennel bulbs, stalks discarded, bulbs halved, each half cut into 4 wedges
- 2 tablespoons extra-virgin olive oil
- 2 teaspoons grated orange zest plus 1 tablespoon juice
- 1 teaspoon minced fresh tarragon
- Salt and pepper

Directions:
1. Combine 1 cup water, garlic, thyme sprigs, and juniper berries in oval slow cooker. Place fennel wedges cut side down in cooker (wedges may overlap). Cover and cook until fennel is tender, 8 to 9 hours on low or 5 to 6 hours on high.
2. Whisk oil, orange zest and juice, tarragon, ¼ teaspoon salt, and ¼ teaspoon pepper together in bowl. Using slotted spoon, transfer fennel to serving dish, brushing away any garlic cloves, thyme sprigs, or juniper berries that stick to fennel. Drizzle fennel with dressing. Serve.

Nutrition Info:
- 100 cal., 7g fat (1g sag. fat), 0mg chol, 210mg sod., 9g carb (5g sugars, 4g fiber), 2g pro.

Pork Loin With Fennel, Oranges, And Olives

Servings:8 | Cooking Time: 2 Hours

Ingredients:
- 1 (2-pound) boneless center-cut pork loin roast, fat trimmed to ⅛ inch
- 1 teaspoon herbes de Provence
- Salt and pepper
- 1 tablespoon extra-virgin olive oil
- 3 fennel bulbs, stalks discarded, bulbs halved, cored, and sliced thin
- ½ cup dry white wine
- 2 garlic cloves, minced
- 4 oranges, plus 1 tablespoon grated orange zest
- ½ cup pitted kalamata olives, chopped
- 2 tablespoons minced fresh tarragon

Directions:
1. Pat roast dry with paper towels and sprinkle with herbes de Provence, ½ teaspoon salt, and ¼ teaspoon pepper. Heat oil in 12-inch skillet over medium-high heat until just smoking. Brown roast on all sides, 7 to 10 minutes; transfer to plate.
2. Add fennel and wine to now-empty skillet, cover, and cook, stirring occasionally, until fennel begins to soften, about 5 minutes. Uncover and continue to cook until fennel

is dry and lightly browned, about 5 minutes. Stir in garlic and cook until fragrant, about 30 seconds; transfer to oval slow cooker. Nestle roast fat side up into slow cooker. Cover and cook until pork registers 140 degrees, 1 to 2 hours on low.
3. Transfer roast to carving board, tent with aluminum foil, and let rest for 15 minutes. Meanwhile, cut away peel and pith from oranges. Quarter oranges, then slice crosswise into ½-inch-thick pieces. Stir orange segments, orange zest, olives, and ¼ teaspoon salt into fennel mixture and let sit until heated through, about 5 minutes. Stir in tarragon and season with pepper to taste. Slice pork ½ inch thick and serve with fennel-orange mixture.

Nutrition Info:
- 240 cal., 7g fat (1g sag. fat), 70mg chol, 350mg sod., 15g carb (10g sugars, 4g fiber), 27g pro.

Chicken With Warm Potato And Radish Salad

Servings:4 | Cooking Time:3 Hours

Ingredients:
- 1¾ pounds small Yukon Gold potatoes, unpeeled, quartered
- 2 (12-ounce) bone-in split chicken breasts, skin removed, trimmed of all visible fat, and halved crosswise
- 1 tablespoon minced fresh thyme or 1 teaspoon dried
- Salt and pepper
- 3 tablespoons extra-virgin olive oil
- 3 tablespoons minced fresh parsley
- 1 shallot, minced
- 1 tablespoon Dijon mustard
- 2 teaspoons grated lemon zest plus 2 tablespoons juice
- 5 radishes, trimmed and sliced thin

Directions:
1. Microwave potatoes and ¼ cup water in covered bowl, stirring occasionally, until almost tender, about 15 minutes; transfer to oval slow cooker. Sprinkle chicken with thyme, ¼ teaspoon salt, and ⅛ teaspoon pepper and nestle into slow cooker. Cover and cook until chicken registers 160 degrees, 2 to 3 hours on low.
2. Transfer chicken to serving platter. Whisk oil, parsley, shallot, 2 tablespoons water, mustard, lemon zest and juice, and ⅛ teaspoon salt together in large bowl. Measure out and reserve ¼ cup dressing. Drain potatoes and transfer to bowl with remaining dressing. Add radishes and toss to combine. Season with pepper to taste. Serve chicken with potato salad and reserved dressing.

Nutrition Info:
- 440 cal., 14g fat (2g sag. fat), 100mg chol, 320mg sod., 38g carb (1g sugars, 3g fiber), 36g pro.

Slow-cooked Chicken Chili

Servings:6 | Cooking Time: 4 Hours

Ingredients:
- 1 medium onion, chopped
- 1 each medium sweet yellow, red and green pepper, chopped
- 2 tablespoons olive oil
- 3 garlic cloves, minced
- 1 pound ground chicken
- 2 cans (14 1/2 ounces each) diced tomatoes, undrained
- 1 can (15 ounces) cannellini beans, rinsed and drained
- 1/4 cup lime juice
- 1 tablespoon all-purpose flour
- 1 tablespoon baking cocoa
- 1 tablespoon ground cumin
- 1 tablespoon chili powder
- 2 teaspoons ground coriander
- 1 teaspoon grated lime peel
- 1/2 teaspoon salt
- 1/2 teaspoon garlic pepper blend
- 1/4 teaspoon pepper
- 2 flour tortillas (8 inches), cut into 1/4-inch strips
- 6 tablespoons reduced-fat sour cream

Directions:
1. In a large skillet, saute onion and peppers in oil for 7-8 minutes or until crisp-tender. Add garlic; cook 1 minute longer. Add chicken; cook and stir over medium heat for 8-9 minutes or until meat is no longer pink.
2. Transfer to a 3-qt. slow cooker. Stir in the tomatoes, beans, lime juice, flour, cocoa, cumin, chili powder, coriander, lime peel, salt, garlic pepper and pepper.
3. Cover and cook on low for 4-5 hours or until heated through.
4. Place tortilla strips on a baking sheet coated with cooking spray. Bake at 400° for 8-10 minutes or until crisp. Serve chili with sour cream and tortilla strips.

Nutrition Info:
- 356 cal., 14g fat (3g sat. fat), 55mg chol., 644mg sod., 39g carb. (5g sugars, 8g fiber), 21g pro.

Beef And Garden Vegetable Soup

Servings:6 | Cooking Time: 5 Minutes

Ingredients:
- 2 onions, chopped fine
- 3 tablespoons no-salt-added tomato paste
- 4 garlic cloves, minced
- 1 tablespoon minced fresh thyme or 1 teaspoon dried
- ¼ ounce dried porcini mushrooms, rinsed and minced
- 1 tablespoon canola oil
- Salt and pepper
- 6 cups unsalted chicken broth
- 4 carrots, peeled and cut into ½-inch pieces
- 1 (14.5-ounce) can no-salt-added diced tomatoes
- 2 teaspoons low-sodium soy sauce
- 2 pounds beef blade steaks, ¾ to 1 inch thick, trimmed of all visible fat and gristle
- 8 ounces green beans, trimmed and cut on bias into 1-inch lengths
- ¼ cup chopped fresh basil

Directions:
1. Microwave onions, tomato paste, garlic, thyme, porcini, oil, and ½ teaspoon salt in bowl, stirring occasionally, until onions are softened, about 5 minutes; transfer to slow cooker. Stir in broth, carrots, tomatoes and their juice, and soy sauce. Nestle steaks into slow cooker. Cover and cook until beef is tender, 9 to 10 hours on low or 6 to 7 hours on high.
2. Transfer steaks to cutting board, let cool slightly, then shred into bite-size pieces using 2 forks; discard gristle.
3. Microwave green beans with 1 tablespoon water in covered bowl, stirring occasionally, until crisp-tender, 4 to 6 minutes. Drain green beans, then stir into soup along with beef; let sit until heated through, about 5 minutes. Stir in basil and season with pepper to taste. Serve.

Nutrition Info:
- 330 cal., 12g fat (4g sag. fat), 105mg chol, 560mg sod., 19g carb (10g sugars, 6g fiber), 38g pro.

Spiced Pork Tenderloin With Carrots And Radishes

Servings:4 | Cooking Time: 2 Hours

Ingredients:
- 1½ pounds carrots, peeled and sliced ¼ inch thick on bias
- 10 radishes, trimmed and sliced ¼ inch thick
- ¼ cup unsalted chicken broth
- 3 tablespoons extra-virgin olive oil
- 1 teaspoon ground cumin
- 1 teaspoon paprika
- 1 (1-pound) pork tenderloin, trimmed of all visible fat
- Salt and pepper
- 2 tablespoons lime juice
- 2 tablespoons minced fresh cilantro
- 1 teaspoon minced canned chipotle chile in adobo sauce

Directions:
1. Microwave carrots and ¼ cup water in covered bowl, stirring occasionally, until crisp-tender, about 8 minutes. Drain carrots and transfer to oval slow cooker. Stir in radishes and broth.
2. Microwave 1 teaspoon oil, cumin, and paprika in bowl until fragrant, about 30 seconds; let cool slightly. Rub tenderloin with spice mixture and sprinkle with ¼ teaspoon salt and ⅛ teaspoon pepper. Nestle tenderloin into slow cooker, cover, and cook until pork registers 145 degrees, 1 to 2 hours on low.
3. Transfer tenderloin to carving board, tent with aluminum foil, and let rest for 5 minutes.
4. Whisk remaining 8 teaspoons oil, lime juice, cilantro, and chipotle together in bowl, then season dressing with pepper to taste. Drain vegetables from cooker and transfer to large bowl. Stir in 2 tablespoons of dressing and season with pepper to taste. Slice tenderloin ½ inch thick and serve with vegetables and remaining dressing.

Nutrition Info:
• 300 cal., 14g fat (2g sag. fat), 75mg chol, 350mg sod., 20g carb (9g sugars, 6g fiber), 26g pro.

No-fuss Quinoa With Lemon

Servings:6 | Cooking Time:3hours

Ingredients:
• 1½ cups prewashed white quinoa, rinsed
• 1 onion, chopped fine
• 1 tablespoon extra-virgin olive oil
• 1¾ cups water
• 2 (2-inch) strips lemon zest plus 1 tablespoon juice
• Salt and pepper
• 2 tablespoons minced fresh parsley

Directions:
1. Lightly coat slow cooker with vegetable oil spray. Microwave quinoa, onion, and 1 teaspoon oil in bowl, stirring occasionally, until quinoa is lightly toasted and onion is softened, about 5 minutes; transfer to prepared slow cooker. Stir in water, lemon zest, and ½ teaspoon salt. Cover and cook until quinoa is tender and all water is absorbed, 3 to 4 hours on low or 2 to 3 hours on high.
2. Discard lemon zest. Fluff quinoa with fork, then gently fold in lemon juice, parsley, and remaining 2 teaspoons oil. Season with pepper to taste. Serve.

Nutrition Info:
• 190 cal., 5g fat (0g sag. fat), 0mg chol, 200mg sod., 30g carb (3g sugars, 4g fiber), 6g pro.

Mediterranean Pot Roast Dinner

Servings:8 | Cooking Time: 8 Hours

Ingredients:
• 2 pounds potatoes (about 6 medium), peeled and cut into 2-inch pieces
• 5 medium carrots (about 3/4 pound), cut into 1-inch pieces
• 2 tablespoons all-purpose flour
• 1 boneless beef chuck roast (3 to 4 pounds)
• 1 tablespoon olive oil
• 8 large fresh mushrooms, quartered
• 2 celery ribs, chopped
• 1 medium onion, thinly sliced
• 1/4 cup sliced Greek olives
• 1/2 cup minced fresh parsley, divided
• 1 can (14 1/2 ounces) fire-roasted diced tomatoes, undrained
• 1 tablespoon minced fresh oregano or 1 teaspoon dried oregano
• 1 tablespoon lemon juice
• 2 teaspoons minced fresh rosemary or 1/2 teaspoon dried rosemary, crushed
• 2 garlic cloves, minced
• 3/4 teaspoon salt
• 1/4 teaspoon pepper
• 1/4 teaspoon crushed red pepper flakes, optional

Directions:

1. Place potatoes and carrots in a 6-qt. slow cooker. Sprinkle the flour over all surfaces of roast. In a large skillet, heat oil over medium-high heat. Brown roast on all sides. Place over vegetables.
2. Add mushrooms, celery, onion, olives and 1/4 cup parsley to slow cooker. In a small bowl, mix the remaining ingredients; pour over top.
3. Cook, covered, on low for 8-10 hours or until meat and vegetables are tender. Remove beef. Stir remaining parsley into vegetables. Serve the beef with the vegetables.

Nutrition Info:
• 422 cal., 18g fat (6g sat. fat), 111mg chol., 538mg sod., 28g carb. (6g sugars, 4g fiber), 37g pro.

Spring Vegetable And Barley Soup

Servings:6 | Cooking Time: 5 Hours

Ingredients:
• 1 tablespoon extra-virgin olive oil
• 4 shallots, minced
• 4 garlic cloves, minced
• ¼ teaspoon red pepper flakes
• 8 cups unsalted chicken broth
• ¾ cup pearled barley
• 2 (2-inch) strips lemon zest
• Salt and pepper
• 8 ounces thin asparagus, trimmed and cut on bias into 1-inch lengths
• 1 yellow summer squash, quartered lengthwise and sliced ½ inch thick
• 2 ounces (2 cups) baby arugula
• ¼ cup grated Parmesan cheese

Directions:

1. Heat oil in 12-inch skillet over medium heat until shimmering. Add shallots and cook until softened and lightly browned, about 5 minutes. Stir in garlic and pepper flakes and cook until fragrant, about 30 seconds. Stir in 1 cup broth, scraping up any browned bits; transfer to slow cooker. Stir in remaining 7 cups broth, barley, lemon zest, and ½ teaspoon salt. Cover and cook until barley is tender, 4 to 6 hours on low or 3 to 5 hours on high.
2. Stir asparagus and squash into soup, cover, and cook on high until tender, 20 to 30 minutes. Stir in arugula and let sit until slightly wilted, about 3 minutes. Season with pepper to taste. Sprinkle individual portions with Parmesan before serving.

Nutrition Info:
• 190 cal., 4g fat (1g sag. fat), 5mg chol, 460mg sod., 28g carb (5g sugars, 7g fiber), 12g pro.

Shredded Beef Tacos With Cabbage-carrot Slaw

Servings:6 | Cooking Time:4 Hours

Ingredients:
- ½ onion, chopped fine
- 1 ounce (2 to 3) dried ancho chiles, stemmed, seeded, and torn into 1-inch pieces (½ cup)
- 3 garlic cloves, minced
- 1 tablespoon no-salt-added tomato paste
- 1 tablespoon canola oil
- 1 teaspoon minced canned chipotle chile in adobo sauce
- ½ teaspoon ground cinnamon
- ¾ cup water, plus extra as needed
- Salt
- 2 pounds boneless beef chuck-eye roast, trimmed of all visible fat and cut into 1½-inch pieces
- ½ head napa cabbage, cored and sliced thin (6 cups)
- 1 carrot, peeled and shredded
- 1 jalapeño chile, stemmed, seeded, and sliced thin
- ¼ cup lime juice (2 limes), plus lime wedges for serving
- ¼ cup chopped fresh cilantro
- 12 (6-inch) corn tortillas, warmed
- 1 ounce queso fresco, crumbled (¼ cup)

Directions:
1. Microwave onion, anchos, garlic, tomato paste, oil, chipotle, and cinnamon in bowl, stirring occasionally, until onion is softened, about 5 minutes; transfer to slow cooker. Stir in water and ½ teaspoon salt. Stir beef into slow cooker. Cover and cook until beef is tender, 7 to 8 hours on low or 4 to 5 hours on high.
2. Combine cabbage, carrot, jalapeño, lime juice, cilantro, and ¼ teaspoon salt in large bowl. Cover slaw and refrigerate until ready to serve.
3. Using slotted spoon, transfer beef to another large bowl. Using 2 forks, shred beef into bite-size pieces; cover to keep warm.
4. Process cooking liquid in blender until smooth, about 1 minute. Adjust sauce consistency with hot water as needed. Toss beef with 1 cup sauce. Toss slaw to recombine. Divide beef evenly among tortillas and top with slaw and queso fresco. Serve, passing lime wedges and remaining sauce separately.

Nutrition Info:
- 420 cal., 14g fat (3g sag. fat), 100mg chol, 500mg sod., 36g carb (6g sugars, 7g fiber), 39g pro.

Italian Meatball And Escarole Soup

Servings:6 | Cooking Time:5 Hours

Ingredients:
- 2 slices 100 percent whole-wheat sandwich bread, torn into quarters
- ¼ cup 1 percent low-fat milk
- 1 ounce Parmesan cheese, grated (½ cup)
- 3 tablespoons minced fresh parsley
- 1 large egg yolk
- 1½ teaspoons minced fresh oregano or ½ teaspoon dried
- 4 garlic cloves, minced
- Salt and pepper
- 1 pound ground turkey
- 2 teaspoons canola oil
- 1 onion, chopped fine
- ¼ teaspoon red pepper flakes
- 6 cups unsalted chicken broth
- 1 (15-ounce) can no-salt-added cannellini beans, rinsed
- 1 head escarole (1 pound), trimmed and sliced 1 inch thick
- 1 tablespoon lemon juice

Directions:
1. Mash bread, milk, Parmesan, parsley, egg yolk, oregano, half of garlic, and ½ teaspoon pepper into paste in large bowl using fork. Add ground turkey and hand-knead until well combined. Pinch off and roll turkey mixture into tablespoon-size meatballs (about 24 meatballs).
2. Heat 1 teaspoon oil in 12-inch nonstick skillet over medium heat until shimmering. Brown half of meatballs on all sides, about 5 minutes; transfer to slow cooker. Repeat with remaining 1 teaspoon oil and remaining meatballs; transfer to slow cooker.
3. Add onion and ½ teaspoon salt to fat left in skillet and cook over medium heat until onion is softened, about 5 minutes. Stir in pepper flakes and remaining garlic and cook until fragrant, about 30 seconds; transfer to slow cooker. Gently stir in broth and beans, cover, and cook until meatballs are tender, 4 to 6 hours on low or 3 to 5 hours on high.
4. Stir escarole into soup, 1 handful at a time, cover, and cook on high until tender, 15 to 20 minutes. Stir in lemon juice and season with pepper to taste. Serve.

Nutrition Info:
- 250 cal., 6g fat (2g sag. fat), 65mg chol, 540mg sod., 14g carb (5g sugars, 7g fiber), 30g pro.

Thai-style Pork

Servings:6 | Cooking Time: 6 1/4 Hours

Ingredients:
- 1/4 cup teriyaki sauce
- 2 tablespoons rice vinegar
- 1 teaspoon crushed red pepper flakes
- 1 teaspoon minced garlic
- 2 pounds boneless pork loin chops
- 1 tablespoon cornstarch
- 1/4 cup cold water
- 1/4 cup creamy peanut butter
- Hot cooked rice
- 1/2 cup chopped green onions
- 1/2 cup dry roasted peanuts
- Lime juice, optional

Directions:
1. Mix first four ingredients. Place pork chops in a 3-qt. slow cooker; top with sauce. Cook, covered, on low until meat is tender, 6-8 hours.
2. Remove pork and cut into bite-size pieces; keep warm.

Transfer cooking juices to a saucepan; bring to a boil. cornstarch and water until smooth; gradually stir into juices. Bring to a boil; cook and stir until thickened, 1-2 minutes. Stir in peanut butter. Add pork.

3. Serve with rice. Sprinkle with green onions and peanuts. If desired, drizzle with lime juice.

Nutrition Info:
• 2/3 cup: 357 cal., 20g fat (5g sat. fat), 73mg chol., 598mg sod., 9g carb. (3g sugars, 2g fiber), 35g pro.

Chicken Thighs With Black-eyed Pea Ragout

Servings:6 | Cooking Time:7minutes

Ingredients:
• 1 pound kale, stemmed and chopped coarse
• 1 onion, chopped fine
• 4 garlic cloves, minced
• 1 tablespoon extra-virgin olive oil
• 1 teaspoon dry mustard
• 2 teaspoons minced fresh thyme or ½ teaspoon dried
• 2 (15-ounce) cans no-salt-added black-eyed peas, rinsed
• ½ cup unsalted chicken broth
• Salt and pepper
• 6 (5-ounce) bone-in chicken thighs, skin removed, trimmed of all visible fat
• 2 teaspoons hot sauce, plus extra for serving
• Lemon wedges

Directions:
1. Lightly coat oval slow cooker with vegetable oil spray. Microwave kale, onion, garlic, oil, mustard, and thyme in covered bowl, stirring occasionally, until vegetables are softened, 5 to 7 minutes; transfer to prepared slow cooker.
2. Process one-third of peas, broth, and ¼ teaspoon salt in food processor until smooth, about 30 seconds; transfer to slow cooker. Stir in remaining peas. Sprinkle chicken with ¼ teaspoon salt and ¼ teaspoon pepper and nestle into slow cooker. Cover and cook until chicken is tender, 4 to 5 hours on low.
3. Transfer chicken to serving platter. Stir hot sauce into ragout and season with pepper to taste. Serve chicken with ragout and lemon wedges, passing extra hot sauce separately.

Nutrition Info:
• 240 cal., 8g fat (1g sag. fat), 80mg chol, 380mg sod., 20g carb (4g sugars, 6g fiber), 24g pro.

Slow Cooker Mushroom Chicken & Peas

Servings:4 | Cooking Time: 3 Hours 10 Minutes

Ingredients:
• 4 boneless skinless chicken breast halves (6 ounces each)
• 1 envelope onion mushroom soup mix
• 1 cup water
• 1/2 pound sliced baby portobello mushrooms
• 1 medium onion, chopped
• 4 garlic cloves, minced

• 2 cups frozen peas, thawed

Directions:
1. Place chicken in a 3-qt. slow cooker. Sprinkle with soup mix, pressing to help seasonings adhere to chicken. Add water, mushrooms, onion and garlic.
2. Cook, covered, on low 3-4 hours or until chicken is tender (a thermometer inserted in chicken should read at least 165°). Stir in peas; cook, covered, 10 minutes longer or until heated through.

Nutrition Info:
• 292 cal., 5g fat (1g sat. fat), 94mg chol., 566mg sod., 20g carb. (7g sugars, 5g fiber), 41g pro.

Teriyaki Beef Stew

Servings:8 | Cooking Time: 6 1/2 Hours

Ingredients:
• 2 pounds beef stew meat
• 1 bottle (12 ounces) ginger beer or ginger ale
• 1/4 cup teriyaki sauce
• 2 garlic cloves, minced
• 2 tablespoons sesame seeds
• 2 tablespoons cornstarch
• 2 tablespoons cold water
• 2 cups frozen peas, thawed
• Hot cooked rice, optional

Directions:
1. In a nonstick skillet, brown beef in batches. Transfer to a 3-qt. slow cooker.
2. In a small bowl, combine the ginger beer, teriyaki sauce, garlic and sesame seeds; pour over beef. Cover and cook on low for 6-8 hours or until the meat is tender.
3. Combine cornstarch and cold water until smooth; gradually stir into stew. Stir in peas. Cover and cook on high for 30 minutes or until thickened. Serve with rice if desired.

Nutrition Info:
• 310 cal., 12g fat (4g sat. fat), 94mg chol., 528mg sod., 17g carb. (9g sugars, 2g fiber), 33g pro.

POULTRY RECIPES

◇ Poultry Recipes ◇

Sausage-topped White Pizza
Servings:6 | Cooking Time: 30 Minutes

Ingredients:
- 2 hot Italian turkey sausage links, casings removed
- 1 cup reduced-fat ricotta cheese
- 1/4 teaspoon garlic powder
- 1 prebaked 12-inch thin whole wheat pizza crust
- 1 medium sweet red pepper, julienned
- 1 small onion, halved and thinly sliced
- 1/2 teaspoon Italian seasoning
- 1/4 teaspoon freshly ground pepper
- 1/4 teaspoon crushed red pepper flakes, optional
- 1/2 cup shredded part-skim mozzarella cheese
- 2 cups arugula or baby spinach

Directions:
1. Preheat oven to 450°. In a large skillet, cook and crumble sausage over medium-high heat until no longer pink, 4-6 minutes. Mix ricotta cheese and garlic powder.
2. Place crust on a baking sheet; spread with ricotta cheese mixture. Top with sausage, red pepper and onion; sprinkle with seasonings, then with the shredded mozzarella cheese.
3. Bake on a lower oven rack until edge is lightly browned and cheese is melted, 8-10 minutes. Top with arugula.

Nutrition Info:
- 242 cal., 8g fat (4g sat. fat), 30mg chol., 504mg sod., 28g carb. (5g sugars, 4g fiber), 16g pro.

Cumin-crusted Chicken Thighs With Cauliflower Couscous
Servings:4 | Cooking Time:25 Minutes

Ingredients:
- 8 (3-ounce) boneless, skinless chicken thighs, trimmed of all visible fat
- 2 teaspoons cumin seeds
- Salt and pepper
- 2 tablespoons canola oil
- 1 head cauliflower (2 pounds), cored and cut into ½-inch pieces
- 1 teaspoon paprika
- ½ cup pomegranate seeds
- ½ cup chopped fresh mint
- 1½ teaspoons grated lime zest, plus lime wedges for serving

Directions:
1. Pat chicken thighs dry with paper towels and sprinkle with 1 teaspoon cumin seeds, ¼ teaspoon salt, and ¼ teaspoon pepper. Heat 1 tablespoon oil in 12-inch nonstick skillet over medium-high heat until just smoking. Cook thighs, turning as needed, until well browned and register 175 degrees, about 8 minutes. Transfer chicken to plate, tent with aluminum foil, and let rest while preparing cauliflow-

er.
2. Working in 2 batches, pulse cauliflower in food processor to ¼- to ⅛-inch pieces, about 6 pulses. Heat remaining 1 tablespoon oil in now-empty skillet over medium-high heat until shimmering. Add cauliflower, paprika, ⅛ teaspoon salt, ¼ teaspoon pepper, and remaining 1 teaspoon cumin seeds and cook, stirring occasionally, until just tender, about 7 minutes. Off heat, stir in pomegranate seeds, chopped mint, and lime zest. Serve chicken with couscous and lime wedges.

Nutrition Info:
- 320 cal., 15g fat (2g sag. fat), 160mg chol, 410mg sod., 10g carb (5g sugars, 4g fiber), 36g pro.

Turkey Pinto Bean Salad With Southern Molasses Dressing
Servings:6 | Cooking Time: 35 Minutes

Ingredients:
- 1/2 cup oil-packed sun-dried tomatoes
- 1 garlic clove, peeled and halved
- 1/2 cup molasses
- 3 tablespoons cider vinegar
- 1 teaspoon prepared mustard
- 1/2 teaspoon salt
- 1/4 teaspoon coarsely ground pepper
- 3 cups cubed cooked turkey breast
- 2 cans (15 ounces each) pinto beans, rinsed and drained
- 1 medium green pepper, diced
- 2 celery ribs, diced
- 1 cup chopped sweet onion
- 1/4 cup minced fresh parsley

Directions:
1. Drain the tomatoes, reserving 2 tablespoons oil. Place the garlic and tomatoes in a food processor; cover and process until chopped. Add the molasses, vinegar, mustard, salt, pepper and reserved oil. Cover and process until smooth.
2. In a large bowl, combine the turkey, beans, green pepper, celery, onion and parsley. Add dressing and toss to coat. Cover mixture and refrigerate for at least 2 hours.

Nutrition Info:
- 379 cal., 7g fat (1g sat. fat), 60mg chol., 483mg sod., 49g carb. (19g sugars, 7g fiber), 29g pro.

Bacon & Swiss Chicken Sandwiches
Servings:4 | Cooking Time: 25 Minutes

Ingredients:
- 1/4 cup reduced-fat mayonnaise
- 1 tablespoon Dijon mustard
- 1 tablespoon honey
- 4 boneless skinless chicken breast halves (4 ounces each)

- 1/2 teaspoon Montreal steak seasoning
- 4 slices Swiss cheese
- 4 whole wheat hamburger buns, split
- 2 bacon strips, cooked and crumbled
- Lettuce leaves and tomato slices, optional

Directions:
1. In a small bowl, mix mayonnaise, mustard and honey. Pound chicken with a meat mallet to 1/2-in. thickness. Sprinkle chicken with steak seasoning. Grill chicken, covered, over medium heat or broil 4 in. from heat 4-6 minutes on each side or until a thermometer reads 165°. Top with cheese during the last 1 minute of cooking.
2. Grill buns over medium heat, cut side down, for 30-60 seconds or until toasted. Serve chicken on buns with bacon, mayonnaise mixture and, if desired, lettuce and tomato.

Nutrition Info:
- 410 cal., 17g fat (6g sat. fat), 91mg chol., 667mg sod., 29g carb. (9g sugars, 3g fiber), 34g pro.

Apple-glazed Chicken Thighs
Servings:6 | Cooking Time: 25 Minutes

Ingredients:
- 6 boneless skinless chicken thighs (1 1/2 pounds)
- 3/4 teaspoon seasoned salt
- 1/4 teaspoon pepper
- 1 tablespoon canola oil
- 1 cup unsweetened apple juice
- 1 teaspoon minced fresh thyme or 1/4 teaspoon dried thyme

Directions:
1. Sprinkle chicken with seasoned salt and pepper. In a large skillet, heat oil over medium-high heat. Brown chicken on both sides. Remove from pan.
2. Add juice and thyme to skillet. Bring to a boil, stirring to loosen browned bits from pan; cook until liquid is reduced by half. Return chicken to the pan; cook, covered, over medium heat 3-4 minutes longer or until a thermometer inserted in chicken reads 170°.

Nutrition Info:
- 204 cal., 11g fat (2g sat. fat), 76mg chol., 255mg sod., 5g carb. (4g sugars, 0 fiber), 21g pro.

Strawberry Minutest Chicken
Servings:4 | Cooking Time: 30 Minutes

Ingredients:
- 1 tablespoon cornstarch
- 1 tablespoon sugar
- 1/8 teaspoon ground nutmeg
- 1/8 teaspoon pepper
- 1/2 cup water
- 1 cup fresh strawberries, chopped
- 1/2 cup white wine or grape juice
- 2 teaspoons minced fresh mint
- CHICKEN
- 4 boneless skinless chicken breast halves (6 ounces each)

- 1/2 teaspoon salt
- 1/4 teaspoon pepper
- Sliced green onion

Directions:
1. In a saucepan, mix the first five ingredients until smooth; stir in the strawberries and wine. Bring to a boil. Reduce heat; simmer, uncovered, 3-5 minutes or until thickened, stirring occasionally. Remove from heat; stir in the mint.
2. Sprinkle the chicken with salt and pepper. On a lightly greased grill rack, grill chicken, covered, over medium heat 5-7 minutes on each side or until a thermometer reads 165°; brush occasionally with 1/4 cup sauce during the last 4 minutes. Serve with remaining sauce. Sprinkle with green onion.

Nutrition Info:
- 224 cal., 4g fat (1g sat. fat), 94mg chol., 378mg sod., 8g carb. (5g sugars, 1g fiber), 35g pro.

Spring Chicken & Pea Salad
Servings:4 | Cooking Time: 20 Minutes

Ingredients:
- 1 cup fresh peas
- 2 cups torn curly or Belgian endive
- 2 cups torn radicchio
- 2 cups chopped rotisserie chicken
- 1/2 cup sliced radishes
- 2 tablespoons chopped red onion
- 2 tablespoons fresh mint leaves, torn
- DRESSING
- 2 tablespoons olive oil
- 1/4 teaspoon grated lemon peel
- 1 tablespoon lemon juice
- 1 tablespoon mint jelly
- 1 garlic clove, minced
- 1/4 teaspoon salt
- 1/4 teaspoon pepper
- Toasted pine nuts, optional

Directions:
1. In a large saucepan, bring 1/2 in. of water to a boil. Add peas; cover and cook 5-8 minutes or until tender.
2. Drain the peas and place in a large bowl. Add endive, radicchio, chicken, radishes, onion and mint. In a small saucepan, combine oil, lemon peel, juice, jelly, garlic, salt and pepper; cook and stir over medium-low heat 4-6 minutes or until jelly is melted. Drizzle over the salad; toss to coat. If desired, sprinkle with pine nuts.

Nutrition Info:
- 250 cal., 12g fat (2g sat. fat), 62mg chol., 225mg sod., 12g carb. (6g sugars, 3g fiber), 23g pro.

Chicken Baked In Foil With Tomatoes And Zucchini

Servings:4 | Cooking Time:30 Minutes

Ingredients:
- 2 zucchini, sliced ¼ inch thick
- Salt and pepper
- 2 tablespoons extra-virgin olive oil
- 2 garlic cloves, minced
- 1 teaspoon minced fresh oregano or ¼ teaspoon dried
- ⅛ teaspoon red pepper flakes
- 3 plum tomatoes, cored, seeded, and cut into ½-inch pieces
- 4 (6-ounce) boneless, skinless chicken breasts, trimmed of all visible fat
- ¼ cup chopped fresh basil
- Lemon wedges

Directions:
1. Toss zucchini with ¼ teaspoon salt in colander and let drain for 30 minutes. Spread zucchini out on several layers of paper towels and pat dry; transfer to bowl. Adjust oven rack to middle position and heat oven to 450 degrees. Cut eight 12-inch square sheets of aluminum foil.
2. Combine oil, garlic, oregano, pepper flakes, and ⅛ teaspoon pepper in medium bowl. Toss zucchini with half of oil mixture in separate bowl. Add tomatoes to remaining oil mixture and toss to coat. Pound chicken breasts to uniform thickness as needed. Pat breasts dry with paper towels and sprinkle with ¼ teaspoon salt and ⅛ teaspoon pepper.
3. Arrange zucchini evenly in center of four pieces of foil. Lay breasts over zucchini then spoon tomato mixture over top.
4. Place remaining pieces of foil on top and fold edges over several times to seal. Place packets on rimmed baking sheet and bake until chicken registers 160 degrees, about 25 minutes. (To test doneness of chicken, you will need to open one packet.)
5. Carefully open packets, allowing steam to escape away from you, and let cool briefly. Smooth out edges of foil and, using spatula, gently slide chicken, vegetables, and any accumulated juices onto individual plates. Sprinkle with basil and serve with lemon wedges.

Nutrition Info:
- 300 cal., 12g fat (2g sag. fat), 125mg chol, 310mg sod., 6g carb (3g sugars, 2g fiber), 40g pro.

Chicken Cucumber Boats

Servings:2 | Cooking Time: 15 Minutes

Ingredients:
- 2 medium cucumbers
- 1/2 cup fat-free plain Greek yogurt
- 2 tablespoons mayonnaise
- 1/2 teaspoon garlic salt
- 3 teaspoons snipped fresh dill, divided
- 1 cup chopped cooked chicken breast
- 1 cup chopped seeded tomato (about 1 large), divided
- 1/2 cup fresh or frozen peas, thawed

Directions:
1. Cut each cucumber lengthwise in half; scoop out pulp, leaving a 1/4-in. shell. In a bowl, mix yogurt, mayonnaise, garlic salt and 1 teaspoon dill; gently stir in chicken, 3/4 cup tomato and peas.
2. Spoon into cucumber shells. Top with the remaining tomato and dill.

Nutrition Info:
- 322 cal., 13g fat (2g sat. fat), 59mg chol.,398mg sod., 18g carb. (10g sugars, 6g fiber), 34g pro.

Poached Chicken Breasts With Warm Tomato-ginger Vinaigrette

Servings:4 | Cooking Time:22 Minutes.

Ingredients:
- CHICKEN
- 4 (6-ounce) boneless, skinless chicken breasts, trimmed of all visible fat
- ½ cup low-sodium soy sauce
- 6 garlic cloves, smashed and peeled
- VINAIGRETTE
- 2 tablespoons extra-virgin olive oil
- 1 small shallot, minced
- 1 teaspoon grated fresh ginger
- Pinch ground cumin
- Pinch ground fennel
- 6 ounces cherry tomatoes, halved
- Salt and pepper
- 1 tablespoon chopped fresh cilantro
- 1½ teaspoons red wine vinegar

Directions:
1. FOR THE CHICKEN Pound chicken breasts to uniform thickness as needed. Whisk 4 quarts water, soy sauce, and garlic together in Dutch oven. Arrange breasts, skinned side up, in steamer basket, making sure not to overlap them. Submerge steamer basket in water.
2. Heat pot over medium heat, stirring liquid occasionally to even out hot spots, until water registers 175 degrees, 15 to 20 minutes. Turn off heat, cover pot, remove from burner, and let sit until chicken registers 160 degrees, 17 to 22 minutes. Transfer breasts to plate, tent with aluminum foil, and let rest while preparing vinaigrette.
3. FOR THE VINAIGRETTE Heat 1 tablespoon oil in 10-inch nonstick skillet over medium heat until shimmering. Add shallot, ginger, cumin, and fennel and cook until fragrant, about 15 seconds. Stir in tomatoes and ⅛ teaspoon salt and cook, stirring frequently, until tomatoes have softened, 3 to 5 minutes. Off heat, stir in cilantro, vinegar, and remaining 1 tablespoon oil. Season with pepper to taste. Spoon vinaigrette evenly over each breast before serving.

Nutrition Info:
- 280 cal., 12g fat (2g sag. fat), 125mg chol, 240mg sod., 3g carb (2g sugars, 1g fiber), 39g pro.

In-a-pinch Chicken & Spinach

Servings:4 | Cooking Time: 25 Minutes

Ingredients:
- 4 boneless skinless chicken breast halves (6 ounces each)
- 2 tablespoons olive oil
- 1 tablespoon butter
- 1 package (6 ounces) fresh baby spinach
- 1 cup salsa

Directions:
1. Pound chicken with a meat mallet to 1/2-in. thickness. In a large skillet, heat oil and butter over medium heat. Cook the chicken for 5-6 minutes on each side or until no longer pink. Remove chicken and keep warm.
2. Add spinach and salsa to pan; cook and stir 3-4 minutes or just until spinach is wilted. Serve with chicken.

Nutrition Info:
- 297 cal., 14g fat (4g sat. fat), 102mg chol., 376mg sod., 6g carb. (2g sugars, 1g fiber), 36g pro.

Chicken With Fire-roasted Tomatoes

Servings:4 | Cooking Time: 30 Minutes

Ingredients:
- 2 tablespoons salt-free garlic herb seasoning blend
- 1/2 teaspoon salt
- 1/4 teaspoon Italian seasoning
- 1/4 teaspoon pepper
- 1/8 teaspoon crushed red pepper flakes, optional
- 4 boneless skinless chicken breast halves (6 ounces each)
- 1 tablespoon olive oil
- 1 can (14 1/2 ounces) fire-roasted diced tomatoes, undrained
- 3/4 pound fresh green beans, trimmed
- 2 tablespoons water
- 1 tablespoon butter
- Hot cooked pasta, optional

Directions:
1. Mix the first five ingredients; sprinkle over both sides of chicken breasts. In a large skillet, heat oil over medium heat. Brown the chicken on both sides. Add tomatoes; bring to a boil. Reduce heat; simmer, covered, 10-12 minutes or until a thermometer inserted in chicken reads 165°.
2. Meanwhile, in a 2-qt. microwave-safe dish, combine green beans and water; microwave, covered, on high for 3-4 minutes or just until tender. Drain.
3. Remove chicken from skillet; keep warm. Stir the butter and beans into tomato mixture. Serve with chicken and, if desired, pasta.

Nutrition Info:
- 294 cal., 10g fat (3g sat. fat), 102mg chol., 681mg sod., 12g carb. (5g sugars, 4g fiber), 37g pro.

Feta Chicken Burgers

Servings:6 | Cooking Time: 30 Minutes

Ingredients:
- 1/4 cup finely chopped cucumber
- 1/4 cup reduced-fat mayonnaise
- BURGERS
- 1/2 cup chopped roasted sweet red pepper
- 1 teaspoon garlic powder
- 1/2 teaspoon Greek seasoning
- 1/4 teaspoon pepper
- 1 1/2 pounds lean ground chicken
- 1 cup crumbled feta cheese
- 6 whole wheat hamburger buns, split and toasted
- Lettuce leaves and tomato slices, optional

Directions:
1. Preheat broiler. Mix cucumber and mayonnaise. For burgers, mix red pepper and seasonings. Add chicken and cheese; mix lightly but thoroughly (mixture will be sticky). Shape into six 1/2-in.-thick patties.
2. Broil burgers 4 in. from heat until a thermometer reads 165°, 3-4 minutes per side. Serve in buns with cucumber sauce. If desired, top with the lettuce and tomato.

Nutrition Info:
- 356 cal., 14g fat (5g sat. fat), 95mg chol., 703mg sod., 25g carb. (5g sugars, 4g fiber), 31g pro.

Turkey & Fruit Salad

Servings:5 | Cooking Time: 25 Minutes

Ingredients:
- 1/4 cup fat-free plain yogurt
- 1/4 cup reduced-fat mayonnaise
- 1 tablespoon honey
- 1 tablespoon spicy brown mustard
- 1/2 teaspoon dried marjoram
- 1/8 teaspoon ground ginger
- 3 cups cubed cooked turkey breast
- 1 large red apple, finely chopped
- 2 celery ribs, thinly sliced
- 1/2 cup dried cranberries
- 1/4 cup chopped walnuts, toasted

Directions:
1. Mix first six ingredients. In a large bowl, combine remaining ingredients. Stir in yogurt mixture. Refrigerate, covered, until serving.

Nutrition Info:
- 278 cal., 9g fat (1g sat. fat), 77mg chol., 208mg sod., 23g carb. (17g sugars, 2g fiber), 28g pro.

Seared Chicken With Spicy Chipotle Cream Sauce

Servings: 4 | Cooking Time:14 Minutes

Ingredients:
- 4 (4-ounce) boneless, skinless chicken breasts, rinsed and patted dry
- 1/2 teaspoon salt (divided use)
- 1/3 cup water
- 6 tablespoons fat-free sour cream
- 2 tablespoons reduced-fat mayonnaise
- 1/4–1/2 medium chipotle chili pepper in adobo sauce,

mashed with a fork and then finely chopped (3/4 teaspoon to 1 1/2 teaspoons total)

Directions:

1. Season the chicken with 1/4 teaspoon salt. Place a large nonstick skillet over medium-high heat until hot. Coat the skillet with nonstick cooking spray, add the chicken (smooth side down), and cook 3 minutes or until beginning to richly brown.

2. Turn the chicken and pour the water around the chicken pieces. Reduce the heat to medium, cover tightly, and cook 10 minutes or until the chicken is no longer pink in the center.

3. Meanwhile, stir the sour cream, mayonnaise, chipotle pepper, and 1/4 teaspoon salt together in a small bowl.

4. Remove the skillet from the heat and place the chicken on a serving platter. Cover the chicken with foil to keep warm.

5. Reduce the heat to medium low and return the skillet to the stove. Add the sour cream mixture and stir until well blended. Cook 1 minute or until thoroughly heated, stirring constantly. Be careful not to bring the sauce to a boil, or it will separate. Spoon about 2 tablespoons of sauce over each chicken breast to serve.

Nutrition Info:

- 170 cal., 4g fat (1g sag. fat), 70mg chol, 440mg sod., 5g carb (1g sugars, 0g fiber), 25g pro.

Lime Chicken With Salsa Verde Sour Cream

Servings:4 | Cooking Time: 20 Minutes

Ingredients:

- 3/4 teaspoon ground coriander
- 1/4 teaspoon salt
- 1/4 teaspoon ground cumin
- 1/4 teaspoon pepper
- 4 boneless skinless chicken thighs (about 1 pound)
- 1/3 cup reduced-fat sour cream
- 2 tablespoons salsa verde
- 2 tablespoons minced fresh cilantro, divided
- 1 medium lime

Directions:

1. Preheat broiler. Mix the seasonings; sprinkle over the chicken. Place chicken on a broiler pan. Broil 4 in. from the heat 6-8 minutes on each side or until a thermometer reads 170°.

2. Meanwhile, in a small bowl, mix sour cream, salsa and 1 tablespoon cilantro. Cut lime in half. Squeeze juice from one lime half into sour cream mixture; stir to combine. Cut remaining lime half into four wedges. Serve chicken with sauce and lime wedges. Sprinkle servings with remaining cilantro.

Nutrition Info:

- 199 cal., 10g fat (3g sat. fat), 82mg chol, 267mg sod., 4g carb. (2g sugars, 1g fiber), 23g pro.

Turkey Lo Mein

Servings:8 | Cooking Time: 30 Minutes

Ingredients:

- 8 ounces uncooked linguine
- 2 pounds turkey breast tenderloins, cut into 1/4-inch strips
- 2 tablespoons canola oil, divided
- 1 2/3 cups julienned sweet red, yellow and/or green peppers
- 1/3 cup chopped onion
- 1/2 pound sliced fresh mushrooms
- 2/3 cup stir-fry sauce

Directions:

1. Cook linguine according to package directions. Meanwhile, in a large skillet or wok, stir-fry the turkey in batches in 1 tablespoon hot oil for 5-6 minutes or until no longer pink. Remove turkey and keep warm.

2. In the same pan, stir-fry the peppers and onion in the remaining oil for 4-5 minutes or until crisp-tender. Add the mushrooms; stir-fry for 3-4 minutes or until vegetables are tender. Add turkey and stir-fry sauce; cook and stir for 2-3 minutes or until heated through. Drain linguine; add to turkey mixture and toss to coat.

Nutrition Info:

- 287 cal., 6g fat (1g sat. fat), 56mg chol., 771mg sod., 28g carb. (4g sugars, 2g fiber), 33g pro.

Turkey Burgers

Servings:4 | Cooking Time:22 Minutes.

Ingredients:

- ½ cup red wine vinegar
- ½ teaspoon red pepper flakes
- 1 small red onion, halved and sliced thin
- 1 pound ground turkey
- 3 ounces (⅓ cup) whole-milk ricotta cheese
- ¼ cup minced fresh cilantro, plus ¼ cup leaves
- 2 teaspoons Worcestershire sauce
- 2 teaspoons Dijon mustard
- ¼ teaspoon salt
- ¼ teaspoon pepper
- 1 tablespoon canola oil
- 4 100 percent whole-wheat hamburger buns, lightly toasted (optional)
- 1 avocado, halved, pitted, and sliced ¼ inch thick
- 1 head Bibb lettuce (8 ounces), leaves separated
- 1 tomato, cored and sliced ¼ inch thick

Directions:

1. Microwave vinegar and pepper flakes in medium bowl until steaming, about 2 minutes. Stir in onion and let sit until ready to serve.

2. Break turkey into small pieces in large bowl, then add ricotta, minced cilantro, Worcestershire, mustard, salt, and pepper. Using your hands, lightly knead mixture until combined. Pat turkey mixture into four ¾-inch-thick patties, about 4 inches in diameter.

3. Heat oil in 12-inch nonstick skillet over medium heat until shimmering. Gently place patties in skillet, reshaping them as needed, and cook until browned and register 160 degrees, 5 to 7 minutes per side. Serve burgers on buns, if using, and top with avocado, lettuce, tomato, cilantro leaves, and onions.

Nutrition Info:
- 420 cal., 17g fat (5g sag. fat), 55mg chol, 530mg sod., 31g carb (5g sugars, 8g fiber), 33g pro.

Sausage & Pepper Pizza

Servings:6 | Cooking Time: 20 Minutes

Ingredients:
- 1 package (6 1/2 ounces) pizza crust mix
- 1 can (8 ounces) pizza sauce
- 1 1/4 cups (5 ounces) shredded pizza cheese blend
- 1 medium onion, sliced
- 1 medium green pepper, sliced
- 2 fully cooked Italian chicken sausage links, sliced
- Grated Parmesan cheese, optional

Directions:
1. Preheat oven to 425°. Prepare pizza dough according to package directions. Press dough onto bottom and 1/2 in. up sides of a greased 13x9-in. baking pan.
2. Spread with pizza sauce. Top with 1 cup cheese blend, onion, pepper and sausage; sprinkle with remaining cheese blend.
3. Bake 17-20 minutes or until crust is golden brown. If desired, sprinkle with Parmesan cheese.

Nutrition Info:
- 257 cal., 9g fat (5g sat. fat), 39mg chol., 565mg sod., 28g carb. (3g sugars, 2g fiber), 15g pro.

Almond-crusted Chicken Breasts

Servings:4 | Cooking Time:18 Minutes

Ingredients:
- ½ cup slivered almonds
- 2 tablespoons canola oil
- 1 large shallot, minced
- ¼ teaspoon salt
- 1 garlic clove, minced
- 1 teaspoon minced fresh thyme or ¼ teaspoon dried
- ½ cup 100 percent whole-wheat panko bread crumbs
- ¼ teaspoon pepper
- 2 tablespoons minced fresh parsley
- 1 tablespoon plain low-fat yogurt
- 1 large egg yolk
- ½ teaspoon grated lemon zest, plus lemon wedges for serving
- 4 (6-ounce) boneless, skinless chicken breasts, trimmed of all visible fat

Directions:
1. Adjust oven rack to middle position and heat oven to 300 degrees. Set wire rack in rimmed baking sheet and lightly spray with canola oil spray. Process almonds in food processor until finely chopped, 20 to 30 seconds.
2. Heat oil in 12-inch nonstick skillet over medium heat until shimmering. Add shallot and salt and cook until softened, 1 to 2 minutes. Stir in garlic and thyme and cook until fragrant, about 30 seconds. Reduce heat to medium-low, add almonds, panko, and pepper and cook, stirring frequently, until well browned and crisp, about 8 minutes. Transfer almond mixture to shallow dish and let cool for 10 minutes. Stir in parsley.
3. Whisk yogurt, egg yolk, and lemon zest together in second shallow dish. Pound chicken breasts to uniform thickness as needed. Pat chicken breasts dry with paper towels and brush skinned side of breasts evenly with yogurt mixture. Working with 1 breast at a time, dredge coated side in nut mixture, pressing gently to adhere.
4. Transfer breasts crumb side up to prepared sheet and bake until chicken registers 160 degrees, 20 to 25 minutes, rotating sheet halfway through baking. Serve with lemon wedges.

Nutrition Info:
- 390 cal., 19g fat (2g sag. fat), 170mg chol, 240mg sod., 12g carb (2g sugars, 3g fiber), 43g pro.

Italian Spaghetti With Chicken & Roasted Vegetables

Servings:6 | Cooking Time: 25 Minutes

Ingredients:
- 3 plum tomatoes, seeded and chopped
- 2 medium zucchini, cubed
- 1 medium yellow summer squash, cubed
- 2 tablespoons olive oil, divided
- 2 teaspoons Italian seasoning, divided
- 8 ounces uncooked whole wheat spaghetti
- 1 pound boneless skinless chicken breasts, cubed
- 1/2 teaspoon garlic powder
- 1/2 cup reduced-sodium chicken broth
- 1/3 cup dry red wine or additional reduced-sodium chicken broth
- 4 cans (8 ounces each) no-salt-added tomato sauce
- 1 can (6 ounces) tomato paste
- 1/4 cup minced fresh basil
- 2 tablespoons minced fresh oregano
- 1/4 teaspoon salt
- 6 tablespoons shredded Parmesan cheese

Directions:
1. Preheat oven to 425°. In a large bowl, combine tomatoes, zucchini and squash. Add 1 tablespoon oil and 1 teaspoon Italian seasoning. Transfer to a 15x10x1-in. baking pan coated with cooking spray. Bake 15-20 minutes or until tender.
2. Meanwhile, cook the spaghetti according to package directions. Sprinkle chicken with garlic powder and remaining Italian seasoning. In a large nonstick skillet, heat remaining oil over medium heat. Add chicken; cook until no longer pink. Remove from skillet.
3. Add broth and wine to skillet, stirring to loosen browned

bits from pan. Stir in the tomato sauce, tomato paste, basil, oregano and salt. Bring to a boil. Return chicken to skillet. Reduce heat; simmer, covered, 4-6 minutes or until sauce is slightly thickened.

4. Drain spaghetti. Add spaghetti and vegetables to the tomato mixture; heat through. Sprinkle with cheese.

Nutrition Info:
• 379 cal., 9g fat (2g sat. fat), 45mg chol., 345mg sod., 49g carb. (14g sugars, 8g fiber), 26g pro.

Wild Rice Salad

Servings:4 | Cooking Time: 1 1/4 Hours

Ingredients:
• 3 cups water
• 1 cup uncooked wild rice
• 2 chicken bouillon cubes
• 4 1/2 teaspoons butter
• 1 cup cut fresh green beans
• 1 cup cubed cooked chicken breast
• 1 medium tomato, chopped
• 1 bunch green onions, sliced
• 1/4 cup rice vinegar
• 1 tablespoon sesame oil
• 1 garlic clove, minced
• 1/2 teaspoon dried tarragon
• 1/4 teaspoon pepper

Directions:
1. In a large saucepan, bring water, rice, bouillon and butter to a boil. Reduce heat; cover and simmer for 45-60 minutes or until rice is tender. Drain if necessary; transfer to a large bowl and cool completely.

2. Place the green beans in a steamer basket; place in a small saucepan over 1 in. of water. Bring to a boil; cover and steam for 8-10 minutes or until beans are crisp-tender.

3. Add chicken, tomato, onions and green beans to the rice; stir until blended. Combine the remaining ingredients; drizzle over mixture and toss to coat. Refrigerate until chilled.

Nutrition Info:
• 330 cal., 10g fat (4g sat. fat), 39mg chol., 618mg sod., 43g carb. (3g sugars, 4g fiber), 18g pro.

Cool & Crunchy Chicken Salad

Servings:6 | Cooking Time: 25 Minutes

Ingredients:
• 1/2 cup reduced-fat mayonnaise
• 2 tablespoons minced fresh parsley
• 1 tablespoon lemon juice
• 1 tablespoon cider vinegar
• 1 teaspoon spicy brown mustard
• 1/2 teaspoon sugar
• 1/4 teaspoon salt
• 1/4 teaspoon pepper
• 3 cups cubed cooked chicken
• 1 cup seedless red grapes, halved
• 1 cup thinly sliced celery
• 1 cup pecan halves, toasted

• Lettuce leaves

Directions:
1. In a large bowl, mix the first eight ingredients until blended. Add chicken, grapes, celery and pecans; toss to coat. Serve on lettuce.

Nutrition Info:
• 340 cal., 24g fat (3g sat. fat), 69mg chol., 311mg sod., 10g carb. (7g sugars, 2g fiber), 22g pro.

Easy Roast Turkey Breast

Servings:12 | Cooking Time:30 Minutes

Ingredients:
• 1 (5-pound) bone-in turkey breast
• ¼ cup salt
• 1 teaspoon pepper

Directions:
1. To remove backbone, use kitchen shears to cut through ribs following vertical line of fat where breast meets back, from tapered end of breast to wing joint. Using your hands, bend back away from breast to pop shoulder joint out of socket. With paring knife, cut through joint between bones to separate back from breast; discard backbone. Trim excess fat from breast. Dissolve salt in 4 quarts cold water in large container. Submerge turkey breast in brine, cover, and refrigerate for at least 3 hours or up to 6 hours.

2. Adjust oven rack to middle position and heat oven to 425 degrees. Set V-rack inside roasting pan and spray with vegetable oil spray. Remove turkey from brine, pat dry with paper towels, and sprinkle with pepper. Place turkey, skin side up, on prepared V-rack and add 1 cup water to pan. Roast turkey for 30 minutes.

3. Reduce oven temperature to 325 degrees and continue to roast until turkey registers 160 degrees, about 1 hour. Transfer turkey to carving board and let rest for 20 minutes. Carve turkey, discard skin, and serve.

Nutrition Info:
• 170 cal., 2g fat (0g sag. fat), 85mg chol, 310mg sod., 0g carb (0g sugars, 0g fiber), 35g pro.

SOUPS, STEWS, AND CHILIS RECIPES

◇ Soups, Stews, And Chilis Recipes ◇

Creamy Butternut Soup

Servings:10 | Cooking Time: 20 Minutes

Ingredients:
- 1 medium butternut squash, peeled, seeded and cubed (about 6 cups)
- 3 medium potatoes (about 1 pound), peeled and cubed
- 1 large onion, diced
- 2 chicken bouillon cubes
- 2 garlic cloves, minced
- 5 cups water
- Sour cream and minced fresh chives, optional

Directions:
1. In a 6-qt. stockpot, combine first six ingredients; bring to a boil. Reduce heat; simmer, covered, until vegetables are tender, 15-20 minutes.
2. Puree soup using an immersion blender. Or, cool slightly and puree soup in batches in a blender; return to pan and heat through. If desired, serve with sour cream and chives.

Nutrition Info:
- 112 cal., 0 fat (0 sat. fat), 0 chol., 231mg sod., 27g carb. (5g sugars, 4g fiber), 3g pro.

Creamy Carrot-ginger Soup

Servings:4 | Cooking Time:16 Minutes

Ingredients:
- 2 tablespoons canola oil
- 1½ pounds carrots, peeled and chopped
- 1 onion, chopped fine
- Salt and pepper
- 1½ tablespoons grated fresh ginger
- 3 cups unsalted chicken broth
- ½ cup 1 percent low-fat milk
- 2 tablespoons orange juice
- 1 tablespoon minced fresh chives

Directions:
1. Heat oil in Dutch oven over medium heat until shimmering. Add carrots, onion, and ⅛ teaspoon salt and cook until softened, 8 to 10 minutes.
2. Stir in ginger and cook until fragrant, about 30 seconds. Stir in broth and bring to simmer. Reduce heat to medium-low, cover, and cook until carrots are very tender, about 16 minutes.
3. Working in batches, process soup in blender until smooth, about 1 minute. Return soup to clean pot, stir in milk and orange juice, and bring to brief simmer over medium-low heat. Season with pepper to taste. Sprinkle individual portions with chives before serving.

Nutrition Info:
- 170 cal., 8g fat (1g sag. fat), 0mg chol, 280mg sod., 20g carb (11g sugars, 5g fiber), 6g pro.

Sweet Corn And Peppers Soup

Servings: 5 | Cooking Time:20 Minutes

Ingredients:
- 1 cup water
- 1 pound frozen pepper and onion stir-fry
- 10 ounces frozen corn kernels, thawed
- 1 1/4 cups fat-free milk
- 2 ounces reduced-fat processed cheese (such as Velveeta), cut in small cubes
- 1/8 teaspoon black pepper

Directions:
1. In a large saucepan, bring the water to boil over high heat. Add the peppers and return to a boil. Reduce the heat, cover tightly, and simmer 15 minutes or until onions are tender.
2. Add the corn and milk. Increase the heat to high, bring just to a boil, and remove from the heat.
3. Add the remaining ingredients and 1/2 teaspoon salt, if desired, cover, and let stand 5 minutes to melt the cheese and develop flavors.

Nutrition Info:
- 120 cal., 2g fat (0g sag. fat), 5mg chol, 220mg sod., 21g carb (10g sugars, 3g fiber), 6g pro.

Turkish Tomato, Bulgur, And Red Pepper Soup

Servings:8 | Cooking Time: 20 Minutes

Ingredients:
- 2 tablespoons extra-virgin olive oil
- 2 red bell peppers, stemmed, seeded, and chopped
- 1 onion, chopped
- Salt and pepper
- 3 garlic cloves, minced
- 1 tablespoon no-salt-added tomato paste
- 1 teaspoon dried mint, crumbled
- ½ teaspoon smoked paprika
- ⅛ teaspoon red pepper flakes
- ½ cup dry white wine
- 1 (28-ounce) can no-salt-added diced fire-roasted tomatoes
- 4 cups unsalted chicken broth
- 2 cups water
- ¾ cup medium-grind bulgur, rinsed
- ⅓ cup chopped fresh mint

Directions:
1. Heat oil in Dutch oven over medium heat until shimmering. Add bell peppers, onion, ¾ teaspoon salt, and ¼ teaspoon pepper and cook until softened and lightly browned, 6 to 8 minutes. Stir in garlic, tomato paste, dried mint, smoked paprika, and pepper flakes and cook until fragrant, about 1 minute.

2. Stir in wine, scraping up any browned bits, and cook until reduced by half, about 1 minute. Add tomatoes and their juice and cook, stirring occasionally, until tomatoes soften and begin to break apart, about 10 minutes.

3. Stir in broth, water, and bulgur and bring to simmer. Reduce heat to low, cover, and cook until bulgur is tender, about 20 minutes. Season with pepper to taste. Sprinkle individual portions with fresh mint before serving.

Nutrition Info:
• 140 cal., 4g fat (0g sag. fat), 0mg chol, 300mg sod., 20g carb (5g sugars, 5g fiber), 5g pro.

Vegetarian Chili

Servings:6 | Cooking Time:45 Minutes

Ingredients:
• 4 teaspoons canola oil
• 1 (8-ounce) package 5-grain tempeh, crumbled into ¼-inch pieces
• 1 tablespoon cumin seeds
• 2 carrots, peeled and cut into ½-inch pieces
• 1 onion, chopped fine
• 1 red bell pepper, stemmed, seeded, and cut into ½-inch pieces
• 9 garlic cloves, minced
• 2 tablespoons chili powder
• 1 teaspoon minced canned chipotle chile in adobo sauce
• Salt and pepper
• 3 cups water
• 1 (28-ounce) can no-salt-added crushed tomatoes
• 1 (15-ounce) can no-salt-added kidney beans, rinsed
• 1 teaspoon dried oregano
• 1 cup frozen corn
• 1 zucchini, halved lengthwise, seeded, and cut into ½-inch pieces
• ½ cup minced fresh cilantro
• Lime wedges

Directions:
1. Heat 1 teaspoon oil in Dutch oven over medium-high heat until shimmering. Add tempeh and cook until browned, about 5 minutes; transfer to plate and set aside.

2. Add cumin seeds to now-empty pot and cook over medium heat, stirring often, until fragrant, about 1 minute. Stir in remaining 1 tablespoon oil, carrots, onion, bell pepper, garlic, chili powder, chipotle, and ¼ teaspoon salt and cook until vegetables are softened, 8 to 10 minutes.

3. Stir in water, tomatoes, beans, and oregano, scraping up any browned bits. Bring to simmer and cook until chili is slightly thickened, about 45 minutes.

4. Stir in corn, zucchini, and tempeh and cook until zucchini is tender, 5 to 10 minutes. Stir in cilantro and season with pepper to taste. Serve with lime wedges.

Nutrition Info:
• 240 cal., 6g fat (0g sag. fat), 0mg chol, 220mg sod., 35g carb (9g sugars, 10g fiber), 13g pro.

Creamy Butternut Squash Soup

Servings:8 | Cooking Time:40 Minutes

Ingredients:
• 3 pounds butternut squash, peeled, seeded, and cut into ½-inch pieces (8 cups)
• 1 onion, halved and sliced ½ inch thick
• 4 teaspoons canola oil
• ¼ teaspoon salt
• 3 garlic cloves, minced
• ¼ cup dry white wine
• 7½ cups low-sodium vegetable broth
• 1 bay leaf
• ½ cup half-and-half
• 4 teaspoons balsamic vinegar

Directions:
1. Adjust oven racks to upper-middle and lower-middle positions and heat oven to 450 degrees. Toss squash and onion with 1 tablespoon oil and salt and spread into even layer on two rimmed baking sheets. Roast, stirring occasionally, until vegetables are softened and lightly browned, 30 to 40 minutes.

2. Heat remaining 1 teaspoon oil in Dutch over medium heat until shimmering. Add squash and onion and cook, stirring often, until squash begins to break down, 3 to 5 minutes. Stir in garlic and cook until fragrant, about 30 seconds.

3. Stir in wine, scraping up any browned bits, and cook until nearly evaporated, about 1 minute. Stir in broth and bay leaf and bring to simmer. Reduce heat to medium-low, cover, and cook until flavors meld, about 5 minutes.

4. Discard bay leaf. Working in batches, process soup in blender until smooth, about 1 minute. Return soup to clean pot, stir in half-and-half, and bring to brief simmer over medium-low heat. Drizzle individual portions with vinegar before serving.

Nutrition Info:
• 120 cal., 5g fat (1g sag. fat), 5mg chol, 210mg sod., 18g carb (4g sugars, 3g fiber), 2g pro.

Autumn Bisque

Servings:12 | Cooking Time: 50 Minutes

Ingredients:
• 1/4 cup buttery spread
• 2 teaspoons minced fresh chives
• 2 teaspoons minced fresh parsley
• 1/2 teaspoon grated lemon peel
• BISQUE
• 2 tablespoons olive oil
• 2 large rutabagas, peeled and cubed (about 9 cups)
• 1 large celery root, peeled and cubed (about 3 cups)
• 3 medium leeks (white portion only), chopped (about 2 cups)
• 1 large carrot, cubed (about 2/3 cup)
• 3 garlic cloves, minced
• 7 cups vegetable stock
• 2 teaspoons minced fresh thyme

- 1 1/2 teaspoons minced fresh rosemary
- 1 teaspoon salt
- 1/2 teaspoon coarsely ground pepper
- 2 cups almond milk
- 2 tablespoons minced fresh chives

Directions:
1. Mix first four ingredients. Using a melon baller or 1-teaspoon measuring spoon, shape mixture into 12 balls. Freeze on a waxed paper-lined baking sheet until firm. Transfer to a freezer container; freeze up to 2 months.
2. In a 6-qt. stock pot, heat oil over medium heat; saute rutabagas, celery root, leeks and carrot 8 minutes. Add garlic; cook and stir 2 minutes. Stir in stock, herbs, salt and pepper; bring to a boil. Reduce heat; simmer the soup, covered, until vegetables are tender, 30-35 minutes.
3. Puree soup using an immersion blender. Or, cool slightly and puree soup in batches in a blender; return to pan. Stir in milk; heat through. Top each serving with chives and herbed buttery spread ball.

Nutrition Info:
- 146 cal., 7g fat (2g sat. fat), 0 chol., 672mg sod., 20g carb. (9g sugars, 5g fiber), 3g pro.

Garlic-chicken And Wild Rice Soup

Servings:6 | Cooking Time:50 Minutes

Ingredients:
- 3 tablespoons extra-virgin olive oil
- ½ cup minced garlic (about 25 cloves)
- 2 carrots, peeled and sliced ¼ inch thick
- 1 onion, chopped fine
- 1 celery rib, minced
- Salt and pepper
- 2 teaspoons minced fresh thyme or ½ teaspoon dried
- 1 teaspoon no-salt-added tomato paste
- 6 cups unsalted chicken broth
- 2 bay leaves
- ⅔ cup wild rice, rinsed
- 8 ounces boneless, skinless chicken breasts, trimmed of all visible fat and cut into ¾-inch pieces
- 3 ounces (3 cups) baby spinach
- ¼ cup chopped fresh parsley

Directions:
1. Heat oil and garlic in Dutch oven over medium-low heat, stirring occasionally, until garlic is light golden and fragrant, 3 to 5 minutes. Increase heat to medium and add carrots, onion, celery, and ¼ teaspoon salt. Cook, stirring occasionally, until vegetables are softened and lightly browned, 10 to 12 minutes.
2. Stir in thyme and tomato paste and cook until fragrant, about 30 seconds. Stir in broth and bay leaves, scraping up any browned bits. Stir in rice and bring to simmer. Reduce heat to medium-low, cover, and cook until rice is tender, 40 to 50 minutes.
3. Discard bay leaves. Reduce heat to low and stir in chicken and spinach. Cook, stirring occasionally, until chicken is cooked through and spinach is wilted, 3 to 5 minutes. Off

heat, stir in parsley and season with pepper to taste. Serve.

Nutrition Info:
- 240 cal., 9g fat (1g sag. fat), 30mg chol, 280mg sod., 25g carb (3g sugars, 4g fiber), 17g pro.

Quick Beef And Vegetable Soup

Servings:6 | Cooking Time:18minutes

Ingredients:
- 1 pound 93 percent lean ground beef
- 2 carrots, peeled and cut into ½-inch pieces
- 1 onion, chopped
- 2 garlic cloves, minced
- 1 tablespoon no-salt-added tomato paste
- 2 teaspoons minced fresh thyme or ½ teaspoon dried
- Salt and pepper
- 4 cups low-sodium beef broth
- 2 cups water
- 1 (14.5-ounce) can no-salt-added diced tomatoes
- 8 ounces Yukon Gold potatoes, peeled and cut into ½-inch pieces
- 6 ounces green beans, trimmed and cut into 1-inch lengths
- 2 tablespoons chopped fresh parsley

Directions:
1. Cook beef, carrots, onion, garlic, tomato paste, thyme, ⅛ teaspoon salt, and ¼ teaspoon pepper in Dutch oven over medium-high heat, breaking up beef with wooden spoon, until beef is no longer pink, about 6 minutes. Stir in broth, water, tomatoes and their juice, and potatoes. Bring to simmer, then reduce heat to low, cover, and cook until potatoes are almost tender, about 10 minutes.
2. Stir in green beans and cook, uncovered, until vegetables are tender and soup has thickened slightly, 10 to 12 minutes. Stir in parsley and season with pepper to taste. Serve.

Nutrition Info:
- 200 cal., 5g fat (2g sag. fat), 50mg chol, 470mg sod., 18g carb (5g sugars, 4g fiber), 19g pro.

New England Fish Stew

Servings:4 | Cooking Time:15 Minutes

Ingredients:
- 1 teaspoon canola oil
- 1 slice bacon, chopped fine
- 1 onion, chopped
- Salt and pepper
- 4½ teaspoons all-purpose flour
- ½ teaspoon minced fresh thyme or ⅛ teaspoon dried
- 2 (8-ounce) bottles clam juice
- ½ cup water
- ¼ cup dry white wine
- 8 ounces red potatoes, unpeeled, cut into 1-inch pieces
- 1 bay leaf
- 1½ pounds skinless cod fillets, ¾ to 1 inch thick, cut into 1½-inch pieces
- ⅓ cup half-and-half
- 2 tablespoons chopped fresh parsley

Directions:

1. Heat oil in Dutch oven over medium heat until shimmering. Add bacon and cook until rendered and crisp, 5 to 7 minutes. Stir in onion and ⅛ teaspoon salt and cook until softened, about 5 minutes. Stir in flour and thyme and cook until fragrant, about 1 minute. Slowly whisk in clam juice, water, and wine, scraping up any browned bits and smoothing out any lumps.

2. Stir in potatoes and bay leaf and bring to simmer. Cover, reduce heat to medium-low, and cook until potatoes are almost tender, about 15 minutes.

3. Nestle cod pieces into stew, cover, and cook until fish flakes apart when gently prodded with paring knife and registers 140 degrees, 8 to 10 minutes.

4. Discard bay leaf. Off heat, stir in half-and-half and parsley and season with pepper to taste. Serve.

Nutrition Info:
• 280 cal., 7g fat (2g sag. fat), 90mg chol, 480mg sod., 15g carb (3g sugars, 2g fiber), 34g pro.

Chicken Tortilla Soup With Greens

Servings:8 | Cooking Time:7 Minutes

Ingredients:
• 8 (6-inch) corn tortillas, cut into ½-inch strips
• 2 tablespoons canola oil
• Salt
• 1½ pounds bone-in split chicken breasts, trimmed
• 12 ounces Swiss chard, stems chopped, leaves cut into 1-inch pieces
• 1 onion, chopped fine
• 1 tablespoon no-salt-added tomato paste
• 1–3 tablespoons minced canned chipotle chile in adobo sauce
• 1 (14.5-ounce) can no-salt-added diced tomatoes, drained
• 2 garlic cloves, minced
• 8 cups unsalted chicken broth
• 1 avocado, halved, pitted, and cut into ½-inch pieces
• 1 cup fresh cilantro leaves

Directions:

1. Adjust oven rack to middle position and heat oven to 425 degrees. Toss tortilla strips with 1 tablespoon oil and spread evenly onto rimmed baking sheet. Bake, stirring occasionally, until strips are deep golden brown and crisp, 8 to 12 minutes. Sprinkle tortillas with ¼ teaspoon salt and transfer to paper towel–lined plate.

2. Pat chicken dry with paper towels. Heat remaining 1 tablespoon oil in Dutch oven over medium-high heat until just smoking. Brown chicken, 3 to 5 minutes per side; transfer to plate and discard skin.

3. Add chard stems, onion, and ½ teaspoon salt to fat left in pot and cook until softened, about 5 minutes. Stir in tomato paste, chipotle plus sauce, and tomatoes and cook until mixture is dry and slightly darkened, 5 to 7 minutes. Stir in garlic and cook until fragrant, about 30 seconds.

4. Stir in broth, scraping up any browned bits. Nestle chicken into pot along with any accumulated juices and bring to simmer. Reduce heat to medium-low, cover, and cook until chicken registers 160 degrees, 16 to 18 minutes. Transfer chicken to plate, let cool slightly, then shred into bite-size pieces using 2 forks.

5. Return soup to simmer, stir in chard leaves, and cook until mostly tender, about 5 minutes. Off heat, stir in chicken and let sit until heated through, about 5 minutes. Divide tortilla strips among individual serving bowls and ladle soup over top. Top with avocado and cilantro before serving.

Nutrition Info:
• 270 cal., 10g fat (1g sag. fat), 60mg chol, 500mg sod., 19g carb (3g sugars, 5g fiber), 26g pro.

Tomato-orange Soup

Servings:6 | Cooking Time: 1 Hour

Ingredients:
• 3 pounds tomatoes, halved
• 2 tablespoons canola oil, divided
• 2 medium onions, chopped
• 2 garlic cloves, minced
• 3 cups reduced-sodium chicken broth
• 1 cup orange juice
• 2 tablespoons tomato paste
• 4 teaspoons grated orange peel
• 1 tablespoon butter
• 1 tablespoon minced fresh cilantro
• 1 tablespoon honey
• 1/4 teaspoon salt

Directions:

1. Preheat oven to 450°. Place the tomatoes in a 15x10x1-in. baking pan, cut side down; brush tomato tops with 1 tablespoon oil. Roast 20-25 minutes or until skins are blistered and charred. Remove and discard skins.

2. In a 6-qt. stockpot, heat remaining oil over medium-high heat. Add onions; cook and stir until tender. Add garlic; cook 1 minute longer. Stir in broth, orange juice, tomato paste and roasted tomatoes; bring to a boil. Reduce heat; simmer, uncovered, 45 minutes.

3. Stir in orange peel, butter, cilantro, honey and salt. Remove from heat; cool slightly. Process soup in batches in a blender until smooth. Return to pot; heat through.

Nutrition Info:
• 160 cal., 7g fat (2g sat. fat), 5mg chol., 419mg sod., 22g carb. (15g sugars, 4g fiber), 5g pro.

Black Bean-tomato Chili

Servings:6 | Cooking Time: 35 Minutes

Ingredients:
• 2 tablespoons olive oil
• 1 large onion, chopped
• 1 medium green pepper, chopped
• 3 garlic cloves, minced
• 1 teaspoon ground cinnamon
• 1 teaspoon ground cumin
• 1 teaspoon chili powder
• 1/4 teaspoon pepper

- 3 cans (14 1/2 ounces each) diced tomatoes, undrained
- 2 cans (15 ounces each) black beans, rinsed and drained
- 1 cup orange juice or juice from 3 medium oranges

Directions:

1. In a Dutch oven, heat the oil over medium-high heat. Add onion and green pepper; cook and stir for 8-10 minutes or until tender. Add garlic and seasonings; cook 1 minute longer.

2. Stir in remaining ingredients; bring to a boil. Reduce heat; simmer, covered, 20-25 minutes to allow flavors to blend, stirring occasionally.

Nutrition Info:

- 232 cal., 5g fat (1g sat. fat), 0 chol., 608mg sod., 39g carb. (13g sugars, 10g fiber), 9g pro.

Hearty Cabbage Soup

Servings:8 | Cooking Time: 20 Minutes

Ingredients:

- 3 tablespoons canola oil
- 1 pound ground chicken
- 1 onion, chopped fine
- 2 teaspoons caraway seeds, toasted
- Salt and pepper
- 5 garlic cloves, minced
- 1 teaspoon minced fresh thyme or ¼ teaspoon dried
- ½ teaspoon hot smoked paprika
- ¼ cup dry white wine
- 1 head green cabbage (2 pounds), cored and cut into ¾-inch pieces
- 8 cups unsalted chicken broth
- 1 bay leaf
- 12 ounces red potatoes, unpeeled, cut into ¾-inch pieces
- ½ cup low-fat sour cream
- 1 tablespoons minced fresh dill

Directions:

1. Heat oil in Dutch oven over medium heat until shimmering. Add chicken, onion, caraway seeds, and ¼ teaspoon salt and cook, breaking up chicken with wooden spoon, until chicken is no longer pink and onion is softened, 7 to 9 minutes.

2. Stir in garlic, thyme, and paprika and cook until fragrant, about 30 seconds. Stir in wine, scraping up any browned bits, and cook until nearly evaporated. Stir in cabbage, broth, and bay leaf and bring to simmer. Reduce heat to medium-low, cover, and cook for 15 minutes. Stir in potatoes and continue to cook until vegetables are tender, 15 to 20 minutes.

3. Discard bay leaf. Stir a few tablespoons of hot broth into sour cream to temper, then stir sour cream mixture and ½ teaspoon salt into pot. Stir in dill and season with pepper to taste. Serve.

Nutrition Info:

- 240 cal., 11g fat (2g sag. fat), 40mg chol, 430mg sod., 18g carb (7g sugars, 5g fiber), 17g pro.

Chinese Starter Soup

Servings: 4 | Cooking Time:10 Minutes

Ingredients:

- 3 cups low-fat, low-sodium chicken broth
- 8 ounces frozen stir-fry vegetables, such as a mix of broccoli, carrots, water chestnuts, and onion
- 2 teaspoons grated gingerroot
- 2 teaspoons lite soy sauce

Directions:

1. In a medium saucepan, bring the broth to boil over high heat. Add the vegetables and return to a boil.

2. Reduce the heat, cover tightly, and simmer 3–4 minutes or until vegetables are tender-crisp.

3. Remove from the heat and add the remaining ingredients. Top with red pepper flakes, if desired. Cover and let stand 3 minutes to develop flavors, then serve.

Nutrition Info:

- 50 cal., 0g fat (0g sag. fat), 0mg chol, 210mg sod., 7g carb (3g sugars, 1g fiber), 4g pro.

Butternut Squash And White Bean Soup With Sage Pesto

Servings:8 | Cooking Time: 20 Minutes

Ingredients:

- PESTO
- ⅓ cup walnuts, toasted
- 2 garlic cloves, minced
- ¾ cup fresh parsley leaves
- ⅓ cup fresh sage leaves
- ⅓ cup extra-virgin olive oil
- 1 ounce Parmesan cheese, grated (½ cup)
- SOUP
- 1 (2- to 2½-pound) butternut squash
- 4 cups unsalted chicken broth
- 3 cups water
- 1 tablespoon extra-virgin olive oil
- 1 pound leeks, white and light green parts only, halved lengthwise, sliced thin, and washed thoroughly
- 1 tablespoon no-salt-addcd tomato paste
- 2 garlic cloves, minced
- Salt and pepper
- 2 (15-ounce) cans no-salt-added cannellini beans
- 1 teaspoon white wine vinegar

Directions:

1. FOR THE PESTO Pulse walnuts and garlic in food processor until coarsely chopped, about 5 pulses. Add parsley and sage. With processor running, slowly add oil and process until smooth, about 1 minute, scraping down sides of bowl as needed. Transfer pesto to bowl and stir in Parmesan; set aside. (Pesto can be refrigerated for up to 3 days. To prevent browning, press plastic wrap flush to surface or top with thin layer of olive oil. Bring to room temperature before using.)

2. FOR THE SOUP Using sharp vegetable peeler or chef's knife, remove skin and fibrous threads just below skin

from squash (peel until squash is completely orange with no white flesh remaining, roughly ⅛ inch deep). Cut round bulb section off squash and cut in half lengthwise. Scoop out and discard seeds; cut each half into 4 wedges.

3. Bring broth, water, and squash wedges to boil in medium saucepan over high heat. Reduce heat to medium, partially cover, and simmer vigorously until squash is very tender and starting to fall apart, about 20 minutes. Using potato masher, mash squash, still in broth, until completely broken down. Cover to keep warm; set aside.

4. Meanwhile, cut neck of squash into ⅓-inch cubes. Heat oil in Dutch oven over medium heat until shimmering. Add leeks and tomato paste and cook, stirring occasionally, until leeks are softened and tomato paste is darkened, about 5 minutes. Stir in garlic and cook until fragrant, about 30 seconds. Add squash pieces, ¼ teaspoon salt, and ¼ teaspoon pepper and cook, stirring occasionally, for 5 minutes. Add squash broth and bring to simmer. Partially cover and cook for 10 minutes.

5. Stir in beans and their liquid, partially cover, and cook, stirring occasionally, until squash is just tender, 15 to 20 minutes. Stir in vinegar. Top each individual portion with 1 tablespoon pesto before serving.

Nutrition Info:
• 270 cal., 16g fat (2g sag. fat), 5mg chol, 240mg sod., 26g carb (5g sugars, 6g fiber), 9g pro.

Hearty Ten Vegetable Stew
Servings:8 | Cooking Time:45 Minutes

Ingredients:
• 2 tablespoons canola oil
• 1 pound white mushrooms, trimmed and sliced thin
• Salt and pepper
• 8 ounces Swiss chard, stems chopped fine, leaves cut into ½-inch pieces
• 2 onions, chopped fine
• 1 celery rib, cut into ½-inch pieces
• 1 carrot, peeled, halved lengthwise, and sliced 1 inch thick
• 1 red bell pepper, stemmed, seeded, and cut into ½-inch pieces
• 6 garlic cloves, minced
• 2 tablespoons all-purpose flour
• 1 tablespoon no-salt added tomato paste
• 2 teaspoons minced fresh thyme or ½ teaspoon dried
• ½ cup dry white wine
• 6 cups low-sodium vegetable broth
• 1 tablespoon low-sodium soy sauce
• 8 ounces red potatoes, unpeeled, cut into 1-inch pieces
• 8 ounces celery root, peeled and cut into 1-inch pieces
• 2 parsnips, peeled and cut into 1-inch pieces
• 2 bay leaves
• 1 zucchini, halved lengthwise, seeded, and cut into ½-inch pieces
• 1 tablespoon lemon juice

Directions:

1. Heat oil in Dutch oven over medium heat until shimmering. Add mushrooms and ¼ teaspoon salt, cover, and cook until mushrooms have released their liquid, about 3 minutes. Uncover, increase heat to medium-high, and continue to cook, stirring occasionally, until mushrooms are dry and well browned, 8 to 12 minutes.

2. Stir in chard stems, onions, celery, carrot, bell pepper, and ⅛ teaspoon salt and cook until vegetables are softened and well browned, 7 to 10 minutes. Stir in garlic, flour, tomato paste, and thyme and cook until fragrant, about 1 minute. Slowly whisk in wine, scraping up any browned bits and smoothing out any lumps, and cook until nearly evaporated, about 2 minutes.

3. Stir in broth, soy sauce, potatoes, celery root, parsnips, and bay leaves and bring to simmer. Reduce heat to medium-low, partially cover, and cook until stew is thickened and vegetables are tender, about 45 minutes.

4. Stir in chard leaves and zucchini, cover, and cook until tender, 5 to 10 minutes. Discard bay leaves. Stir in lemon juice and ¼ teaspoon salt and season with pepper to taste. Serve.

Nutrition Info:
• 160 cal., 5g fat (0g sag. fat), 0mg chol, 460mg sod., 23g carb (6g sugars, 4g fiber), 4g pro.

Creamy Chicken Rice Soup
Servings:4 | Cooking Time: 30 Minutes

Ingredients:
• 1 tablespoon canola oil
• 1 medium carrot, chopped
• 1 celery rib, chopped
• 1/2 cup chopped onion
• 1/2 teaspoon minced garlic
• 1/3 cup uncooked long grain rice
• 3/4 teaspoon dried basil
• 1/4 teaspoon pepper
• 2 cans (14 1/2 ounces each) reduced-sodium chicken broth
• 3 tablespoons all-purpose flour
• 1 can (5 ounces) evaporated milk
• 2 cups cubed cooked chicken

Directions:

1. In a large saucepan, heat oil over medium-high heat; saute carrot, celery and onion until tender. Add garlic; cook and stir 1 minute. Stir in rice, seasonings and broth; bring to a boil. Reduce heat; simmer, covered, until rice is tender, about 15 minutes.

2. Mix flour and milk until smooth; stir into soup. Bring to a boil; cook and stir until thickened, about 2 minutes. Stir in chicken; heat through.

Nutrition Info:
• 322 cal., 11g fat (3g sat. fat), 73mg chol., 630mg sod., 26g carb. (6g sugars, 1g fiber), 28g pro.

Italian Vegetable Soup

Servings:6 | Cooking Time: 18minutes

Ingredients:
- 2 tablespoons extra-virgin olive oil
- 1 onion, chopped fine
- ¼ teaspoon salt
- 1 teaspoon minced fresh thyme or ¼ teaspoon dried
- 6 garlic cloves, minced
- 8 cups unsalted chicken broth
- 3 bay leaves
- 8 ounces (3¼ cups) medium whole-wheat shells
- 1 zucchini, halved lengthwise, seeded, and cut into ½-inch pieces
- 12 ounces curly-leaf spinach, stemmed and chopped coarse
- 2 cups frozen peas
- ¼ cup chopped fresh basil
- ¼ teaspoon grated lemon zest
- 6 tablespoons grated Parmesan cheese

Directions:
1. Heat 1 tablespoon oil in Dutch oven over medium heat until simmering. Add onion and salt and cook until softened, about 5 minutes. Stir in thyme and two-thirds of garlic and cook until fragrant, about 30 seconds. Stir in broth and bay leaves, scraping up any browned bits, and bring to simmer.
2. Stir in pasta and cook for 8 minutes. Stir in zucchini and cook until pasta and zucchini are just tender, 3 to 5 minutes. Stir in spinach and peas and cook until spinach is wilted, about 3 minutes.
3. Discard bay leaves. Stir in basil, lemon zest, remaining 1 tablespoon oil, and remaining garlic. Sprinkle individual portions with Parmesan before serving.

Nutrition Info:
- 280 cal., 8g fat (1g sag. fat), 5mg chol, 440mg sod., 36g carb (6g sugars, 9g fiber), 18g pro.

Spicy Pumpkin & Corn Soup

Servings:8 | Cooking Time: 20 Minutes

Ingredients:
- 1 can (15 ounces) solid-pack pumpkin
- 1 can (15 ounces) black beans, rinsed and drained
- 1 1/2 cups frozen corn
- 1 can (10 ounces) diced tomatoes and green chilies
- 2 cans (14 1/2 ounces each) reduced-sodium chicken broth
- 1/4 teaspoon pepper

Directions:
1. In a large saucepan, mix all ingredients. Bring to a boil. Reduce heat; simmer, uncovered, 10-15 minutes or until slightly thickened, stirring occasionally.

Nutrition Info:
- 100 cal., 0 fat (0 sat. fat), 0 chol., 542mg sod., 20g carb. (3g sugars, 5g fiber), 6g pro.

Roasted Cauliflower & Red Pepper Soup

Servings:6 | Cooking Time: 25 Minutes

Ingredients:
- 2 medium sweet red peppers, halved and seeded
- 1 large head cauliflower, broken into florets (about 7 cups)
- 4 tablespoons olive oil, divided
- 1 cup chopped sweet onion
- 2 garlic cloves, minced
- 2 1/2 teaspoons minced fresh rosemary or 3/4 teaspoon dried rosemary, crushed
- 1/2 teaspoon paprika
- 1/4 cup all-purpose flour
- 4 cups chicken stock
- 1 cup 2% milk
- 1/2 teaspoon salt
- 1/4 teaspoon pepper
- 1/8 to 1/4 teaspoon cayenne pepper
- Shredded Parmesan cheese, optional

Directions:
1. Preheat broiler. Place peppers on a foil-lined baking sheet, skin side up. Broil 4 in. from heat until skins are blistered, about 5 minutes. Transfer to a bowl; let stand, covered, 20 minutes. Change oven setting to bake; preheat oven to 400°.
2. Toss cauliflower with 2 tablespoons oil; spread in a 15x10x1-in. pan. Roast until tender, 25-30 minutes, stirring occasionally. Remove skin and seeds from peppers; chop peppers.
3. In a 6-qt. stockpot, heat remaining oil over medium heat. Add onion; cook until golden and softened, 6-8 minutes, stirring occasionally. Add the garlic, rosemary and paprika; cook and stir 1 minute. Stir in flour until blended; cook and stir 1 minute. Gradually stir in stock. Bring to a boil, stirring constantly; cook and stir until thickened.
4. Stir in cauliflower and peppers. Puree soup using an immersion blender. Or, cool slightly and puree in batches in a blender; return to pot. Stir in milk and remaining seasonings; heat through. If desired, serve with cheese.

Nutrition Info:
- 193 cal., 10g fat (2g sat. fat), 3mg chol., 601mg sod., 19g carb. (8g sugars, 4g fiber), 8g pro.

Beef And Vegetable Stew

Servings:6 | Cooking Time: 1 Hour

Ingredients:
- 2 pounds boneless beef chuck-eye roast, trimmed of all visible fat and cut into 1½-inch pieces
- Salt and pepper
- 5 teaspoons canola oil
- 1 portobello mushroom cap, cut into ½-inch pieces
- 2 onions, chopped fine
- 3 tablespoons all-purpose flour
- 3 garlic cloves, minced
- 1 tablespoon no-salt-added tomato paste
- 1 tablespoon minced fresh thyme or 1 teaspoon dried

- 1½ cups dry red wine
- 4 cups unsalted chicken broth
- 2 bay leaves
- 4 carrots, peeled and cut into 1-inch pieces
- 12 ounces red potatoes, unpeeled, cut into 1-inch pieces
- 12 ounces parsnips, peeled and cut into 1-inch pieces
- 1 pound kale, stemmed and cut into ½-inch pieces
- ½ cup frozen peas
- ¼ cup minced fresh parsley

Directions:

1. Adjust oven rack to lower-middle position and heat oven to 300 degrees. Pat beef dry with paper towels and sprinkle with ½ teaspoon salt and ¼ teaspoon pepper. Heat 1 teaspoon oil in Dutch oven over medium-high heat until just smoking. Brown half of beef on all sides, 5 to 7 minutes; transfer to bowl. Repeat with 1 teaspoon oil and remaining beef; transfer to bowl.

2. Add mushroom and ¼ teaspoon salt to fat left in pot, cover, and cook until mushroom has released its liquid, about 3 minutes. Uncover, increase heat to medium-high, and continue to cook, stirring occasionally, until mushroom is dry and well browned, about 10 minutes.

3. Stir in onions and remaining 1 tablespoon oil and cook until softened, about 5 minutes. Stir in flour, garlic, tomato paste, and thyme and cook until fragrant, about 1 minute. Slowly whisk in wine, scraping up any browned bits and smoothing out any lumps. Stir in broth, bay leaves, and beef and any accumulated juices and bring to simmer. Cover, transfer pot to oven, and cook for 1½ hours.

4. Stir in carrots, potatoes, and parsnips, cover, and cook until meat and vegetables are tender, about 1 hour.

5. Stir in kale, cover, and cook until tender, about 10 minutes. Remove pot from oven and discard bay leaves. Stir in peas and let sit until heated through, about 5 minutes. Stir in parsley and serve.

Nutrition Info:

- 480 cal., 12g fat (3g sag. fat), 100mg chol, 570mg sod., 39g carb (10g sugars, 9g fiber), 42g pro.

Golden Summer Peach Gazpacho

Servings:8 | Cooking Time: 20 Minutes

Ingredients:

- 3 cups sliced peeled fresh or frozen peaches, thawed
- 3 medium yellow tomatoes, chopped
- 1 medium sweet yellow pepper, chopped
- 1 medium cucumber, peeled and chopped
- 1/2 cup chopped sweet onion
- 1 garlic clove, minced
- 1/3 cup lime juice
- 2 tablespoons rice vinegar
- 1 tablespoon marinade for chicken
- 1 teaspoon salt
- 1/4 teaspoon hot pepper sauce
- 1 to 3 teaspoons sugar, optional
- Chopped peaches, cucumber and tomatoes

Directions:

1. Place the first six ingredients in a food processor; process until blended. Add lime juice, vinegar, marinade for chicken, salt and pepper sauce; process until smooth. If desired, stir in sugar.

2. Refrigerate, covered, for at least 4 hours. Top individual servings with additional chopped peaches, cucumber and tomatoes.

Nutrition Info:

- 56 cal., 0 fat (0 sat. fat), 0 chol., 342mg sod., 13g carb. (8g sugars, 2g fiber), 2g pro.

Creamy Potato Soup With Green Onions

Servings: 3 | Cooking Time:15 Minutes

Ingredients:

- 2 cups fat-free milk
- 1 pound baking potatoes, peeled and diced
- 3 tablespoons no-trans-fat margarine (35% vegetable oil)
- 1/4 teaspoon salt
- 1/4 teaspoon black pepper
- 3 tablespoons finely chopped green onions, green and white parts

Directions:

1. Bring the milk just to a boil in a large saucepan over high heat (catch it before it comes to a full boil).

2. Add the potatoes and return just to a boil. Reduce the heat, cover tightly, and simmer 12 minutes or until the potatoes are tender.

3. Remove from the heat and add the margarine, salt, and pepper. Using a whisk or potato masher or handheld electric mixer, mash the mixture until thickened, but still lumpy.

4. Spoon into individual bowls and sprinkle each serving with 1 tablespoon onions.

Nutrition Info:

- 200 cal., 5g fat (1g sag. fat), 5mg chol, 360mg sod., 32g carb (9g sugars, 2g fiber), 8g pro.

FISH & SEA-FOOD RECIPES

Crispy Fish & Chips

Servings:4 | Cooking Time: 30 Minutes

Ingredients:
- 4 cups frozen steak fries
- 4 salmon fillets (6 ounces each)
- 1 to 2 tablespoons prepared horseradish
- 1 tablespoon grated Parmesan cheese
- 1 tablespoon Worcestershire sauce
- 1 teaspoon Dijon mustard
- 1/4 teaspoon salt
- 1/2 cup panko (Japanese) bread crumbs
- Cooking spray

Directions:
1. Preheat oven to 450°. Arrange steak fries in a single layer on a baking sheet. Bake on lowest oven rack 18-20 minutes or until light golden brown.
2. Meanwhile, place salmon on a foil-lined baking sheet coated with cooking spray. In a small bowl, mix horseradish, cheese, Worcestershire sauce, mustard and salt; stir in panko. Press mixture onto fillets. Spritz tops with cooking spray.
3. Bake salmon on middle oven rack 8-10 minutes or until fish just begins to flake easily with a fork. Serve with fries.

Nutrition Info:
- 419 cal., 20g fat (4g sat. fat), 86mg chol., 695mg sod., 26g carb. (2g sugars, 2g fiber), 32g pro.

Grilled Swordfish With Eggplant, Tomato, And Chickpea Salad

Servings:4 | Cooking Time:30minutes

Ingredients:
- 1 cup fresh cilantro leaves
- ½ red onion, chopped coarse
- 5 tablespoons extra-virgin olive oil
- 3 tablespoons lemon juice
- 4 garlic cloves, chopped
- 1 teaspoon ground cumin
- 1 teaspoon paprika
- ¼ teaspoon cayenne pepper
- ⅛ teaspoon ground cinnamon
- Salt and pepper
- 4 (6-ounce) skin-on swordfish steaks, 1 to 1½ inches thick
- 1 large eggplant, sliced into ½-inch-thick rounds
- 6 ounces cherry tomatoes, halved
- 1 (15-ounce) can no-salt added chickpeas, rinsed

Directions:
1. Process cilantro, onion, 3 tablespoons oil, lemon juice, garlic, cumin, paprika, cayenne, cinnamon, and ¼ teaspoon salt in food processor until smooth, about 2 minutes, scraping down sides of bowl as needed. Measure out and reserve ½ cup cilantro mixture. Transfer remaining cilantro mixture to large bowl and set aside.
2. Brush swordfish with reserved ½ cup cilantro mixture. Brush eggplant with remaining 2 tablespoons oil and sprinkle with ⅛ teaspoon salt and ⅛ teaspoon pepper.
3. FOR A CHARCOAL GRILL Open bottom vent completely. Light large chimney starter filled with charcoal briquettes (6 quarts). When top coals are partially covered with ash, pour two-thirds evenly over half of grill, then pour remaining coals over other half of grill. Set cooking grate in place, cover, and open lid vent completely. Heat grill until hot, about 5 minutes.
4. FOR A GAS GRILL Turn all burners to high, cover, and heat grill until hot, about 15 minutes. Leave primary burner on high and turn other burner(s) to medium-high.
5. Clean cooking grate, then repeatedly brush grate with well-oiled paper towels until black and glossy, 5 to 10 times. Place swordfish and eggplant on hotter part of grill. Cook swordfish, uncovered, until streaked with dark grill marks, 6 to 9 minutes, gently flipping steaks using 2 spatulas halfway through cooking. Cook eggplant, flipping as needed, until softened and lightly charred, about 8 minutes; transfer to bowl and cover with aluminum foil.
6. Gently move swordfish to cooler part of grill and continue to cook, uncovered, until swordfish flakes apart when gently prodded with paring knife and registers 140 degrees, 1 to 3 minutes per side; transfer to serving platter and tent loosely with foil.
7. Coarsely chop eggplant and add to bowl with cilantro mixture along with tomatoes and chickpeas. Gently toss to combine and season with pepper to taste. Serve.

Nutrition Info:
- 530 cal., 30g fat (5g sag. fat), 110mg chol, 380mg sod., 25g carb (7g sugars, 8g fiber), 40g pro.

Pesto Grilled Salmon

Servings:12 | Cooking Time: 30 Minutes

Ingredients:
- 1 salmon fillet (3 pounds)
- 1/2 cup prepared pesto
- 2 green onions, finely chopped
- 1/4 cup lemon juice
- 2 garlic cloves, minced

Directions:
1. Moisten a paper towel with cooking oil; using long-handled tongs, lightly coat the grill rack. Place salmon skin side down on grill rack. Grill, covered, over medium heat or broil 4 in. from the heat for 5 minutes.
2. In a small bowl, combine the pesto, onions, lemon juice and garlic. Carefully spoon some of the pesto mixture over salmon. Grill for about15-20 minutes longer or until the fish flakes easily with a fork, basting occasionally with the

remaining pesto mixture.

Nutrition Info:
• 262 cal., 17g fat (4g sat. fat), 70mg chol., 147mg sod., 1g carb. (0 sugars, 0 fiber), 25g pro.

Cilantro Shrimp & Rice

Servings:8 | Cooking Time: 30 Minutes

Ingredients:
• 2 packages (8 1/2 ounces each) ready-to-serve basmati rice
• 2 tablespoons olive oil
• 2 cups frozen corn, thawed
• 2 medium zucchini, quartered and sliced
• 1 large sweet red pepper, chopped
• 1/2 teaspoon crushed red pepper flakes
• 3 garlic cloves, minced
• 1 pound peeled and deveined cooked large shrimp, tails removed
• 1/2 cup chopped fresh cilantro
• 1 tablespoon grated lime peel
• 2 tablespoons lime juice
• 3/4 teaspoon salt
• Lime wedges, optional

Directions:
1. Prepare the rice according to the package directions.
2. Meanwhile, in a large skillet, heat oil over medium-high heat. Add the corn, zucchini, red pepper and pepper flakes; cook and stir 3-5 minutes or until the zucchini is crisp-tender. Add garlic; cook 1 minute longer. Add shrimp; cook and stir 3-5 minutes or until heated through.
3. Stir in the rice, cilantro, lime peel, lime juice and salt. If desired, serve with lime wedges.

Nutrition Info:
• 243 cal., 6g fat (1g sat. fat), 86mg chol., 324mg sod., 28g carb. (3g sugars, 3g fiber), 16g pro.

Lemon-peppered Shrimp

Servings: 4 | Cooking Time:7 Minutes

Ingredients:
• 1 pound peeled raw shrimp, rinsed and patted dry
• 1 tablespoon salt-free steak seasoning blend
• 1 teaspoon lemon zest
• 2–3 tablespoons lemon juice
• 3 tablespoons no-trans-fat margarine (35% vegetable oil)
• 1/4 teaspoon salt

Directions:
1. Place a large nonstick skillet over medium heat until hot. Coat the skillet with nonstick cooking spray, add the shrimp, sprinkle evenly with the steak seasoning, and cook 5 minutes or until the shrimp is opaque in the center, stirring frequently.
2. Stir in the lemon zest, juice, margarine, and salt and cook 1 minute.

Nutrition Info:
• 140 cal., 4g fat (0g sag. fat), 190mg chol, 320mg sod., 2g

carb (0g sugars, 1g fiber), 24g pro.

Lime-cilantro Tilapia

Servings:4 | Cooking Time: 25 Minutes

Ingredients:
• 1/3 cup all-purpose flour
• 3/4 teaspoon salt
• 1/2 teaspoon pepper
• 1/2 teaspoon ground cumin, divided
• 4 tilapia fillets (6 ounces each)
• 1 tablespoon olive oil
• 1/2 cup reduced-sodium chicken broth
• 2 tablespoons minced fresh cilantro
• 1 teaspoon grated lime peel
• 2 tablespoons lime juice

Directions:
1. In a shallow bowl, mix flour, salt, pepper and 1/4 teaspoon cumin. Dip fillets in flour mixture to coat both sides; shake off excess.
2. In a large nonstick skillet, heat oil over medium heat. Add fillets; cook, uncovered, 3-4 minutes on each side or until the fish flakes easily with a fork. Remove and keep warm.
3. To the same pan, add broth, cilantro, lime peel, lime juice and the remaining cumin; bring to a boil. Reduce the heat; simmer, uncovered, 2-3 minutes or until slightly thickened. Serve with tilapia.

Nutrition Info:
• 198 cal., 5g fat (1g sat. fat), 83mg chol., 398 mg sod., 6g carb. (1g sugars, 0 fiber), 33g pro.

Salmon & Spud Salad

Servings:4 | Cooking Time: 30 Minutes

Ingredients:
• 1 pound fingerling potatoes
• 1/2 pound fresh green beans
• 1/2 pound fresh asparagus
• 4 salmon fillets (6 ounces each)
• 1 tablespoon plus 1/3 cup red wine vinaigrette, divided
• 1/4 teaspoon salt
• 1/4 teaspoon pepper
• 4 cups fresh arugula or baby spinach
• 2 cups cherry tomatoes, halved
• 1 tablespoon minced fresh chives

Directions:
1. Cut potatoes lengthwise in half. Trim and cut green beans and asparagus into 2-in. pieces. Place potatoes in a 6-qt. stockpot; add water to cover. Bring to a boil. Reduce heat; cook, uncovered, 10-15 minutes or until tender, adding green beans and asparagus during the last 4 minutes of cooking. Drain.
2. Meanwhile, brush salmon with 1 tablespoon vinaigrette; sprinkle with salt and pepper. Place fish on oiled grill rack, skin side down. Grill it, covered, over medium-high heat or broil 4 in. from heat 6-8 minutes or until fish just begins to flake easily with a fork.

3. In a large bowl, combine potato mixture, arugula, tomatoes and chives. Drizzle with remaining vinaigrette; toss to coat. Serve with salmon.

Nutrition Info:
• 480 cal., 23g fat (4g sat. fat), 85mg chol., 642mg sod., 33g carb. (8g sugars, 6g fiber), 34g pro.

Halibut Baked In Foil With Tomatoes And Zucchini

Servings:4 | Cooking Time:25 Minutes

Ingredients:
• 1 pound zucchini, sliced crosswise into ¼-inch-thick rounds
• Salt and pepper
• 3 plum tomatoes, cored, seeded, and cut into ½-inch pieces
• 2 tablespoons extra-virgin olive oil
• 2 garlic cloves, minced
• 1 teaspoon minced fresh oregano or ¼ teaspoon dried
• ⅛ teaspoon red pepper flakes
• 4 (6-ounce) skinless halibut fillets, 1 to 1½ inches thick
• ¼ cup dry white wine
• ¼ cup chopped fresh basil
• Lemon wedges

Directions:
1. Toss zucchini with ⅛ teaspoon salt and let drain in colander for 30 minutes; pat zucchini dry with paper towels, pressing firmly to remove as much liquid as possible. Adjust oven rack to middle position and heat oven to 450 degrees.
2. Combine tomatoes, oil, garlic, oregano, pepper flakes, and ⅛ teaspoon pepper in bowl. Pat halibut dry with paper towels and sprinkle with ¼ teaspoon salt and ⅛ teaspoon pepper.
3. Cut eight 12-inch sheets of aluminum foil; arrange 4 flat on counter. Shingle zucchini in center of foil sheets and sprinkle with wine. Place halibut on top of zucchini, then top halibut with tomato mixture. Place remaining pieces of foil on top. Press edges of foil together and fold together several times until each packet is well sealed and measures about 7 inches square. (Packets can be refrigerated for up to 3 hours before cooking. Increase baking time to 20 to 25 minutes when made ahead.)
4. Place packets on rimmed baking sheet, overlapping as needed, and bake until halibut flakes apart when gently prodded with paring knife and registers 140 degrees, 15 to 20 minutes. (To check temperature, poke thermometer through foil into halibut.)
5. Carefully open packets, allowing steam to escape away from you, and gently slide halibut, vegetables, and any accumulated juices onto individual serving plates. Sprinkle with basil and serve with lemon wedges.

Nutrition Info:
• 260 cal., 10g fat (1g sag. fat), 85mg chol, 320mg sod., 7g carb (4g sugars, 2g fiber), 34g pro.

Mustard Vinaigrette With Lemon And Parsley

Servings:1 | Cooking Time:10 Minutes

Ingredients:
• 3 tablespoons extra-virgin olive oil
• 2 tablespoons lemon juice
• 5 teaspoons whole-grain mustard
• 1 small shallot, minced
• 1 tablespoon water
• 2 teaspoons minced fresh parsley
• Pepper

Directions:
1. Whisk oil, lemon juice, mustard, shallot, water, and parsley together in bowl and season with pepper to taste. Let sit for 10 minutes. (Vinaigrette can be refrigerated for up to 24 hours; whisk to recombine before serving.)

Nutrition Info:
• 110 cal., 11g fat (1g sag. fat), 0mg chol, 125mg sod., 1g carb (0g sugars, 0g fiber), 0g pro.

Pan-roasted Sea Bass With Wild Mushrooms

Servings:4 | Cooking Time:10 Minutes

Ingredients:
• ½ cup water
• ⅓ ounce dried porcini mushrooms, rinsed
• 4 (6-ounce) skinless sea bass fillets, 1 to 1½ inches thick
• ¼ cup extra virgin olive oil
• Salt and pepper
• 1 sprig fresh rosemary
• 1 pound cremini mushrooms, trimmed and halved if small or quartered if large
• 12 ounces portobello mushroom caps, halved and sliced ½ inch thick
• 1 red onion, halved and sliced thin
• 2 garlic cloves, minced
• 1 tablespoon minced fresh parsley
• Lemon wedges

Directions:
1. Adjust oven rack to lower-middle position and heat oven to 475 degrees. Microwave water and porcini mushrooms in covered bowl until steaming, about 1 minute. Let sit until softened, about 5 minutes. Drain mushrooms in fine-mesh strainer lined with coffee filter, reserving porcini liquid, and mince mushrooms.
2. Pat sea bass dry with paper towels, rub with 2 tablespoons oil, and sprinkle with ¼ teaspoon salt and ⅛ teaspoon pepper.
3. Heat remaining 2 tablespoons oil and rosemary in 12-inch ovensafe skillet over medium-high heat until shimmering. Add cremini mushrooms, portobello mushrooms, onion, and ¼ teaspoon salt. Cook, stirring occasionally, until mushrooms have released their liquid and are beginning to brown, 8 to 10 minutes. Stir in garlic and minced porcini mushrooms and cook until fragrant, about 30 seconds.

4. Off heat, stir in reserved porcini liquid. Nestle sea bass skinned side down into skillet, transfer to oven, and roast until sea bass flakes apart when gently prodded with paring knife and registers 140 degrees, 10 to 12 minutes. Sprinkle with parsley. Serve with lemon wedges.

Nutrition Info:
• 360 cal., 18g fat (3g sag. fat), 70mg chol., 430mg sod., 11g carb (6g sugars, 2g fiber), 36g pro.

Tuna & White Bean Lettuce Wraps

Servings:4 | Cooking Time: 20 Minutes

Ingredients:
• 1 can (12 ounces) light tuna in water, drained and flaked
• 1 can (15 ounces) cannellini beans, rinsed and drained
• 1/4 cup chopped red onion
• 2 tablespoons olive oil
• 1 tablespoon minced fresh parsley
• 1/8 teaspoon salt
• 1/8 teaspoon pepper
• 12 Bibb or Boston lettuce leaves (about 1 medium head)
• 1 medium ripe avocado, peeled and cubed

Directions:
1. In a small bowl, combine the first seven ingredients; toss lightly to combine. Serve tuna mixture in lettuce leaves; top with avocado.

Nutrition Info:
• 279 cal., 13g fat (2g sat. fat), 31mg chol., 421mg sod., 19g carb. (1g sugars, 7g fiber), 22g pro.

Oven-roasted Salmon

Servings:4 | Cooking Time:10 Minutes

Ingredients:
• 1 (1½-pound) skin-on salmon fillet, 1 inch thick
• 1 teaspoon extra-virgin olive oil
• ¼ teaspoon salt
• ⅛ teaspoon pepper

Directions:
1. Adjust oven rack to lowest position, place aluminum foil–lined rimmed baking sheet on rack, and heat oven to 500 degrees. Cut salmon crosswise into 4 fillets, then make 4 or 5 shallow slashes about an inch apart along skin side of each piece, being careful not to cut into flesh. Pat fillets dry with paper towels, rub with oil, and sprinkle with salt and pepper.
2. Once oven reaches 500 degrees, reduce oven temperature to 275 degrees. Remove sheet from oven and carefully place salmon, skin-side down, on hot sheet. Roast until centers are still translucent when checked with tip of paring knife and register 125 degrees (for medium-rare), 4 to 6 minutes.
3. Slide spatula along underside of fillets and transfer to individual serving plates or serving platter, leaving skin behind; discard skin. Serve.

Nutrition Info:
• 360 cal., 24g fat (5g sag. fat), 95mg chol, 250mg sod., 0g carb (0g sugars, 0g fiber), 35g pro.

Cajun Baked Catfish

Servings:2 | Cooking Time: 25 Minutes

Ingredients:
• 2 tablespoons yellow cornmeal
• 2 teaspoons Cajun or blackened seasoning
• 1/2 teaspoon dried thyme
• 1/2 teaspoon dried basil
• 1/4 teaspoon garlic powder
• 1/4 teaspoon lemon-pepper seasoning
• 2 catfish or tilapia fillets (6 ounces each)
• 1/4 teaspoon paprika

Directions:
1. Preheat oven to 400°. In a shallow bowl, mix the first six ingredients.
2. Dip the fillets in cornmeal mixture to evenly coat both sides. Place them on a baking sheet coated with cooking spray. Sprinkle with paprika.
3. Bake 20-25 minutes or until fish just begins to flake easily with a fork.

Nutrition Info:
• 242 cal., 10g fat (2g sat. fat), 94mg chol., 748mg sod., 8g carb. (0 sugars, 1g fiber), 27g pro.

Tomato-poached Halibut

Servings:4 | Cooking Time: 30 Minutes

Ingredients:
• 1 tablespoon olive oil
• 2 poblano peppers, finely chopped
• 1 small onion, finely chopped
• 1 can (14 1/2 ounces) fire-roasted diced tomatoes, undrained
• 1 can (14 1/2 ounces) no-salt-added diced tomatoes, undrained
• 1/4 cup chopped pitted green olives
• 3 garlic cloves, minced
• 1/4 teaspoon pepper
• 1/8 teaspoon salt
• 4 halibut fillets (4 ounces each)
• 1/3 cup chopped fresh cilantro
• 4 lemon wedges
• Crusty whole grain bread, optional

Directions:
1. In a large nonstick skillet, heat oil over medium-high heat. Add poblano peppers and onion; cook and stir about 4-6 minutes or until tender.
2. Stir in tomatoes, olives, garlic, pepper and salt. Bring to a boil. Adjust heat to maintain a gentle simmer. Add fillets. Cook, covered, 8-10 minutes or until fish just begins to flake easily with a fork. Sprinkle with cilantro. Serve with lemon wedges and, if desired, bread.

Nutrition Info:
• 224 cal., 7g fat (1g sat. fat), 56mg chol., 651mg sod., 17g carb. (8g sugars, 4g fiber), 24g pro.

Two-sauce Cajun Fish

Servings: 4 | Cooking Time:12–15 Minutes

Ingredients:
- 4 (4-ounce) tilapia filets (or any mild, lean white fish filets), rinsed and patted dry
- 1/2 teaspoon seafood seasoning
- 1 (14.5-ounce) can stewed tomatoes with Cajun seasonings, well drained
- 2 tablespoons no-trans-fat margarine (35% vegetable oil)

Directions:
1. Preheat the oven to 400°F.
2. Coat a broiler rack and pan with nonstick cooking spray, arrange the fish filets on the rack about 2 inches apart, and sprinkle them evenly with the seafood seasoning.
3. Place the tomatoes in a blender and puree until just smooth. Set aside 1/4 cup of the mixture in a small glass bowl.
4. Spoon the remaining tomatoes evenly over the top of each filet and bake 12–15 minutes or until the filets are opaque in the center.
5. Meanwhile, add the margarine to the reserved 1/4 cup tomato mixture and microwave on HIGH 20 seconds or until the mixture is just melted. Stir to blend well.
6. Place the filets on a serving platter, spoon the tomato-margarine mixture over the center of each filet, and sprinkle each lightly with chopped fresh parsley, if desired.

Nutrition Info:
- 150 cal., 5g fat (1g sag. fat), 50mg chol, 250mg sod., 4g carb (3g sugars, 1g fiber), 23g pro.

Salmon With Mango-citrus Salsa

Servings:4 | Cooking Time: 30 Minutes

Ingredients:
- 1 large navel orange
- 1 medium lemon
- 2 tablespoons olive oil
- 1 tablespoon capers, drained and coarsely chopped
- 1 1/2 teaspoons minced fresh mint
- 1 1/2 teaspoons minced fresh parsley
- 1/4 teaspoon crushed red pepper flakes
- 1/8 teaspoon plus 1/2 teaspoon salt, divided
- 1/8 teaspoon plus 1/4 teaspoon pepper, divided
- 1 medium mango, peeled and chopped
- 1 green onion, thinly sliced
- 4 salmon fillets (6 ounces each)
- 1 tablespoon canola oil

Directions:
1. For salsa, finely grate enough peel from orange to measure 2 teaspoons; finely grate enough peel from lemon to measure 1/2 teaspoon. Place citrus peels in a small bowl. Cut lemon crosswise in half; squeeze 2 tablespoons lemon juice and add to bowl.
2. Cut a thin slice from the top and bottom of orange; stand orange upright on a cutting board. With a knife, cut off the peel and outer membrane from the orange. Cut along the membrane of each segment to remove fruit.
3. Add olive oil, capers, mint, parsley, pepper flakes and 1/8 teaspoon each salt and pepper to lemon juice mixture. Gently stir in mango, green onion and orange sections.
4. Sprinkle salmon with the remaining salt and pepper. In a large skillet, heat canola oil over medium heat. Add the salmon; cook 5-6 minutes on each side or until fish just begins to flake easily with a fork. Serve with salsa.

Nutrition Info:
- 433 cal., 26g fat (4g sat. fat), 85mg chol., 516mg sod., 19g carb. (16g sugars, 3g fiber), 30g pro.

Seared Scallops With Snap Pea And Edamame Slaw

Servings:4 | Cooking Time: 10 Minutes

Ingredients:
- 3 tablespoons chopped fresh chives
- 2 tablespoons plain low-fat yogurt
- 2 tablespoons mayonnaise
- ½ teaspoon grated lemon zest plus 1 tablespoon juice
- Salt and pepper
- 12 ounces sugar snap peas, strings removed and sliced thin on bias
- 10 ounces frozen edamame, thawed
- 1 English cucumber, halved lengthwise, seeded, and sliced thin
- 6 radishes, trimmed, halved lengthwise, and sliced thin
- 1½ pounds large sea scallops, tendons removed
- 2 tablespoons canola oil

Directions:
1. Whisk chives, yogurt, mayonnaise, lemon zest and juice, and ⅛ teaspoon salt together in large bowl. Add snap peas, edamame, cucumber, and radishes and stir to coat; set aside.
2. Place scallops in rimmed baking sheet lined with clean kitchen towel. Place second clean kitchen towel on top of scallops and press gently on towel to blot liquid. Let scallops sit at room temperature, covered with towel, for 10 minutes. Sprinkle scallops with ⅛ teaspoon salt and ⅛ teaspoon pepper.
3. Heat 1 tablespoon oil in 12-inch nonstick skillet over medium heat until just smoking. Add half of scallops and cook, without moving them, until well browned on first side, about 1½ minutes. Flip scallops and continue to cook, without moving them, until well browned on second side, sides are firm, and centers are opaque, about 1½ minutes. Transfer scallops to serving platter and tent loosely with aluminum foil. Repeat with remaining 1 tablespoon oil and remaining scallops. Serve scallops with slaw.

Nutrition Info:
- 360 cal., 16g fat (1g sag. fat), 45mg chol, 480mg sod., 22g carb (8g sugars, 6g fiber), 32g pro.

Pomegranate Roasted Salmon With Lentils And Chard

Servings:4 | Cooking Time:60 Minutes

Ingredients:
- 1 tablespoon plus 1 teaspoon extra-virgin olive oil
- 12 ounces Swiss chard, stemmed, ½ cup stems chopped fine, leaves cut into 2-inch pieces
- 1 small onion, chopped fine
- 2 garlic cloves, minced
- 4 sprigs fresh thyme
- Salt and pepper
- 1½ cups unsalted chicken broth
- ¾ cup lentilles du Puy, picked over and rinsed
- 1 (1½-pound) skin-on salmon fillet, 1 inch thick
- 2 tablespoons pomegranate molasses
- ½ cup pomegranate seeds

Directions:
1. Heat 1 tablespoon oil in large saucepan over medium-high heat until shimmering. Add chard stems, onion, garlic, thyme, and ⅛ teaspoon salt and cook, stirring frequently, until softened, about 5 minutes. Stir in broth and lentils and bring to boil. Reduce heat to low, cover, and simmer, stirring occasionally, until lentils are mostly tender but still intact, 45 to 55 minutes.
2. Adjust oven rack to lowest position, place aluminum foil–lined rimmed baking sheet on rack, and heat oven to 500 degrees. Uncover lentils and stir in chard leaves. Increase heat to medium-low and continue to cook until chard leaves are tender and lentils are completely tender, about 4 minutes. Off heat, discard thyme sprigs and season with pepper to taste; cover to keep warm.
3. Cut salmon crosswise into 4 fillets. Pat dry with paper towels. Brush with remaining 1 teaspoon oil, then brush with 1 tablespoon pomegranate molasses and sprinkle with ¼ teaspoon salt and ⅛ teaspoon pepper. Once oven reaches 500 degrees, reduce oven temperature to 275 degrees. Remove sheet from oven and carefully place salmon skin-side down on hot sheet. Roast until centers are still translucent when checked with tip of paring knife and register 125 degrees (for medium-rare), 4 to 6 minutes.
4. Brush salmon with remaining 1 tablespoon pomegranate molasses. Slide spatula under fillets and transfer to individual serving plates or serving platter, leaving skin behind; discard skin. Stir pomegranate seeds into lentil mixture and serve with salmon.

Nutrition Info:
- 580 cal., 29g fat (6g sag. fat), 95mg chol, 540mg sod., 35g carb (9g sugars, 8g fiber), 46g pro.

Cod With Bacon & Balsamic Tomatoes

Servings:4 | Cooking Time: 30 Minutes

Ingredients:
- 4 center-cut bacon strips, chopped
- 4 cod fillets (5 ounces each)
- 1/2 teaspoon salt
- 1/4 teaspoon pepper
- 2 cups grape tomatoes, halved
- 2 tablespoons balsamic vinegar

Directions:
1. In a large skillet, cook the bacon over medium heat until crisp, stirring occasionally. Remove with a slotted spoon; drain on paper towels.
2. Sprinkle fillets with salt and pepper. Add fillets to the bacon drippings; cook over medium-high heat 4-6 minutes on each side or until fish just begins to flake easily with a fork. Remove from pan and keep warm.
3. Add tomatoes to skillet; cook and stir 2-4 minutes or until tomatoes are softened. Stir in vinegar; reduce heat to medium-low. Cook 1-2 minutes longer or until sauce is thickened. Serve cod with tomato mixture and bacon.

Nutrition Info:
- 178 cal., 6g fat (2g sat. fat), 64mg chol., 485mg sod., 5g carb. (4g sugars, 1g fiber), 26g pro.

Halibut En Cocotte With Cherry Tomatoes

Servings:8 | Cooking Time:40 Minutes

Ingredients:
- 2 tablespoons extra-virgin olive oil
- 2 garlic cloves, sliced thin
- ⅛ teaspoon red pepper flakes
- 12 ounces cherry tomatoes, quartered
- 1 tablespoon capers, rinsed
- 1 teaspoon minced fresh thyme or ¼ teaspoon dried
- 2 (1½-pound) skin-on full halibut steaks, 1 to 1½ inches thick and 10 to 12 inches long, trimmed of cartilage at both ends
- Salt and pepper

Directions:
1. Adjust oven rack to lowest position and heat oven to 250 degrees. Cook 1 tablespoon oil, garlic, and pepper flakes in Dutch oven over medium-low heat until garlic is light golden, 2 to 4 minutes. Off heat, stir in tomatoes, capers, and thyme.
2. Pat halibut steaks dry with paper towels and sprinkle with ⅛ teaspoon salt and ⅛ teaspoon pepper. Lay halibut on top of tomatoes in pot. Place large sheet of aluminum foil over pot and press to seal, then cover with lid. Transfer pot to oven and cook until halibut flakes apart when gently prodded with paring knife and registers 140 degrees, 35 to 40 minutes.
3. Gently transfer halibut to serving platter and tent loosely with foil. Simmer tomato mixture over medium-high heat until thickened slightly, about 2 minutes. Off heat, stir in remaining 1 tablespoon oil and season with pepper to taste. Spoon sauce evenly over halibut and serve.

Nutrition Info:
- 170 cal., 5g fat (1g sag. fat), 70mg chol, 160mg sod., 2g carb (1g sugars, 1g fiber), 27g pro.

Fresh Tomato Relish

Servings:1 | Cooking Time: 15 Minutes

Ingredients:
- Be sure to use super-ripe tomatoes in this simple relish.
- 2 tomatoes, cored, seeded, and cut into ¼-inch pieces
- 1 small shallot, minced
- 1 small garlic clove, minced
- 2 tablespoons chopped fresh basil
- 1 tablespoon extra-virgin olive oil
- 1 teaspoon red wine vinegar
- Pepper

Directions:
1. Combine all ingredients in bowl, let sit for 15 minutes, and season with pepper to taste.

Nutrition Info:
- 45 cal., 3g fat (0g sag. fat), 0mg chol, 0mg sod., 3g carb (2g sugars, 1g fiber), 1g pro.

Salmon Tacos With Super Slaw

Servings:6 | Cooking Time:10 Minutes

Ingredients:
- ¼ teaspoon grated lime zest plus 2 tablespoons juice, plus lime wedges for serving
- Salt and pepper
- 4 ounces collard greens, stemmed and sliced thin (2 cups)
- 4 ounces jícama, peeled and cut into 2-inch-long matchsticks
- 4 radishes, trimmed and cut into 1-inch-long matchsticks
- ½ small red onion, halved and sliced thin
- ¼ cup fresh cilantro leaves
- 1½ teaspoons chili powder
- 1 (1½-pound) skin-on salmon fillet, 1 inch thick
- 1 tablespoon canola oil
- 1 avocado, halved, pitted, and cut into ½-inch pieces
- 12 (6-inch) corn tortillas, warmed
- Hot sauce

Directions:
1. Whisk lime zest and juice and ¼ teaspoon salt together in large bowl. Add collards, jícama, radishes, onion, and cilantro and toss to combine.
2. Combine chili powder, ¾ teaspoon salt, and ¼ teaspoon pepper in small bowl. Cut salmon crosswise into 4 fillets. Pat dry with paper towels and sprinkle evenly with spice mixture. Heat oil in 12-inch nonstick skillet over medium-high heat until shimmering. Cook salmon, skin side up, until well browned, 3 to 5 minutes. Gently flip salmon using 2 spatulas and continue to cook until salmon is still translucent when checked with tip of paring knife and registers 125 degrees (for medium-rare), 3 to 5 minutes. Transfer salmon to plate and let cool slightly, about 2 minutes. Using 2 forks, flake fish into 2-inch pieces, discarding skin.
3. Divide fish, collard slaw, and avocado evenly among tortillas, and drizzle with hot sauce to taste. Serve.

Nutrition Info:
- 440 cal., 24g fat (4g sag. fat), 60mg chol, 490mg sod., 29g carb (1g sugars, 6g fiber), 27g pro.

Teriyaki Salmon

Servings:4 | Cooking Time: 30 Minutes

Ingredients:
- 3/4 cup reduced-sodium teriyaki sauce
- 1/2 cup maple syrup
- 4 salmon fillets (6 ounces each)
- Mixed salad greens, optional

Directions:
1. In a small bowl, whisk teriyaki sauce and syrup. Pour 1 cup marinade into a large resealable plastic bag. Add salmon; seal bag and turn to coat. Refrigerate 15 minutes. Cover and refrigerate any of the remaining marinade.
2. Drain the salmon, discarding the marinade in bag. Moisten a paper towel with cooking oil; using long-handled tongs, rub on grill rack to coat lightly.
3. Place salmon on grill rack, skin side down. Grill, covered, over medium heat or broil 4 in. from heat 8-12 minutes or until fish just begins to flake easily with a fork, basting frequently with reserved marinade. If desired, serve over mixed salad greens.

Nutrition Info:
- 362 cal., 18g fat (4g sat. fat), 100mg chol., 422mg sod., 12g carb. (12g sugars, 0 fiber), 35g pro.

MEAT RECIPES

Stir-fried Beef With Bok Choy And Green Beans

Servings:4 | Cooking Time:30 Seconds

Ingredients:
- SAUCE
- ¼ cup water
- 2 tablespoons dry sherry or Chinese rice wine
- 1 tablespoon low-sodium soy sauce
- 1½ teaspoons cornstarch
- 1 tablespoon oyster sauce
- 2 teaspoons rice vinegar
- 2 teaspoons coarsely ground pepper
- 1½ teaspoons toasted sesame oil
- STIR-FRY
- 1 tablespoon dry sherry or Chinese rice wine
- 1 tablespoon low-sodium soy sauce
- 1½ teaspoons cornstarch
- 12 ounces flank steak, trimmed of all visible fat, sliced thin against grain into 2-inch-long pieces
- 2 tablespoons canola oil
- 3 garlic cloves, minced
- 1 tablespoon grated fresh ginger
- 1 pound bok choy, stalks and greens separated, stalks cut on bias into ¼-inch slices and greens cut into ½-inch strips
- 8 ounces green beans, trimmed and cut into 2-inch lengths
- 1 carrot, peeled and shredded

Directions:
1. FOR THE SAUCE Whisk all ingredients together in bowl.
2. FOR THE STIR-FRY Whisk sherry, soy sauce, and cornstarch together in large bowl. Add beef to soy sauce mixture, tossing to coat, and set aside for 15 to 30 minutes. Combine 2 teaspoons oil, garlic, and ginger in separate bowl; set aside.
3. Heat 1 teaspoon oil in 12-inch nonstick skillet over high heat until just smoking. Add half of beef in single layer and cook without stirring for 1 minute. Continue to cook, stirring occasionally, until spotty brown on both sides, about 1 minute; transfer to clean bowl. Repeat with remaining beef and 1 teaspoon oil; transfer to bowl.
4. Heat remaining 2 teaspoons oil in now-empty skillet over high heat until just smoking. Add bok choy stalks and green beans and cook, stirring occasionally, until vegetables are spotty brown and crisp-tender, about 5 minutes. Push vegetables to sides of skillet. Add garlic mixture to center and cook, mashing mixture into skillet, until fragrant, 30 to 60 seconds. Stir mixture into vegetables. Stir in bok choy greens, carrot, and beef.
5. Whisk sauce to recombine, then add to skillet and cook, stirring constantly, until sauce has thickened, about 30 seconds. Serve immediately.

Nutrition Info:
- 270 cal., 15g fat (3g sag. fat), 60mg chol, 520mg sod., 12g carb (4g sugars, 3g fiber), 22g pro.

Chard & Bacon Linguine

Servings:4 | Cooking Time: 30 Minutes

Ingredients:
- 8 ounces uncooked whole wheat linguine
- 4 bacon strips, chopped
- 4 garlic cloves, minced
- 1/2 cup reduced-sodium chicken broth
- 1/2 cup dry white wine or additional chicken broth
- 1/4 teaspoon salt
- 6 cups chopped Swiss chard (about 6 ounces)
- 1/3 cup shredded Parmesan cheese

Directions:
1. Cook linguine according to package directions; drain. Meanwhile, in a large skillet, cook bacon over medium heat until crisp, stirring occasionally. Add garlic; cook 1 minute longer.
2. Add the broth, wine, salt and Swiss chard to skillet; bring to a boil. Cook and stir 4-5 minutes or until chard is tender.
3. Add linguine; heat through, tossing to combine. Sprinkle with cheese.

Nutrition Info:
- 353 cal., 14g fat (5g sat. fat), 23mg chol., 633mg sod., 47g carb. (2g sugars, 7g fiber), 14g pro.

Grapefruit-zested Pork

Servings: 4 | Cooking Time:6 Minutes

Ingredients:
- 3 tablespoons lite soy sauce
- 1/2–1 teaspoon grapefruit zest
- 3 tablespoons grapefruit juice
- 1 jalapeño pepper, seeded and finely chopped, or 1/8–1/4 teaspoon dried red pepper flakes
- 4 thin lean pork chops with bone in (about 1 1/4 pounds total)

Directions:
1. Combine all ingredients in a large zippered plastic bag. Seal tightly and toss back and forth to coat evenly. Refrigerate overnight or at least 8 hours.
2. Preheat the broiler.
3. Coat the broiler rack and pan with nonstick cooking spray, arrange the pork chops on the rack (discarding the marinade), and broil 2 inches away from the heat source for 3 minutes. Turn and broil 3 minutes longer or until the pork is no longer pink in the center.

Nutrition Info:
- 130 cal., 3g fat (1g sag. fat), 60mg chol, 270mg sod., 2g

carb (1g sugars, 0g fiber), 23g pro.

Roast Butterflied Leg Of Lamb With Coriander, Cumin, And Mustard Seeds

Servings:12 | Cooking Time:30 Seconds

Ingredients:
- 1 (2½-pound) boneless half leg of lamb
- 1½ teaspoons kosher salt
- ⅓ cup extra-virgin olive oil
- 3 shallots, sliced thin
- 4 garlic cloves, peeled and smashed
- 1 (1-inch) piece ginger, peeled, sliced into ½-inch-thick rounds, and smashed
- 1 tablespoon coriander seeds
- 1 tablespoon cumin seeds
- 1 tablespoon mustard seeds
- 3 bay leaves
- 2 (2-inch) strips lemon zest

Directions:
1. Place lamb on cutting board with fat cap facing down. Using sharp knife, trim any pockets of fat and connective tissue from underside of lamb. Flip lamb over, trim fat cap to ⅛ inch, and pound roast to even 1-inch thickness. Cut slits, spaced ½ inch apart, in fat cap in crosshatch pattern, being careful to cut down to but not into meat. Rub salt over entire roast and into slits. Let sit, uncovered, at room temperature for 1 hour.
2. Meanwhile, adjust oven rack to lower-middle position and second rack 4 to 5 inches from broiler element and heat oven to 250 degrees. Stir together oil, shallots, garlic, ginger, coriander seeds, cumin seeds, mustard seeds, bay leaves, and lemon zest in rimmed baking sheet and bake on lower rack until spices are softened and fragrant and shallots and garlic turn golden, about 1 hour. Remove sheet from oven and discard bay leaves.
3. Pat lamb dry with paper towels and transfer fat side up to sheet (directly on top of spices). Roast on lower rack until lamb registers 120 degrees, 20 to 25 minutes. Remove sheet from oven and heat broiler. Broil lamb on upper rack until surface is well browned and charred in spots and lamb registers 120 to 125 degrees (for medium-rare), 3 to 8 minutes.
4. Remove sheet from oven and transfer lamb to carving board (some spices will cling to bottom of roast). Tent loosely with aluminum foil and let rest for 20 minutes.
5. Slice lamb with grain into 2 equal pieces. Turn each piece and slice against grain into ¼-inch-thick slices. Serve.

Nutrition Info:
- 150 cal., 7g fat (2g sag. fat), 60mg chol, 220mg sod., 0g carb (0g sugars, 0g fiber), 19g pro.

Pork With Pineapple Ginger Salsa

Servings: 4 | Cooking Time:12 Minutes

Ingredients:
- 1 (8-ounce) can pineapple tidbits packed in juice, drained, reserve juice
- 2 teaspoons grated gingerroot
- 1/2–1 medium jalapeño, seeded and minced
- 1 teaspoon pourable sugar substitute (optional)
- 4 (4-ounce) boneless pork chops, trimmed of fat
- 1/4 teaspoon salt
- 1/4 teaspoon black pepper

Directions:
1. Stir the pineapple, 1 tablespoon of the reserved pineapple juice, gingerroot, jalapeño, and 1 teaspoon sugar substitute (if desired), together in a small bowl and set aside.
2. Sprinkle both sides of the pork evenly with salt and pepper.
3. Place a large nonstick skillet over medium-high heat until hot. Coat the skillet with nonstick cooking spray, add the pork, and cook 4 minutes. Turn and cook 4 minutes longer or until the pork is barely pink in the center.
4. Add the remaining pineapple juice to the pork in the skillet and cook 2 minutes. Turn and cook 1 minute longer or until the liquid has evaporated. Remove the skillet from the heat, turn the pork several times to lightly glaze with the salsa, and serve.

Nutrition Info:
- 170 cal., 3g fat (1g sag. fat), 65mg chol, 210mg sod., 10g carb (8g sugars, 1g fiber), 25g pro.

Harissa-rubbed Roast Boneless Leg Of Lamb With Warm Cauliflower Salad

Servings:12 | Cooking Time:20 Minutes

Ingredients:
- ½ cup extra-virgin olive oil
- 6 garlic cloves, minced
- 2 tablespoons paprika
- 1 tablespoon ground coriander
- 1 tablespoon ground dried Aleppo pepper
- 1 teaspoon ground cumin
- ¾ teaspoon caraway seeds
- Salt and pepper
- 1 (2½-pound) boneless half leg of lamb
- 1 head cauliflower (2 pounds), cored and cut into 1-inch florets
- ½ red onion, sliced ¼ inch thick
- 1 cup shredded carrots
- ½ cup raisins
- ¼ cup fresh cilantro leaves
- 2 tablespoons sliced almonds, toasted
- 1 tablespoon lemon juice, plus extra for seasoning

Directions:
1. Combine 6 tablespoons oil, garlic, paprika, coriander, Aleppo pepper, cumin, caraway seeds, and ¾ teaspoon salt in bowl and microwave until bubbling and very fragrant, about 1 minute, stirring halfway through microwaving. Let cool to room temperature.
2. Adjust oven rack to lower-middle position and heat oven to 375 degrees. Set V-rack in large roasting pan and spray with vegetable oil spray. Place lamb on cutting board with fat cap facing up. Using sharp knife, trim fat cap to ⅛ inch.

Flip lamb over and trim any pockets of fat and connective tissue from underside of lamb (side that was closest to bone). Pound roast to even 1-inch thickness, then rub with 2 tablespoons spice paste. Roll roast tightly into cylinder, tie at 1½-inch intervals with kitchen twine, then rub exterior with 1 tablespoon oil.

3. Heat remaining 1 tablespoon oil in 12-inch skillet over medium-high heat until just smoking. Brown lamb on all sides, about 8 minutes. Brush lamb all over with remaining spice paste and place fat side down in prepared V-rack. Roast until lamb registers 120 to 125 degrees (for medium-rare), about 1 hour, flipping lamb halfway through roasting. Transfer lamb to carving board, tent with aluminum foil, and let rest while making salad.

4. Increase oven temperature to 475 degrees. Pour off all but 3 tablespoons fat from pan; discard any charred drippings. Add cauliflower, ½ teaspoon salt, and ½ teaspoon pepper to fat left in pan and toss to coat. Cover with foil and roast until cauliflower is softened, about 5 minutes.

5. Remove foil and spread onion evenly over cauliflower. Roast until vegetables are tender and cauliflower is golden brown, 10 to 15 minutes, stirring halfway through roasting. Transfer vegetable mixture to serving bowl, add carrots, raisins, cilantro, almonds, and lemon juice and toss to combine. Season with pepper and lemon juice to taste. Slice lamb ½ inch thick and serve with salad.

Nutrition Info:
• 260 cal., 15g fat (3g sag. fat), 60mg chol, 340mg sod., 10g carb (6g sugars, 2g fiber), 21g pro.

Egg Roll Noodle Bowl
Servings:4 | Cooking Time: 30 Minutes

Ingredients:
• 1 tablespoon sesame oil
• 1/2 pound ground pork
• 1 tablespoon soy sauce
• 1 garlic clove, minced
• 1 teaspoon ground ginger
• 1/2 teaspoon salt
• 1/4 teaspoon ground turmeric
• 1/4 teaspoon pepper
• 6 cups shredded cabbage (about 1 small head)
• 2 large carrots, shredded (about 2 cups)
• 4 ounces rice noodles
• 3 green onions, thinly sliced
• Additional soy sauce, optional

Directions:
1. In a large skillet, heat the oil over medium-high heat; cook and crumble pork until browned, 4-6 minutes. Stir in soy sauce, garlic and seasonings. Add cabbage and carrots; cook 4-6 minutes longer or until vegetables are tender, stirring occasionally.

2. Cook rice noodles according to the package directions; drain and add immediately to pork mixture, tossing to combine. Sprinkle with green onions. If desired, serve with additional soy sauce.

Nutrition Info:
• 302 cal., 12g fat (4g sat. fat), 38mg chol., 652mg sod., 33g carb. (2g sugars, 4g fiber), 14g pro.

Spice-rubbed Pork Tenderloin With Fennel, Tomatoes, Artichokes, And Olives
Servings:4 | Cooking Time:30 Seconds

Ingredients:
• 2 large fennel bulbs, stalks discarded, bulbs halved, cored, and sliced ½ inch thick
• 12 ounces frozen artichoke hearts, thawed and patted dry
• ½ cup pitted kalamata olives, halved
• 3 tablespoons extra-virgin olive oil
• 1 teaspoon herbes de Provence
• Salt and pepper
• 1 (1-pound) pork tenderloin, trimmed of all visible fat
• 1 pound cherry tomatoes, halved
• 1 tablespoon grated lemon zest
• 2 tablespoons minced fresh parsley

Directions:
1. Adjust oven rack to lower-middle position and heat oven to 450 degrees. Microwave fennel and 2 tablespoons water in covered bowl until softened, about 5 minutes. Drain fennel well, then toss with artichoke hearts, olives, and 2 tablespoons oil.

2. Combine herbes de Provence, ¼ teaspoon salt, and ¼ teaspoon pepper in bowl. Pat tenderloin dry with paper towels, then rub with remaining 1 tablespoon oil and sprinkle with herb mixture. Spread vegetables into even layer on rimmed baking sheet, then lay tenderloin on top. Roast until pork registers 145 degrees, 25 to 30 minutes, rotating sheet halfway through roasting.

3. Remove sheet from oven. Transfer tenderloin to carving board, tent with aluminum foil, and let rest while vegetables finish cooking. Stir tomatoes and lemon zest into vegetables and continue to roast until fennel is tender and tomatoes have softened, about 10 minutes. Stir in parsley and season with pepper to taste. Slice pork ½ inch thick and serve with vegetables.

Nutrition Info:
• 330 cal., 15g fat (2g sag. fat), 75mg chol, 400mg sod., 22g carb (8g sugars, 11g fiber), 28g pro.

Roast Beef Tenderloin
Servings:12 | Cooking Time:30 Seconds

Ingredients:
• HORSERADISH SAUCE
• ½ cup mayonnaise
• ¼ cup sour cream
• 3 tablespoons prepared horseradish
• 2 tablespoons lemon juice
• ½ teaspoon garlic powder
• Salt and pepper
• BEEF TENDERLOIN
• ¾ teaspoon salt
• 1 (3-pound) center-cut beef tenderloin roast, trimmed of

all visible fat and tied at 1½-inch intervals
- ½ teaspoon pepper
- 2 teaspoons canola oil

Directions:

1. FOR THE HORSERADISH SAUCE Combine mayonnaise, sour cream, horseradish, lemon juice, garlic powder, ¼ teaspoon salt, and ⅛ teaspoon pepper in bowl. Adjust consistency with water as needed and season with pepper to taste. Cover and refrigerate until ready to serve. (Sauce can be refrigerated for up to 2 days.)

2. FOR THE BEEF TENDERLOIN Sprinkle salt evenly over roast, cover loosely with plastic wrap, and let sit at room temperature for 1 hour.

3. Adjust oven rack to middle position and heat oven to 300 degrees. Pat roast dry with paper towels. Sprinkle roast evenly with pepper and transfer to wire rack set in rimmed baking sheet. Roast until meat registers 120 to 125 degrees (for medium-rare), 40 to 55 minutes, flipping roast halfway through roasting.

4. Heat oil in 12-inch skillet over medium-high heat until just smoking. Brown roast on all sides, 4 to 8 minutes. Transfer roast to carving board, tent with aluminum foil, and let rest for 15 minutes. Discard twine and slice roast thin. Serve with sauce.

Nutrition Info:
- 250 cal., 16g fat (4g sag. fat), 80mg chol, 330mg sod., 1g carb (1g sugars, 0g fiber), 25g pro.

Tempting Pork Tenderloin Burgers

Servings:4 | Cooking Time: 30 Minutes

Ingredients:
- 1 large egg white, lightly beaten
- 1/3 cup panko (Japanese) bread crumbs
- 3 tablespoons dried cranberries, chopped
- 1/2 teaspoon poultry seasoning
- 1 pork tenderloin (1 pound), cubed
- 3 tablespoons Dijon mustard
- 3 tablespoons mayonnaise
- 1 1/2 teaspoons maple syrup
- 4 whole wheat hamburger buns, split and lightly toasted
- Arugula or baby spinach

Directions:

1. In a bowl, mix first four ingredients. In a food processor, pulse pork until finely chopped. Add to the egg white mixture; mix lightly but thoroughly. Shape into four 1/2-in.-thick patties. Mix mustard, mayonnaise and syrup.

2. Place patties on an oiled grill rack; grill, covered, over medium heat until a thermometer reads 160°, 4-6 minutes per side. Serve in buns with arugula and mustard mixture.

Nutrition Info:
- 378 cal., 14g fat (3g sat. fat), 64mg chol., 620mg sod., 33g carb. (11g sugars, 4g fiber), 28g pro.

Grilled Balsamic Beef Skewers With Tomatoes And Salad

Servings:8 | Cooking Time:20 Minutes

Ingredients:
- ½ cup balsamic vinegar
- 7 tablespoons extra-virgin olive oil
- 2 tablespoons Dijon mustard
- 4 garlic cloves, minced
- ½ teaspoon red pepper flakes
- Salt and pepper
- 2 pounds sirloin steak tips, trimmed of all visible fat and cut into 1-inch pieces
- 1 red onion, peeled and cut through root end into 8 wedges
- 2 tablespoons lemon juice
- 8 ounces (8 cups) arugula
- 1 ounce Parmesan cheese, shaved
- 2 large heirloom tomatoes, cored and sliced thin

Directions:

1. Whisk vinegar, ¼ cup oil, mustard, garlic, pepper flakes, ½ teaspoon salt, and ½ teaspoon pepper together in large bowl. Transfer ½ cup vinegar mixture to small saucepan. Toss steak with remaining vinegar mixture and let marinate for 10 minutes.

2. Meanwhile, cook reserved ½ cup vinegar mixture over medium heat until slightly thickened, about 2 minutes; set aside basting sauce. Working with 1 skewer at a time, thread 1 onion wedge, followed by one-quarter of marinated steak, then 1 onion wedge onto each skewer.

3. FOR A CHARCOAL GRILL Open bottom grill vent completely. Light large chimney starter filled with charcoal briquettes (6 quarts). When top coals are partially covered with ash, pour evenly over grill. Set cooking grate in place, cover, and open lid vent completely. Heat grill until hot, about 5 minutes.

4. FOR A GAS GRILL Turn all burners to high, cover, and heat grill until hot, about 15 minutes. Leave all burners on high.

5. Clean and oil cooking grate. Place skewers on grill and cook (covered if using gas), turning and basting with sauce every 2 minutes, until well charred and meat registers 120 to 125 degrees (for medium-rare), 10 to 12 minutes. Transfer to plate, tent with aluminum foil, and let rest for 5 minutes.

6. Whisk lemon juice, ¼ teaspoon salt, and ⅛ teaspoon pepper, and 2 tablespoons oil in large bowl. Add arugula and gently toss to coat. Sprinkle salad with Parmesan. Arrange tomatoes on serving platter, then drizzle with remaining 1 tablespoon oil and season with pepper. Using tongs, slide steak and onions off skewers onto platter with tomatoes and season with pepper to taste. Serve with salad.

Nutrition Info:
- 340 cal., 23g fat (6g sag. fat), 80mg chol, 430mg sod., 6g carb (4g sugars, 1g fiber), 26g pro.

Pork With Kalamata Rice

Servings: 4 | Cooking Time: 8 Minutes

Ingredients:
- 1/3 cup medium salsa
- 12 small kalamata olives, pitted and coarsely chopped
- 2 cups cooked brown rice, warm (omit added salt or fat)
- 4 (4-ounce) boneless pork chops, trimmed of fat
- 1/4 teaspoon salt
- 1/4 teaspoon black pepper
- 1/2 cup water

Directions:
1. Add the salsa and olives to the cooked rice and toss gently. Place on a serving platter and cover with a sheet of foil to keep warm.
2. Place a large nonstick skillet over medium-high heat until hot. Coat the skillet with nonstick cooking spray. Sprinkle the pork with salt and pepper. Place the pork in the skillet, immediately reduce the heat to medium, and cook 4 minutes. Turn and cook 4 minutes longer or until the pork is barely pink in the center. Place the pork on top of the rice, cover with foil, and set aside.
3. Add the water to the skillet, stir, and bring to a boil over medium-high heat. Boil 2 minutes or until the liquid is reduced to 1/4 cup. Pour the sauce over the pork and rice.

Nutrition Info:
- 270 cal., 6g fat (1g sag. fat), 65mg chol, 430mg sod., 24g carb (1g sugars, 2g fiber), 28g pro.

One-pot Beef & Pepper Stew

Servings: 8 | Cooking Time: 30 Minutes

Ingredients:
- 1 pound lean ground beef (90% lean)
- 3 cans (14 1/2 ounces each) diced tomatoes, undrained
- 4 large green peppers, coarsely chopped
- 1 large onion, chopped
- 2 cans (4 ounces each) chopped green chilies
- 3 teaspoons garlic powder
- 1 teaspoon pepper
- 1/4 teaspoon salt
- 2 cups uncooked instant rice
- Hot pepper sauce, optional

Directions:
1. In a 6-qt. stockpot, cook beef over medium heat 6-8 minutes or until no longer pink, breaking into crumbles; drain. Add tomatoes, green peppers, onion, chilies and seasonings; bring to a boil. Reduce heat; simmer, covered, for 20-25 minutes or until vegetables are tender.
2. Prepare rice according to package directions. Serve with the stew and, if desired, pepper sauce.

Nutrition Info:
- 244 cal., 5g fat (2g sat. fat), 35mg chol., 467mg sod., 35g carb. (8g sugars, 5g fiber), 15g pro.

Vegetable Steak Kabobs

Servings: 6 | Cooking Time: 10 Minutes

Ingredients:
- 1/2 cup olive oil
- 1/3 cup red wine vinegar
- 2 tablespoons ketchup
- 2 to 3 garlic cloves, minced
- 1 teaspoon Worcestershire sauce
- 1/2 teaspoon each dried marjoram, basil and oregano
- 1/2 teaspoon dried rosemary, crushed
- 1 beef top sirloin steak (1 1/2 pounds), cut into 1-inch cubes
- 1/2 pound whole fresh mushrooms
- 2 medium onions, cut into wedges
- 1 1/2 cups cherry tomatoes
- 2 small green peppers, cut into 1-inch pieces

Directions:
1. In a small bowl, whisk oil, vinegar, ketchup, garlic, Worcestershire sauce and seasonings. Pour 1/2 cup marinade into a large resealable plastic bag. Add beef; seal bag and turn to coat. Pour remaining marinade into another large resealable plastic bag. Add mushrooms, onions, tomatoes and peppers; seal bag and turn to coat. Refrigerate beef and vegetables 8 hours or overnight.
2. Drain beef, discarding marinade. Drain vegetables, reserving marinade. On six metal or soaked wooden skewers, thread beef and vegetables.
3. Grill kabobs, covered, over medium heat or broil 4 in. from heat 10-15 minutes or until beef reaches desired doneness and vegetables are crisp-tender, turning occasionally. Baste with reserved marinade the last 5 minutes.

Nutrition Info:
- 234 cal., 10g fat (2g sat. fat), 69mg chol., 99mg sod., 10g carb. (0 sugars, 2g fiber), 26g pro.

Philly Cheesesteak Rolls

Servings: 4 | Cooking Time: 15 Minutes

Ingredients:
- 1/2 pound sliced fresh mushrooms
- 1 medium onion, halved and sliced
- 1 small green pepper, cut into thin strips
- 1 beef top round steak (1 pound)
- 4 wedges The Laughing Cow light Swiss cheese
- 1/4 teaspoon pepper
- 3 cups hot mashed potatoes (made with fat-free milk)

Directions:
1. Preheat oven to 450°. Place a large nonstick skillet coated with cooking spray over medium-high heat. Add mushrooms, onion and green pepper; cook and stir until tender, 8-10 minutes. Remove from pan; cool slightly.
2. Cut steak into four pieces; pound with a meat mallet to 1/4-in. thickness. Spread wedges with cheese. Sprinkle with pepper; top with the mushroom mixture. Roll up from a short side; secure with toothpicks. Place rolls in a foil-lined 15x10x1-in. baking pan.

3. Bake until meat reaches desired doneness (for medium-rare, a thermometer should read 145°; medium, 160°), for 12-17 minutes. Let stand 5 minutes before serving. Serve with mashed potatoes.

Nutrition Info:
• 364 cal., 10g fat (3g sat. fat), 68mg chol., 822mg sod., 34g carb. (5g sugars, 4g fiber), 33g pro.

Italian Crumb-crusted Beef Roast

Servings:8 | Cooking Time: 1 3/4 Hours

Ingredients:
• 1 beef sirloin tip roast (3 pounds)
• 1/4 teaspoon salt
• 3/4 cup Italian-style panko (Japanese) bread crumbs
• 1/4 cup mayonnaise
• 3 tablespoons dried minced onion
• 1/2 teaspoon Italian seasoning
• 1/4 teaspoon pepper

Directions:
1. Preheat oven to 325°. Place roast on a rack in a shallow roasting pan; sprinkle with salt. In a small bowl, mix remaining ingredients; press onto top and sides of roast.
2. Roast 1 3/4-2 1/4 hours or until meat reaches desired doneness (for medium-rare, a thermometer should read 145°; medium, 160°; well-done, 170°). Remove roast from oven; tent with foil. Let roast stand 10 minutes before slicing.

Nutrition Info:
• 319 cal., 15g fat (3g sat. fat), 111mg chol., 311mg sod., 7g carb. (0 sugars, 0 fiber), 35g pro.

Farmers Market Pasta

Servings:6 | Cooking Time: 20 Minutes

Ingredients:
• 9 ounces uncooked whole wheat linguine
• 1 pound fresh asparagus, trimmed and cut into 2-inch pieces
• 2 medium carrots, thinly sliceed
• 1 small red onion, chopped
• 2 medium zucchini or yellow summer squash, thinly sliced
• 1/2 pound sliced fresh mushrooms
• 2 garlic cloves, minced
• 1 cup half-and-half cream
• 2/3 cup reduced-sodium chicken broth
• 1 cup frozen petite peas
• 2 cups cubed fully cooked ham
• 2 tablespoons julienned fresh basil
• 1/4 teaspoon pepper
• 1/2 cup grated Parmesan cheese
• Additonal fresh basil and Parmesan cheese, optional

Directions:
1. In a 6-qt. stockpot, cook linguine according to package directions, adding asparagus and carrots during the last 3-5 minutes of cooking. Drain; return to the pot.
2. Place a large skillet coated with cooking spray over medium heat. Add onion; cook and stir 3 minutes. Add squash, mushrooms, and garlic; cook and stir until crisp-tender, 4-5 minutes.
3. Add the cream and broth; bring to a boil, stirring to loosen browned bits from the pan. Reduce heat; simmer, uncovered, until the sauce is thickened slightly, for about 5 minutes. Stir in the peas, ham, basil and pepper; heat mixture through.
4. Add to linguine mixture; stir in 1/2 cup cheese. If desired, top with additional basil and cheese.

Nutrition Info:
• 338 cal., 9g fat (4g sat. fat), 53mg chol., 817mg sod., 46g carb. (8g sugars, 8g fiber), 23g pro.

Pork Tenderloin With Fennel & Cranberries

Servings:8 | Cooking Time: 20 Minutes

Ingredients:
• 1 teaspoon kosher salt
• 1 teaspoon fennel seeds, crushed
• 1 teaspoon paprika
• 1/4 teaspoon cayenne pepper
• 2 pork tenderloins (1 pound each)
• 2 tablespoons olive oil, divided
• 2 medium fennel bulbs, halved and thinly sliced
• 2 shallots, thinly sliced
• 3 garlic cloves, minced
• 1 1/2 cups dry white wine or chicken broth
• 1 cup dried cranberries
• 2 tablespoons minced fresh rosemary or 2 teaspoons dried rosemary, crushed
• Fennel fronds, optional

Directions:
1. Preheat oven to 425°. In a small bowl, mix salt, fennel seeds, paprika and cayenne. Rub over pork.
2. In a large skillet, heat 1 tablespoon oil over medium-high heat. Brown the pork on all sides. Transfer to a rack in a shallow roasting pan. Roast for 20-25 minutes or until a thermometer reads 145°. Remove tenderloins from oven; tent with foil. Let stand for 5 minutes before slicing.
3. Meanwhile, in same skillet, heat remaining oil over medium-high heat. Add fennel and shallots; cook and stir 4-6 minutes or until tender. Add garlic; cook 1 minute longer.
4. Stir in the wine, cranberries and rosemary. Bring to a boil. Reduce heat; simmer, uncovered, 10 minutes.
5. To serve, spoon fennel mixture onto a serving platter. Using a slotted spoon, top with tenderloin slices and, if desired, fennel fronds.

Nutrition Info:
• 273 cal., 7g fat (2g sat. fat), 63mg chol., 374mg sod., 20g carb. (11g sugars, 3g fiber), 24g pro.

Italian Pork Stew

Servings:8 | Cooking Time: 2 1/4 Hours

Ingredients:
- 2/3 cup all-purpose flour
- 2 pounds boneless pork loin, cut into 1-inch pieces
- 4 tablespoons olive oil, divided
- 1 large onion, chopped
- 5 garlic cloves, crushed
- 1 can (28 ounces) diced tomatoes, undrained
- 1 cup dry red wine or beef broth
- 3 bay leaves
- 1 cinnamon stick (3 inches)
- 1 tablespoon tomato paste
- 1 tablespoon red wine vinegar
- 1 teaspoon anchovy paste
- 1 teaspoon each dried oregano, basil and sage leaves
- 1/2 teaspoon salt
- 1/2 teaspoon crushed red pepper flakes
- 1/4 teaspoon pepper
- 1/4 cup minced fresh parsley
- Hot cooked bow tie pasta
- Grated Parmesan cheese

Directions:
1. Place flour in a large resealable plastic bag. Add pork, a few pieces at a time, and shake to coat. In a Dutch oven, brown pork in 3 tablespoons oil in batches. Remove and keep warm.
2. In the same pan, saute onion in remaining oil until crisp-tender. Add garlic; cook 1 minute longer. Stir in the tomatoes, wine, bay leaves, cinnamon, tomato paste, vinegar, anchovy paste, herbs, salt, pepper flakes, pepper and pork; bring to a boil.
3. Reduce heat; cover and simmer for 1 1/2 hours, stirring occasionally. Stir in parsley. Cover and cook 30-40 minutes longer or until meat is tender. Skim fat; discard bay leaves and cinnamon.
4. Serve stew with the pasta; sprinkle with the cheese.

Nutrition Info:
- 256 cal., 12g fat (3g sat. fat), 59mg chol., 349mg sod., 12g carb. (4g sugars, 2g fiber), 24g pro.

Special Occasion Beef Bourguignon

Servings:8 | Cooking Time: 2 Hours

Ingredients:
- 4 bacon strips, chopped
- 1 beef sirloin tip roast (2 pounds), cut into 1 1/2-inch cubes and patted dry
- 1/4 cup all-purpose flour
- 1/2 teaspoon salt
- 1/2 teaspoon pepper
- 1 tablespoon canola oil
- 2 medium onions, chopped
- 2 medium carrots, coarsely chopped
- 1/2 pound medium fresh mushrooms, quartered
- 4 garlic cloves, minced
- 1 tablespoon tomato paste

- 2 cups dry red wine
- 1 cup beef stock
- 2 bay leaves
- 1/2 teaspoon dried thyme
- 8 ounces uncooked egg noodles
- Minced fresh parsley

Directions:
1. Preheat oven to 325°. In a Dutch oven, cook bacon over medium-low heat until crisp, stirring occasionally. Remove with a slotted spoon, reserving drippings; drain on paper towels.
2. In batches, brown beef in drippings over medium-high heat; remove from pan. Toss with flour, salt and pepper.
3. In same pan, heat 1 tablespoon oil over medium heat; saute the onions, carrots and mushrooms until onions are tender, 4-5 minutes. Add garlic and tomato paste; cook and stir 1 minute. Add wine and stock, stirring to loosen browned bits from pan. Add herbs, bacon and beef; bring to a boil.
4. Transfer to oven; bake, covered, until meat is tender, 2 to 2 1/4 hours. Remove bay leaves.
5. To serve, cook noodles according to package directions; drain. Serve stew with noodles; sprinkle with parsley.

Nutrition Info:
- 422 cal., 14g fat (4g sat. fat), 105mg chol., 357mg sod., 31g carb. (4g sugars, 2g fiber), 31g pro.

Grilled Lamb Shish Kebabs

Servings:6 | Cooking Time:20 Minutes

Ingredients:
- MARINADE
- 6 tablespoons extra-virgin olive oil
- 7 large fresh mint leaves
- 2 teaspoons chopped fresh rosemary
- 2 garlic cloves, peeled
- ½ teaspoon salt
- ½ teaspoon grated lemon zest plus 2 tablespoons juice
- ¼ teaspoon pepper
- LAMB AND VEGETABLES
- 2 pounds boneless leg of lamb, trimmed of all visible fat and cut into 2-inch pieces
- 2 zucchini or yellow summer squash, halved lengthwise and sliced 1 inch thick
- 2 red or green bell peppers, stemmed, seeded, and cut into 1½-inch pieces
- 2 red onions, cut into 1-inch pieces, 3 layers thick

Directions:
1. FOR THE MARINADE Process all ingredients in food processor until smooth, about 1 minute, scraping down sides of bowl as needed. Transfer 3 tablespoons marinade to large bowl and set aside.
2. FOR THE LAMB AND VEGETABLES Place remaining marinade and lamb in 1-gallon zipper-lock bag and toss to coat. Press out as much air as possible and seal bag. Refrigerate for at least 1 hour or up to 2 hours, flipping bag every 30 minutes.

3. Add zucchini, bell peppers, and onions to bowl with reserved marinade and toss to coat. Cover and let sit at room temperature for at least 30 minutes.

4. Remove lamb from bag and pat dry with paper towels. Thread lamb tightly onto two 12-inch metal skewers. In alternating pattern of zucchini, bell pepper, and onion, thread vegetables onto four 12-inch metal skewers.

5. FOR A CHARCOAL GRILL Open bottom vent completely. Light large chimney starter mounded with charcoal briquettes (7 quarts). When top coals are partially covered with ash, pour evenly over center of grill, leaving 2-inch gap between grill wall and charcoal. Set cooking grate in place, cover, and open lid vent completely. Heat grill until hot, about 5 minutes.

6. FOR A GAS GRILL Turn all burners to high, cover, and heat grill until hot, about 15 minutes. Leave primary burner on high and turn other burner(s) to medium-low.

7. Clean and oil cooking grate. Place lamb skewers on grill (directly over coals if using charcoal or over hotter side of grill if using gas). Place vegetable skewers on grill (near edge of coals but still over coals if using charcoal or on cooler side of grill if using gas). Cook (covered if using gas), turning skewers every 3 to 4 minutes, until lamb is well browned and registers 120 to 125 degrees (for medium-rare), 10 to 15 minutes. Transfer lamb skewers to serving platter, tent loosely with aluminum foil, and let rest while finishing vegetables.

8. Continue to cook vegetable skewers until tender and lightly charred, 5 to 7 minutes; transfer to platter. Using tongs, slide lamb and vegetables off skewers onto serving platter. Serve.

Nutrition Info:
• 300 cal., 17g fat (4g sag. fat), 85mg chol, 270mg sod., 9g carb (5g sugars, 2g fiber), 29g pro.

One-pan Roasted Pork Chops And Vegetables With Parsley Vinaigrette

Servings:4 | Cooking Time:30 Seconds

Ingredients:
• 1 pound Yukon Gold potatoes, unpeeled, halved lengthwise and sliced ½ inch thick
• 1 pound carrots, peeled and cut into 3-inch lengths, thick ends quartered lengthwise
• 1 fennel bulb, stalks discarded, bulb halved, cored, and cut into ½-inch-thick wedges
• 10 garlic cloves, peeled
• 3 tablespoons plus 1 teaspoon extra-virgin olive oil
• 2 teaspoons minced fresh rosemary or ¾ teaspoon dried
• Salt and pepper
• 1 teaspoon paprika
• 1 teaspoon ground coriander
• 2 (10-ounce) bone-in center-cut pork chops, 1 inch thick, trimmed of all visible fat
• 4 teaspoons red wine vinegar
• 2 tablespoons minced fresh parsley
• 1 small shallot, minced

Directions:
1. Adjust oven rack to upper-middle position and heat oven to 450 degrees. Toss potatoes, carrots, fennel, garlic, 1 tablespoon oil, rosemary, ¼ teaspoons salt, and ¼ teaspoon pepper together in bowl. Spread vegetables into single layer on rimmed baking sheet. Roast until beginning to soften, about 25 minutes.

2. Combine 1 teaspoon oil, paprika, coriander, ¼ teaspoon salt, and 1 teaspoon pepper in bowl. Pat pork dry with paper towels, then rub with spice mixture. Lay chops on top of vegetables and continue to roast until pork register 145 degrees and vegetables are tender, 10 to 15 minutes, rotating sheet halfway through roasting.

3. Remove sheet from oven, tent with aluminum foil, and let rest for 5 minutes. Whisk remaining 2 tablespoons oil, vinegar, parsley, shallot, ¼ teaspoon salt, and ¼ teaspoon pepper together in bowl. Transfer chops to carving board, carve meat from bone, and slice ½ inch thick. Drizzle vinaigrette over pork before serving with vegetables.

Nutrition Info:
• 480 cal., 19g fat (4g sag. fat), 80mg chol, 640mg sod., 39g carb (8g sugars, 7g fiber), 36g pro.

Melon Arugula Salad With Ham

Servings:8 | Cooking Time: 20 Minutes

Ingredients:
• 1/4 cup olive oil
• 3 tablespoons white wine vinegar
• 3 tablespoons honey
• 3 cups cubed watermelon
• 2 cups cubed honeydew
• 2 1/2 cups cubed fully cooked ham
• 1 small cucumber, coarsely chopped
• 8 cups fresh arugula
• 3/4 cup crumbled feta cheese

Directions:
1. In a large bowl, whisk together oil, vinegar and honey. Add both melons, ham and cucumber; toss to coat.

2. To serve, arrange the arugula on a platter. Top with the melon mixture; sprinkle with cheese.

Nutrition Info:
• 202 cal., 10g fat (3g sat. fat), 32mg chol., 646mg sod., 17g carb. (15g sugars, 2g fiber), 12g pro.

VEGETARIAN RECIPES

◇ Vegetarian Recipes ◇

Open-faced Grilled Pepper-goat Cheese Sandwiches

Servings: 4 | Cooking Time:25 Minutes

Ingredients:
- 3 large red bell peppers, halved lengthwise
- 1 1/2 tablespoons balsamic vinegar
- 8 ounces whole grain loaf bread, cut in half lengthwise
- 2 ounces crumbled goat cheese

Directions:
1. Heat grill or grill pan over medium-high heat. Flatten pepper halves with palm of hand. Coat both sides with cooking spray and cook 20 minutes or until tender, turning frequently. Place on cutting board and coarsely chop. Combine the peppers with the vinegar and 1/8 teaspoon salt, if desired. Cover to keep warm.
2. Coat both sides of the bread with cooking spray and cook 1 1/2 to 2 minutes on each side or until lightly browned. Cut each bread half crosswise into 4 pieces.
3. Top each bread slice with 1/4 cup pepper mixture and sprinkle cheese evenly over all.

Nutrition Info:
- 250 cal., 7g fat (3g sag. fat), 10mg chol, 280mg sod., 33g carb (10g sugars, 7g fiber), 12g pro.

Tomato & Garlic Butter Bean Dinner

Servings:4 | Cooking Time: 15 Minutes

Ingredients:
- 1 tablespoon olive oil
- 2 garlic cloves, minced
- 2 cans (14 1/2 ounces) no-salt-added petite diced tomatoes, undrained
- 1 can (16 ounces) butter beans, rinsed and drained
- 6 cups fresh baby spinach (about 6 ounces)
- 1/2 teaspoon Italian seasoning
- 1/4 teaspoon pepper
- Hot cooked pasta and grated Parmesan cheese, optional

Directions:
1. In a large skillet, heat oil over medium-high heat. Add garlic; cook and stir 30-45 seconds or until tender. Add tomatoes, beans, spinach, Italian seasoning and pepper; cook until spinach wilts, stirring occasionally. If desired, serve with pasta and cheese.

Nutrition Info:
- 147 cal., 4g fat (1g sat. fat), 0 chol., 353mg sod., 28g carb. (8g sugars, 9g fiber), 8g pro.

"refried" Bean And Rice Casserole

Servings: 4 | Cooking Time:15 Minutes

Ingredients:
- 2 1/4 cups cooked brown rice (omit added salt or fat)
- 1 (15.5-ounce) can dark red kidney beans, rinsed and drained
- 7 tablespoons picante sauce
- 1/4 cup water
- 1/2 cup shredded, reduced-fat, sharp cheddar cheese

Directions:
1. Preheat the oven to 350°F.
2. Coat an 8-inch-square baking pan with nonstick cooking spray. Place the rice in the pan and set aside.
3. Add the beans, picante sauce, and water to a blender and blend until pureed, scraping the sides of the blender frequently.
4. Spread the bean mixture evenly over the rice and sprinkle with cheese. Bake, uncovered, for 15 minutes or until thoroughly heated.

Nutrition Info:
- 260 cal., 3g fat (1g sag. fat), 5mg chol, 430mg sod., 44g carb (1g sugars, 7g fiber), 14g pro.

Tomato Topper Over Anything

Servings: 3 | Cooking Time:22 Minutes

Ingredients:
- 1 (14.5-ounce) can no-salt-added tomatoes with green pepper and onion
- 1/2 cup chopped roasted red peppers
- 2–3 tablespoons chopped fresh basil
- 2 teaspoons extra virgin olive oil

Directions:
1. Bring the tomatoes and peppers to boil in a medium saucepan. Reduce the heat and simmer, uncovered, for 15 minutes or until slightly thickened, stirring occasionally.
2. Remove the mixture from the heat, stir in the basil and oil, and let stand 5 minutes to develop flavors.

Nutrition Info:
- 80 cal., 3g fat (0g sag. fat), 0mg chol, 90mg sod., 12g carb (8g sugars, 2g fiber), 2g pro.

Curried Tempeh With Cauliflower And Peas

Servings:6 | Cooking Time:15 Minutes

Ingredients:
- 1 (14.5-ounce) no-salt-added can diced tomatoes
- ¼ cup canola oil
- 2 tablespoons curry powder
- 1½ teaspoons garam masala
- 2 onions, chopped fine
- Salt and pepper
- 3 garlic cloves, minced
- 1 tablespoon grated fresh ginger
- 1 serrano chile, stemmed, seeded, and minced
- 1 tablespoon no-salt-added tomato paste
- ½ head cauliflower (1 pound), cored and cut into 1-inch

florets
- 8 ounces tempeh, cut into 1-inch pieces
- 1¼ cups water
- 1 cup frozen peas
- ¼ cup light coconut milk
- 2 tablespoons minced fresh cilantro
- Lime wedges

Directions:
1. Pulse diced tomatoes with their juice in food processor until nearly smooth, with some ¼-inch pieces visible, about 3 pulses.
2. Heat oil in Dutch oven over medium-high heat until shimmering. Add curry powder and garam masala and cook until fragrant, about 10 seconds. Add onions and ¼ teaspoon salt and cook, stirring occasionally, until softened and browned, about 10 minutes.
3. Reduce heat to medium. Stir in garlic, ginger, serrano, and tomato paste and cook until fragrant, about 30 seconds. Add cauliflower and tempeh and cook, stirring constantly, until florets are coated with spices, about 2 minutes.
4. Gradually stir in water, scraping up any browned bits. Stir in tomatoes and bring to simmer. Cover, reduce heat to low, and cook until vegetables are tender, 10 to 15 minutes.
5. Stir in peas, coconut milk, and ¾ teaspoon salt and cook until heated through, 1 to 2 minutes. Off heat, stir in cilantro and season with pepper to taste. Serve with lime wedges.

Nutrition Info:
- 240 cal., 15g fat (2g sag. fat), 0mg chol, 430mg sod., 19g carb (6g sugars, 6g fiber), 12g pro.

Speedy Greek Orzo Salad

Servings: 9 | Cooking Time:7 Minutes

Ingredients:
- 8 ounces uncooked whole-wheat orzo pasta
- 1/2 cup reduced-fat olive oil vinaigrette salad dressing (divided use)
- 3 tablespoons salt-free Greek seasoning (sold in jars in the spice aisle)
- 2 ounces crumbled, reduced-fat, sun-dried tomato and basil feta cheese
- 2 tablespoons chopped fresh parsley (optional)

Directions:
1. Cook the pasta according to package directions, omitting any salt and fat.
2. Meanwhile, stir 1/4 cup salad dressing and the Greek seasoning together in a medium bowl.
3. Drain the pasta in a colander and run under cold water until cooled. Shake off excess liquid and add it to the salad dressing mixture. Toss well, then add the feta and toss gently. Cover the bowl with plastic wrap and refrigerate at least 1 hour.
4. At serving time, add 1/4 cup salad dressing and toss to coat. Sprinkle with 2 tablespoons chopped fresh parsley, if desired.

Nutrition Info:
- 130 cal., 4g fat (1g sag. fat), 5mg chol, 180mg sod., 20g

carb (1g sugars, 5g fiber), 4g pro.

Skillet-grilled Meatless Burgers With Spicy Sour Cream

Servings: 4 | Cooking Time:15 Minutes

Ingredients:
- 4 soy protein burgers (preferably the grilled variety)
- 1 1/2 cups thinly sliced onions
- 1/8 teaspoon salt (divided use)
- 1/4 cup fat-free sour cream
- 4–6 drops chipotle-flavored hot sauce

Directions:
1. Place a large nonstick skillet over medium heat until hot. Coat the skillet with nonstick cooking spray, add the patties, and cook 4 minutes on each side. Set the patties aside on a separate plate and cover with foil to keep warm.
2. Coat the skillet with nonstick cooking spray and increase the heat to medium high. Add the onions and 1/16 teaspoon salt. Lightly coat the onions with nonstick cooking spray and cook 5 minutes or until they are richly browned, stirring frequently.
3. Meanwhile, stir the sour cream, hot sauce, and 1/16 teaspoon salt together in a small bowl.
4. When the onions are browned, push them to one side of the skillet and add the patties. Spoon the onions on top of the patties and cook 1–2 minutes longer to heat thoroughly. Top each patty with 1 tablespoon sour cream.

Nutrition Info:
- 120 cal., 2g fat (0g sag. fat), 5mg chol, 440mg sod., 12g carb (2g sugars, 7g fiber), 16g pro.

Mexican-style Spaghetti Squash Casserole

Servings:4 | Cooking Time:45 Minutes

Ingredients:
- 1 (2½- to 3-pound) spaghetti squash, halved lengthwise and seeded
- 3 tablespoons extra-virgin olive oil
- Salt and pepper
- 2 garlic cloves, minced
- ½ teaspoon smoked paprika
- ½ teaspoon ground cumin
- 1 (15-ounce) can no-salt-added black beans, rinsed
- 1 cup frozen corn
- 6 ounces cherry tomatoes, quartered
- 6 scallions (4 minced, 2 sliced thin)
- 1 jalapeño chile, stemmed, seeded, and minced
- 1 avocado, halved, pitted, and cut into ½-inch pieces
- 2 ounces queso fresco, crumbled (½ cup)
- Lime wedges

Directions:
1. Adjust oven rack to middle position and heat oven to 375 degrees. Lightly spray 8-inch square baking dish with vegetable oil spray. Brush cut sides of squash with 1 tablespoon oil and sprinkle with ⅛ teaspoon salt and ¼ teaspoon pepper. Place squash cut side down in prepared dish (squash

will not sit flat in dish) and roast until just tender, 40 to 45 minutes. Flip squash cut side up and let sit until cool enough to handle, about 20 minutes. Do not turn off oven.

2. Combine remaining 2 tablespoons oil, garlic, paprika, cumin, and ½ teaspoon salt in large bowl and microwave until fragrant, about 30 seconds. Stir in beans, corn, tomatoes, minced scallions, and jalapeño.

3. Using fork, scrape squash into strands in bowl with bean mixture. Stir to combine, then spread mixture evenly in now-empty dish and cover tightly with aluminum foil. Bake until heated through, 20 to 25 minutes. Sprinkle with avocado, queso fresco, and sliced scallions. Serve with lime wedges.

Nutrition Info:
• 400 cal., 24g fat (4g sag. fat), 10mg chol, 520mg sod., 41g carb (9g sugars, 11g fiber), 11g pro.

Sweet Potato, Poblano, And Black Bean Tacos

Servings:6 | Cooking Time:30 Minutes

Ingredients:
• ½ cup red wine vinegar
• ½ teaspoon red pepper flakes
• 1 red onion, halved and sliced thin
• 3 tablespoons extra-virgin olive oil
• 3 garlic cloves, minced
• 1½ teaspoons ground cumin
• 1½ teaspoons ground coriander
• 1 teaspoon minced fresh oregano or ¼ teaspoon dried
• Salt and pepper
• 1 pound sweet potatoes, peeled and cut into ½-inch pieces
• 4 poblano chiles, stemmed, seeded, and cut into ½-inch-wide strips
• 1 (15-ounce) can no-salt added black beans, rinsed
• ¼ cup chopped fresh cilantro
• 12 (6-inch) corn tortillas, warmed
• 1 avocado, halved, pitted, and cut into ½-inch pieces

Directions:
1. Adjust oven racks to upper-middle and lower-middle positions and heat oven to 450 degrees. Line 2 rimmed baking sheets with aluminum foil. Microwave vinegar and pepper flakes in medium bowl until steaming, about 2 minutes. Stir in onion and let sit until ready to serve.

2. Whisk oil, garlic, cumin, coriander, oregano, ½ teaspoon salt, and ½ teaspoon pepper together in large bowl. Add potatoes and poblanos to oil mixture and toss to coat.

3. Spread vegetable mixture in even layer in lined baking sheets. Roast vegetables until tender and golden brown, about 30 minutes, stirring vegetables and switching and rotating sheets halfway through baking.

4. Return vegetables to now-empty bowl, add black beans and cilantro, and gently toss to combine. Divide vegetables evenly among warm tortillas and top with avocado and pickled onions. Serve.

Nutrition Info:
• 350 cal., 14g fat (2g sag. fat), 0mg chol, 250mg sod., 51g carb (7g sugars, 11g fiber), 8g pro.

Country Vegetable And Thyme Quiche

Servings: 4 | Cooking Time:35 Minutes

Ingredients:
• 1 pound frozen corn and vegetable blend (or your favorite vegetable blend), thawed
• 1/2 teaspoon dried thyme
• 1/4 teaspoon salt
• 1/4 teaspoon black pepper
• 1 1/2 cups egg substitute
• 1/2 cup shredded, reduced-fat, sharp cheddar cheese

Directions:
1. Preheat the oven to 350°F.
2. Coat a 9-inch deep-dish pie pan with nonstick cooking spray. Place the vegetables in the pan and sprinkle them evenly with thyme, salt, and pepper. Pour egg substitute over the vegetables and bake 35 minutes or until just set.
3. Remove the quiche from the oven, sprinkle evenly with the cheese, and let stand 10 minutes to melt the cheese and let the quiche set.

Nutrition Info:
• 150 cal., 2g fat (1g sag. fat), 5mg chol, 430mg sod., 16g carb (4g sugars, 5g fiber), 16g pro.

Black Bean And Corn Bowl

Servings: 4 | Cooking Time:22 Minutes

Ingredients:
• 1 (10.5-ounce) can mild tomatoes with green chilis
• 1 (15-ounce) can black beans, rinsed and drained
• 2 cups frozen corn kernels
• 1/4 cup reduced-fat sour cream

Directions:
1. Place all ingredients except the sour cream in a large saucepan. Bring to a boil over high heat, then reduce the heat, cover, and simmer 20 minutes.
2. Serve in 4 individual bowls topped with 1 tablespoon sour cream.

Nutrition Info:
• 170 cal., 2g fat (1g sag. fat), 5mg chol, 310mg sod., 31g carb (6g sugars, 7g fiber), 9g pro.

Butternut & Portobello Lasagna

Servings:12 | Cooking Time: 45 Minutes

Ingredients:
• 1 package (10 ounces) frozen cubed butternut squash, thawed
• 2 teaspoons olive oil
• 1 teaspoon brown sugar
• 1/4 teaspoon salt
• 1/8 teaspoon pepper
• MUSHROOMS
• 4 large portobello mushrooms, coarsely chopped
• 2 teaspoons balsamic vinegar
• 2 teaspoons olive oil

- 1/4 teaspoon salt
- 1/8 teaspoon pepper
- SAUCE
- 2 cans (28 ounces each) whole tomatoes, undrained
- 2 teaspoons olive oil
- 2 garlic cloves, minced
- 1 teaspoon crushed red pepper flakes
- 1/2 cup fresh basil leaves, thinly sliced
- 1/4 teaspoon salt
- 1/8 teaspoon pepper
- LASAGNA
- 9 no-cook lasagna noodles
- 4 ounces fresh baby spinach (about 5 cups)
- 3 cups part-skim ricotta cheese
- 1 1/2 cups shredded part-skim mozzarella cheese

Directions:
1. Preheat oven to 350°. In a large bowl, combine the first five ingredients. In another bowl, combine ingredients for mushrooms. Transfer vegetables to separate foil-lined 15x10x1-in. baking pans. Roast 14-16 minutes or until tender, stirring occasionally.
2. Meanwhile, for sauce, drain tomatoes, reserving juices; coarsely chop tomatoes. In a large saucepan, heat oil over medium heat. Add garlic and pepper flakes; cook 1 minute longer. Stir in chopped tomatoes, reserved tomato juices, basil, salt and pepper; bring to a boil. Reduce heat; simmer, uncovered, 35-45 minutes or until thickened, stirring occasionally.
3. Spread 1 cup sauce into a greased 13x9-in. baking dish. Layer with three noodles, 1 cup sauce, spinach and mushrooms. Continue layering with three noodles, 1 cup sauce, ricotta cheese and roasted squash. Top with remaining noodles and sauce. Sprinkle with mozzarella cheese.
4. Bake, covered, 30 minutes. Bake, uncovered, 15-20 minutes longer or until bubbly. Let stand 15 minutes before serving.

Nutrition Info:
- 252 cal., 10g fat (5g sat. fat), 27mg chol., 508mg sod., 25g carb. (5g sugars, 4g fiber), 15g pro.

Avocado & Garbanzo Bean Quinoa Salad

Servings:6 | Cooking Time: 15 Minutes

Ingredients:
- 1 cup quinoa, rinsed
- 1 can (15 ounces) garbanzo beans or chickpeas, rinsed and drained
- 2 cups cherry tomatoes, halved
- 1 cup (4 ounces) crumbled feta cheese
- 1/2 medium ripe avocado, peeled and cubed
- 4 green onions, chopped (about 1/2 cup)
- DRESSING
- 3 tablespoons white wine vinegar
- 1 teaspoon Dijon mustard
- 1/4 teaspoon kosher salt
- 1/4 teaspoon garlic powder
- 1/4 teaspoon freshly ground pepper

- 1/4 cup olive oil

Directions:
1. Cook quinoa according to package directions; transfer to a large bowl and cool slightly.
2. Add beans, tomatoes, cheese, avocado and green onions to quinoa; gently stir to combine. In a small bowl, whisk the first five dressing ingredients. Gradually whisk in oil until blended. Drizzle over salad; gently toss to coat. Refrigerate leftovers.

Nutrition Info:
- 328 cal., 17g fat (4g sat. fat), 10mg chol., 378mg sod., 34g carb. (3g sugars, 7g fiber), 11g pro.

Cheesy Tortilla Rounds

Servings: 4 | Cooking Time:14 Minutes

Ingredients:
- 4 (6-inch) soft corn tortillas
- 1 cup fat-free refried beans
- 1/2 cup shredded, reduced-fat mozzarella cheese
- 1 poblano chili pepper, seeded and thinly sliced, or 2 jalapeño chili peppers, seeded and thinly sliced

Directions:
1. Preheat the broiler.
2. Place a large nonstick skillet over medium-high heat until hot. Coat the skillet with nonstick cooking spray. Place two tortillas in the skillet and cook 1 minute or until they begin to lightly brown on the bottom. Turn them and cook 1 minute, then place on a baking sheet. Repeat with the other two tortillas.
3. Return the skillet to medium-high heat, coat with nonstick cooking spray, and add the peppers. Coat the peppers with nonstick cooking spray and cook 6 minutes or until they are tender and brown, stirring frequently. Remove them from the heat.
4. Spread equal amounts of beans evenly on each tortilla. Broil 4 inches away from the heat source for 1 minute. Sprinkle the cheese and pepper slices evenly over each tortilla and broil another 2 minutes or until the cheese has melted. Serve with lime wedges, if desired.

Nutrition Info:
- 150 cal., 3g fat (1g sag. fat), 10mg chol, 370mg sod., 23g carb (2g sugars, 5g fiber), 9g pro.

Stuffed Eggplant With Bulgur

Servings:4 | Cooking Time: 40 Minutes

Ingredients:
- 4 (10-ounce) Italian eggplants, halved lengthwise
- ¼ cup extra-virgin olive oil
- Salt and pepper
- ½ cup medium-grind bulgur, rinsed
- ¼ cup water
- 1 onion, chopped fine
- 3 garlic cloves, minced
- 2 teaspoons minced fresh oregano or ½ teaspoon dried
- ¼ teaspoon ground cinnamon

- ⅛ teaspoon cayenne pepper
- 1 pound plum tomatoes, cored, seeded, and chopped
- 2 ounces Pecorino Romano cheese, grated (1 cup)
- 2 tablespoons pine nuts, toasted
- ¼ teaspoon grated lemon zest plus 1 tablespoon juice
- 2 tablespoons minced fresh parsley
- Lemon wedges

Directions:

1. Adjust oven racks to upper-middle and lowest positions, place parchment paper–lined rimmed baking sheet on lowest rack, and heat oven to 400 degrees.

2. Score flesh of each eggplant half in 1-inch crosshatch pattern, about 1 inch deep. Brush scored sides of eggplant with 1 tablespoon oil and sprinkle with ⅛ teaspoon salt and ¼ teaspoon pepper. Lay eggplant cut side down on hot sheet and roast until flesh is tender, 40 to 50 minutes. Transfer eggplant cut side down to paper towel–lined baking sheet and let drain. Do not wash rimmed baking sheet.

3. Meanwhile, toss bulgur with water in bowl and let sit until grains are softened and liquid is fully absorbed, 20 to 40 minutes.

4. Heat 1 tablespoon oil in 12-inch skillet over medium heat until shimmering. Add onion and cook until softened, 5 minutes. Stir in garlic, oregano, cinnamon, cayenne, and ¼ teaspoon salt and cook until fragrant, about 30 seconds. Stir in bulgur, tomatoes, ¾ cup Pecorino, pine nuts, and lemon zest and juice and cook until heated through, about 1 minute. Season with pepper to taste.

5. Return eggplant cut side up to rimmed baking sheet. Using 2 forks, gently push eggplant flesh to sides to make room for filling. Mound bulgur mixture into eggplant halves and pack lightly with back of spoon. Sprinkle with remaining ¼ cup Pecorino. Bake on upper-middle rack until cheese is melted, 5 to 10 minutes. Drizzle with remaining 2 tablespoons oil, sprinkle with parsley, and serve with lemon wedges.

Nutrition Info:
- 370 cal., 22g fat (5g sag. fat), 15mg chol, 320mg sod., 39g carb (14g sugars, 12g fiber), 11g pro.

Tasty Lentil Tacos
Servings:6 | Cooking Time: 40 Minutes

Ingredients:
- 1 teaspoon canola oil
- 1 medium onion, finely chopped
- 1 garlic clove, minced
- 1 cup dried lentils, rinsed
- 1 tablespoon chili powder
- 2 teaspoons ground cumin
- 1 teaspoon dried oregano
- 2 1/2 cups vegetable or reduced-sodium chicken broth
- 1 cup salsa
- 12 taco shells
- 1 1/2 cups shredded lettuce
- 1 cup chopped fresh tomatoes
- 1 1/2 cups shredded reduced-fat cheddar cheese

- 6 tablespoons fat-free sour cream

Directions:

1. In a large nonstick skillet, heat oil over medium heat; saute onion and garlic until tender. Add the lentils and seasonings; cook and stir 1 minute. Stir in broth; bring to a boil. Reduce heat; simmer, covered, until lentils are tender, 25-30 minutes.

2. Cook, uncovered, until mixture is thickened, for 6-8 minutes, stirring occasionally. Mash lentils slightly; stir in salsa and heat through. Serve in taco shells. Top with remaining ingredients.

Nutrition Info:
- 365 cal., 12g fat (5g sat. fat), 21mg chol., 777mg sod., 44g carb. (5g sugars, 6g fiber), 19g pro.

Pesto Potatoes And Edamame Bake
Servings: 4 | Cooking Time:1 Hour

Ingredients:
- 1 1/2 pounds red potatoes, cut into 1/4-inch-thick slices
- 1 cup fresh or frozen, thawed shelled edamame
- 1/2 cup prepared basil pesto
- 1/4 cup salted hulled pumpkin seeds

Directions:

1. Preheat oven to 350°F.

2. Coat a 2-quart baking dish with cooking spray. Arrange half of the potatoes on bottom of baking dish, overlapping slightly. Spoon half of the pesto evenly over all, top with the edamame, sprinkle with 1/4 teaspoon pepper. Repeat with remaining potatoes and pesto.

3. Cover and bake 55 minutes or until tender. Sprinkle with pumpkin seeds and bake, uncovered, 5 minutes.

Nutrition Info:
- 370 cal., 22g fat (3g sag. fat), 5mg chol, 380mg sod., 33g carb (3g sugars, 2g fiber), 14g pro.

Vegan Black Bean Burgers
Servings:6 | Cooking Time:15 Minutes

Ingredients:
- 2 (15-ounce) cans no-salt-added black beans, drained, with 6 tablespoons bean liquid reserved, and rinsed
- 2 tablespoons all-purpose flour
- 4 scallions, minced
- 3 tablespoons minced fresh cilantro
- 2 garlic cloves, minced
- 1 teaspoon ground cumin
- 1 teaspoon hot sauce (optional)
- ½ teaspoon ground coriander
- ½ teaspoon salt
- ¼ teaspoon pepper
- 1 ounce corn tortilla chips, crushed (½ cup)
- ¼ cup canola oil
- 6 100 percent whole-wheat burger buns, lightly toasted (optional)
- 2 avocados, halved, pitted, and sliced ¼ inch thick
- 1 head Bibb lettuce (8 ounces), leaves separated

• 2 tomatoes, cored and sliced ¼ inch thick

Directions:

1. Line rimmed baking sheet with triple layer of paper towels, spread beans over towels, and let sit for 15 minutes.
2. Whisk reserved bean liquid and flour in large bowl until well combined and smooth. Stir in scallions, cilantro, garlic, cumin, hot sauce, if using, coriander, salt, and pepper until well combined. Process tortilla chips in food processor until finely ground, about 30 seconds. Add black beans and pulse until beans are coarsely ground, about 5 pulses. Transfer bean mixture to bowl with flour mixture and mix until well combined.
3. Adjust oven rack to middle position and heat oven to 200 degrees. Divide mixture into 6 equal portions and pack firmly into 3½-inch-wide patties.
4. Heat 1 tablespoon oil in 10-inch nonstick skillet over medium heat until shimmering. Gently lay 3 patties in skillet and cook until crisp and well browned on first side, about 5 minutes. Gently flip patties, add 1 tablespoon oil, and cook until crisp and well browned on second side, 3 to 5 minutes.
5. Transfer burgers to wire rack set in rimmed baking sheet and place in oven to keep warm. Wipe out skillet with paper towels and repeat with remaining 2 tablespoons oil and remaining patties. Serve burgers on buns, if using, and top with avocado, lettuce, and tomatoes.

Nutrition Info:
• 450 cal., 24g fat (2g sag. fat), 0mg chol, 460mg sod., 52g carb (6g sugars, 15g fiber), 13g pro.

Cheesy Spinach-stuffed Shells

Servings:12 | Cooking Time: 45 Minutes

Ingredients:
• 1 package (12 ounces) jumbo pasta shells
• 1 tablespoon butter
• 1 cup sliced mushrooms
• 1 small onion, finely chopped
• 4 garlic cloves, minced
• 2 large eggs, lightly beaten
• 1 carton (15 ounces) part-skim ricotta cheese
• 1 package (10 ounces) frozen chopped spinach, thawed and squeezed dry
• 2 tablespoons minced fresh basil or 2 teaspoons dried basil
• 1/4 teaspoon pepper
• 1 can (4 1/4 ounces) chopped ripe olives
• 1 1/2 cups shredded Italian cheese blend, divided
• 1 1/2 cups shredded part-skim mozzarella cheese, divided
• 1 jar (24 ounces) marinara sauce
• Additional minced fresh basil, optional

Directions:
1. Preheat oven to 375°. Cook the pasta shells according to the package directions for al dente. Drain; rinse with cold water.
2. Meanwhile, in a small skillet, heat butter over medium-high heat. Add mushrooms and onion; cook and stir 4-6 minutes or until vegetables are tender. Add garlic; cook 1 minute longer. Remove from heat; cool slightly.
3. In a bowl, mix eggs, ricotta cheese, spinach, basil and pepper. Stir in olives, mushroom mixture and 3/4 cup each cheese blend and mozzarella cheese.
4. Spread 1 cup sauce into a 13x9-in. baking dish coated with cooking spray. Fill shells with cheese mixture; place in baking dish, overlapping ends slightly. Spoon remaining sauce over top.
5. Bake, covered, 40-45 minutes or until heated through. Uncover; sprinkle with remaining cheeses. Bake 5 minutes longer or until cheese is melted. Let stand 5 minutes before serving. If desired, sprinkle with additional basil.

Nutrition Info:
• 313 cal., 13g fat (7g sat. fat), 65mg chol., 642mg sod., 32g carb. (5g sugars, 3g fiber), 18g pro.

Sautéed Spinach With Chickpeas And Garlicky Yogurt

Servings:4 | Cooking Time:45 Minutes

Ingredients:
• 1 cup plain low-fat yogurt
• 2 tablespoons chopped fresh mint
• 5 garlic cloves (4 sliced thin, 1 minced)
• 18 ounces (18 cups) baby spinach
• 2 tablespoons extra-virgin olive oil
• 1 teaspoon ground coriander
• 1 teaspoon ground turmeric
• ¼ teaspoon grated lemon zest
• ⅛ teaspoon red pepper flakes
• 2 (15-ounce) cans no-salt-added chickpeas, rinsed
• ½ cup oil-packed sun-dried tomatoes, sliced thin
• Salt and pepper

Directions:
1. Combine yogurt, mint, and minced garlic in bowl; cover and refrigerate sauce until ready to serve.
2. Microwave spinach and ¼ cup water in covered bowl until spinach is wilted and has reduced in volume by half, 3 to 4 minutes. Remove bowl from microwave and keep covered for 1 minute. Carefully transfer spinach to colander and, using back of rubber spatula, gently press spinach to release excess liquid. Transfer spinach to cutting board and chop coarsely. Return spinach to colander and press again.
3. Cook 1 tablespoon oil and sliced garlic in 12-inch skillet over medium heat, stirring constantly, until garlic is light golden brown and beginning to sizzle, 3 to 6 minutes. Stir in coriander, turmeric, lemon zest, and pepper flakes and cook until fragrant, about 30 seconds. Stir in chickpeas, tomatoes, and 2 tablespoons water. Cook, stirring occasionally, until water evaporates and tomatoes are softened, 1 to 245 minutes.
4. Stir in spinach and ¼ teaspoon salt and cook until uniformly wilted and glossy green, about 2 minutes. Transfer spinach mixture to serving platter, drizzle with remaining 1 tablespoon oil, and season with pepper to taste. Serve with yogurt sauce.

Nutrition Info:
• 310 cal., 11g fat (2g sag. fat), 5mg chol, 360mg sod., 37g carb (5g sugars, 10g fiber), 15g pro.

Cauliflower Steaks With Chimichurri Sauce

Servings:4 | Cooking Time: 10 Minutes

Ingredients:
• 2 heads cauliflower (2 pounds each)
• ¼ cup extra-virgin olive oil
• Salt and pepper
• 1 recipe Chimichurri (this page)
• Lemon wedges

Directions:
1. Adjust oven rack to lowest position and heat oven to 500 degrees. Working with 1 head cauliflower at a time, discard outer leaves and trim stem flush with bottom florets. Halve cauliflower lengthwise through core. Cut one 1½-inch-thick slab lengthwise from each half, trimming any florets not connected to core. Repeat with remaining cauliflower. (You should have 4 steaks; reserve remaining cauliflower for another use.)
2. Place steaks on rimmed baking sheet and drizzle with 2 tablespoons oil. Sprinkle with pinch salt and ⅛ teaspoon pepper and rub to distribute. Flip steaks and repeat.
3. Cover sheet tightly with foil and roast for 5 minutes. Remove foil and continue to roast until bottoms of steaks are well browned, 8 to 10 minutes. Gently flip and continue to roast until cauliflower is tender and second sides are well browned, 6 to 8 minutes.
4. Transfer steaks to serving platter and brush tops evenly with ¼ cup chimichurri. Serve with lemon wedges and remaining chimichurri.

Nutrition Info:
• 370 cal., 29g fat (4g sag. fat), 0mg chol, 300mg sod., 24g carb (9g sugars, 10g fiber), 9g pro.

Black Beans With Bell Peppers & Rice

Servings:6 | Cooking Time: 30 Minutes

Ingredients:
• 1 tablespoon olive oil
• 1 each medium sweet yellow, orange and red pepper, chopped
• 1 large onion, chopped
• 2 garlic cloves, minced
• 2 cans (15 ounces each) black beans, rinsed and drained
• 1 package (8.8 ounces) ready-to-serve brown rice
• 1 1/2 teaspoons ground cumin
• 1/2 teaspoon dried oregano
• 1 1/2 cups (6 ounces) shredded Mexican cheese blend, divided
• 3 tablespoons minced fresh cilantro

Directions:
1. In a large skillet, heat the oil over medium-high heat. Add peppers, onion and garlic; cook and stir 6-8 minutes or until tender. Add beans, rice, cumin and oregano; heat through.

2. Stir in 1 cup cheese; sprinkle with remaining cheese. Remove from heat. Let stand, covered, 5 minutes or until cheese is melted. Sprinkle with cilantro.

Nutrition Info:
• 347 cal., 12g fat (6g sat. fat), 25mg chol., 477mg sod., 40g carb. (4g sugars, 8g fiber), 15g pro.

Summer Squash "spaghetti" With Roasted Cherry Tomato Sauce

Servings:4 | Cooking Time:30 Minutes

Ingredients:
• 6 ounces (¾ cup) whole-milk ricotta cheese
• 6 tablespoons chopped fresh basil
• Salt and pepper
• 3 pounds yellow summer squash, trimmed
• 2 pounds cherry tomatoes, halved
• 1 shallot, sliced thin
• 3 tablespoons extra-virgin olive oil
• 5 garlic cloves, minced
• 1 tablespoon minced fresh oregano or 1 teaspoon dried
• 1 tablespoon no-salt-added tomato paste
• ¼ teaspoon red pepper flakes

Directions:
1. Adjust oven racks to upper-middle and lower-middle positions and heat oven to 375 degrees. Line rimmed baking sheet with aluminum foil. Combine ricotta, 2 tablespoons basil, ⅛ teaspoon salt, and ¼ teaspoon pepper in bowl; set aside for serving. Using spiralizer, cut squash into ⅛-inch-thick noodles, then cut noodles into 12-inch lengths.
2. Toss tomatoes, shallot, 2 tablespoons oil, garlic, oregano, tomato paste, pepper flakes, ⅛ teaspoon salt, and ¼ teaspoon pepper together in bowl. Spread tomato mixture in lined baking sheet and roast, without stirring, on lower rack until tomatoes are softened and skins begin to shrivel, about 30 minutes.
3. Meanwhile, toss squash with ⅛ teaspoon salt and remaining 1 tablespoon oil on second rimmed baking sheet and roast on upper rack until tender, 20 to 25 minutes. Transfer squash to colander and shake to remove any excess liquid; transfer to large serving bowl. (If tomatoes are not finished cooking, cover bowl with aluminum foil to keep warm.)
4. Add roasted tomato mixture and any accumulated juices to bowl with squash and gently toss to combine. Season with ⅛ teaspoon salt and pepper to taste. Dollop individual portions with 3 tablespoons ricotta mixture and sprinkle with remaining ¼ cup basil before serving.

Nutrition Info:
• 280 cal., 17g fat (5g sag. fat), 20mg chol, 390mg sod., 24g carb (15g sugars, 7g fiber), 13g pro.

SALADS RECIPES

◇ Salads Recipes ◇

Cumin'd Salsa Salad

Servings: 4 | Cooking Time: 3 Minutes

Ingredients:
- 3/4 cup mild or medium salsa fresca (pico de gallo)
- 2 tablespoons water
- 1/4 teaspoon ground cumin
- 8 cups shredded lettuce
- 20 baked bite-sized multi-grain tortilla chips, coarsely crumbled (1 ounce)

Directions:
1. Stir the salsa, water, and cumin together in a small bowl.
2. Place 2 cups of lettuce on each of 4 salad plates, spoon 3 tablespoons picante mixture over each salad, and top with chips.

Nutrition Info:
- 60 cal., 2g fat (0g sag. fat), 0mg chol, 40mg sod., 9g carb (3g sugars, 2g fiber), 2g pro.

Chicken Salad With Fennel, Lemon, And Parmesan

Servings:6 | Cooking Time: 30 Minutes

Ingredients:
- Salt and pepper
- 1½ pounds boneless, skinless chicken breasts, trimmed of all visible fat and pounded to ¾-inch thickness
- ⅓ cup mayonnaise
- ¼ cup grated Parmesan cheese
- 1 teaspoon extra-virgin olive oil
- ½ teaspoon grated lemon zest plus 3 tablespoons juice
- ¼ teaspoon celery seeds
- 1 fennel bulb, stalks discarded, bulb halved, cored, and chopped fine
- 2 tablespoons finely chopped red onion
- 2 tablespoons minced fresh basil

Directions:
1. Whisk 4 quarts water and 2 tablespoons salt in Dutch oven until salt is dissolved. Arrange breasts, skinned side up, in steamer basket, making sure not to overlap them. Submerge steamer basket in water.
2. Heat pot over medium heat, stirring liquid occasionally to even out hot spots, until water registers 175 degrees, 15 to 20 minutes. Turn off heat, cover pot, remove from burner, and let sit until meat registers 160 degrees, 17 to 22 minutes. Transfer chicken to paper towel–lined plate and refrigerate until cool, about 30 minutes.
3. Whisk mayonnaise, Parmesan, oil, lemon zest and juice, celery seeds, ¼ teaspoon salt, and ¼ teaspoon pepper in large bowl until combined. Pat chicken dry with paper towels and cut into ½-inch pieces. Add chicken, fennel, onion, and basil to mayonnaise mixture and gently toss to coat. (Salad can be refrigerated for up to 2 days.) Season with

pepper to taste. Serve.

Nutrition Info:
- 260 cal., 14g fat (3g sag. fat), 90mg chol, 380mg sod., 4g carb (2g sugars, 1g fiber), 28g pro.

Warm Spinach Salad With Feta And Pistachios

Servings:6 | Cooking Time:15 Minutes

Ingredients:
- 1½ ounces feta cheese, crumbled (⅓ cup)
- 3 tablespoons extra-virgin olive oil
- 1 (3-inch) strip lemon zest plus 1½ tablespoons juice
- 1 shallot, minced
- 10 ounces curly-leaf spinach, stemmed and torn into bite-size pieces
- 6 radishes, trimmed and sliced thin
- 3 tablespoons chopped toasted pistachios
- Pepper

Directions:
1. Place feta on plate and freeze until slightly firm, about 15 minutes.
2. Cook oil, lemon zest, and shallot in Dutch oven over medium-low heat until shallot is softened, about 5 minutes. Off heat, discard zest and stir in lemon juice. Add spinach, cover, and let sit until just beginning to wilt, about 30 seconds.
3. Transfer spinach mixture and liquid left in pot to large bowl. Add radishes, pistachios, and feta and gently toss to coat. Season with pepper to taste. Serve.

Nutrition Info:
- 120 cal., 10g fat (2g sag. fat), 5mg chol, 105mg sod., 4g carb (1g sugars, 2g fiber), 3g pro.

Brussels Sprout And Kale Salad With Herbs And Peanuts

Servings:4 | Cooking Time: 2 Hours

Ingredients:
- ⅓ cup cider vinegar
- 2 tablespoons extra-virgin olive oil
- 1 tablespoon lime juice
- ½ teaspoon ground coriander
- Salt and pepper
- 1 pound Brussels sprouts, trimmed, halved, and sliced very thin
- 8 ounces Tuscan kale, stemmed and sliced into ¼-inch-wide strips (4½ cups)
- ¼ cup dry-roasted, unsalted peanuts, chopped
- 1 tablespoon chopped fresh cilantro
- 1 tablespoon chopped fresh mint

Directions:

1. Whisk vinegar, oil, lime juice, coriander, ¼ teaspoon salt, and ¼ teaspoon pepper together in large bowl. Add Brussels sprouts and gently toss to coat. Cover and let sit for at least 30 minutes or up to 2 hours.

2. Vigorously squeeze and massage kale with hands until leaves are uniformly darkened and slightly wilted, about 1 minute. Add kale, peanuts, cilantro, and mint to bowl with Brussels sprouts and gently toss to coat. Season with pepper to taste. Serve.

Nutrition Info:
• 190 cal., 12g fat (2g sag. fat), 0mg chol, 190mg sod., 15g carb (4g sugars, 6g fiber), 7g pro.

Mesclun Salad With Goat Cheese And Almonds

Servings:4 | Cooking Time:8minutes

Ingredients:
• 5 ounces (5 cups) mesclun
• 3 tablespoons toasted sliced almonds
• 1 recipe Classic Vinaigrette (this page)
• 2 ounces goat cheese, crumbled (½ cup)

Directions:
1. Gently toss mesclun with almonds and vinaigrette in bowl until well coated. Sprinkle with goat cheese. Serve.

Nutrition Info:
• 170 cal., 16g fat (4g sag. fat), 5mg chol, 160mg sod., 1g carb (0g sugars, 1g fiber), 4g pro.

Summer Buzz Fruit Salad

Servings:6 | Cooking Time: 15 Minutes

Ingredients:
• 2 cups watermelon balls
• 2 cups fresh sweet cherries, pitted and halved
• 1 cup fresh blueberries
• 1/2 cup cubed English cucumber
• 1/2 cup microgreens or torn mixed salad greens
• 1/2 cup crumbled feta cheese
• 3 fresh mint leaves, thinly sliced
• 1/4 cup honey
• 1 tablespoon lemon juice
• 1 teaspoon grated lemon peel

Directions:
1. Combine the first seven ingredients. In a small bowl, whisk together remaining ingredients. Drizzle over salad; toss.

Nutrition Info:
• 131 cal., 2g fat (1g sat. fat), 5mg chol., 94mg sod., 28g carb. (24g sugars, 2g fiber), 3g pro.

Dill-marinated Broccoli

Servings:8 | Cooking Time: 15 Minutes

Ingredients:
• 6 cups fresh broccoli florets
• 1 cup canola oil

• 1 cup cider vinegar
• 2 tablespoons snipped fresh dill
• 2 teaspoons sugar
• 1 teaspoon garlic salt
• 1 teaspoon salt

Directions:
1. Place broccoli in a large resealable plastic bag. Whisk together remaining ingredients; add to broccoli. Seal bag and turn to coat; refrigerate 4 hours or overnight. To serve, drain broccoli, discarding marinade.

Nutrition Info:
• 79 cal., 7g fat (1g sat. fat), 0 chol., 119mg sod., 3g carb. (0 sugars, 2g fiber), 2g pro.

French Potato Salad With Dijon And Fines Herbes

Servings:6 | Cooking Time:10 Minutes

Ingredients:
• 2 pounds small red potatoes, unpeeled, sliced ¼ inch thick
• 2 tablespoons salt
• 1 garlic clove, peeled and threaded on skewer
• ¼ cup extra-virgin olive oil
• 1½ tablespoons white wine or champagne vinegar
• 2 teaspoons Dijon mustard
• ½ teaspoon pepper
• 1 small shallot, minced
• 1 tablespoon minced fresh chervil
• 1 tablespoon minced fresh parsley
• 1 tablespoon minced fresh chives
• 1 teaspoon minced fresh tarragon

Directions:
1. Place potatoes in large saucepan, add water to cover by 1 inch, and bring to boil. Add salt, reduce to simmer, and cook until potatoes are tender and paring knife can be slipped in and out of potatoes with little resistance, about 6 minutes.

2. While potatoes are cooking, lower skewered garlic into simmering water and blanch for 45 seconds. Run garlic under cold running water, then remove from skewer and mince.

3. Reserve ¼ cup cooking water, then drain potatoes and arrange in tight single layer on rimmed baking sheet. Whisk minced garlic, oil, vinegar, mustard, pepper, and reserved potato cooking water together in bowl, then drizzle over potatoes. Let potatoes sit until flavors meld, about 10 minutes. (Potatoes can be refrigerated for up to 8 hours; bring to room temperature before continuing.)

4. Transfer potatoes to large bowl. Sprinkle shallot, chervil, parsley, chives, and tarragon over potatoes and gently toss to coat using rubber spatula. Serve.

Nutrition Info:
• 190 cal., 10g fat (1g sag. fat), 0mg chol, 260mg sod., 25g carb (2g sugars, 3g fiber), 3g pro.

Asparagus, Red Pepper, And Spinach Salad With Goat Cheese

Servings:6 | Cooking Time:8 Minutes

Ingredients:
- 5 tablespoons extra-virgin olive oil
- 1 red bell pepper, stemmed, seeded, and cut into 2-inch-long matchsticks
- 1 pound asparagus, trimmed and cut into 1-inch lengths on bias
- Salt and pepper
- 1 shallot, sliced thin
- 1 tablespoon plus 1 teaspoon sherry vinegar
- 1 garlic clove, minced
- 6 ounces (6 cups) baby spinach
- 2 ounces goat cheese, crumbled (½ cup)

Directions:
1. Heat 1 tablespoon oil in 12-inch nonstick skillet over high heat until just smoking. Add bell pepper and cook until lightly browned, about 2 minutes. Add asparagus, ¼ teaspoon salt, and ⅛ teaspoon pepper and cook, stirring occasionally, until asparagus is browned and almost tender, about 2 minutes. Stir in shallot and cook until softened and asparagus is crisp-tender, about 1 minute. Transfer to bowl and let cool slightly.
2. Whisk remaining ¼ cup oil, vinegar, garlic, ¼ teaspoon salt, and ⅛ teaspoon pepper together in small bowl. Gently toss spinach with 2 tablespoons dressing until coated. Season with pepper to taste. Divide spinach among individual plates. Gently toss asparagus mixture with remaining dressing and arrange over spinach. Sprinkle with goat cheese. Serve.

Nutrition Info:
- 160 cal., 14g fat (3g sag. fat), 5mg chol, 260mg sod., 6g carb (3g sugars, 3g fiber), 4g pro.

Baby Kale Salad With Avocado-lime Dressing

Servings:4 | Cooking Time: 20 Minutes

Ingredients:
- 6 cups baby kale salad blend
- 1 cup julienned zucchini
- 1/2 cup thinly sliced sweet onion
- 1/2 cup fat-free plain yogurt
- 2 tablespoons lime juice
- 1 garlic clove, minced
- 1/4 teaspoon salt
- 1/8 teaspoon pepper
- 1/2 medium ripe avocado, peeled
- 3 green onions, chopped
- 2 tablespoons minced fresh parsley

Directions:
1. In a large bowl, combine salad blend, zucchini and sweet onion. Place the remaining ingredients in a blender; cover and process until smooth. Divide salad mixture among four plates; drizzle with dressing.

Nutrition Info:
- 74 cal., 3g fat (1g sat. fat), 1mg chol., 197mg sod., 10g carb. (4g sugars, 4g fiber), 4g pro.

Red, White & Blue Potato Salad

Servings:12 | Cooking Time: 10 Minutes

Ingredients:
- 1 1/4 pounds small purple potatoes (about 11), quartered
- 1 pound small Yukon Gold potatoes (about 9), quartered
- 1 pound small red potatoes (about 9), quartered
- 1/2 cup chicken stock
- 1/4 cup white wine or additional chicken stock
- 2 tablespoons sherry vinegar
- 2 tablespoons white wine vinegar
- 1 1/2 teaspoons Dijon mustard
- 1 1/2 teaspoons stone-ground mustard
- 3/4 teaspoon salt
- 1/2 teaspoon coarsely ground pepper
- 6 tablespoons olive oil
- 3 celery ribs, chopped
- 1 small sweet red pepper, chopped
- 8 green onions, chopped
- 3/4 pound bacon strips, cooked and crumbled
- 3 tablespoons each minced fresh basil, dill and parsley
- 2 tablespoons toasted sesame seeds

Directions:
1. Place all potatoes in a Dutch oven; add water to cover. Bring to a boil. Reduce heat; cook, uncovered, 10-15 minutes or until tender. Drain; transfer to a large bowl. Drizzle potatoes with stock and wine; toss gently, allowing liquids to absorb.
2. In a small bowl, whisk vinegars, mustards, salt and pepper. Gradually whisk in oil until blended. Add the vinaigrette, vegetables, bacon and herbs to the potato mixture; toss to combine. Sprinkle with sesame seeds. Serve warm.

Nutrition Info:
- 221 cal., 12g fat (2g sat. fat), 10mg chol., 405mg sod., 22g carb. (2g sugars, 3g fiber), 7g pro.

Mediterranean Tuna Salad

Servings:6 | Cooking Time:1week

Ingredients:
- 3 tablespoons lemon juice, plus extra for seasoning
- 2 teaspoons Dijon mustard
- Pepper
- 5 tablespoons extra-virgin olive oil
- ¼ cup minced red onion
- 1 garlic clove, minced
- 4 (5-ounce) cans solid white tuna in water, drained and flaked
- 2 celery ribs, minced
- 1 red bell pepper, stemmed, seeded, and chopped fine
- ¼ cup pitted kalamata olives, minced
- ¼ cup minced fresh parsley

Directions:
1. Whisk lemon juice, mustard, and ½ teaspoon pepper in

large bowl until combined. While whisking constantly, drizzle in oil until completely emulsified. Stir in red onion and garlic and let sit for 5 minutes. Add tuna, celery, bell pepper, olives, and parsley and gently toss to coat. (Salad can be refrigerated for up to 24 hours.) Season with extra lemon juice and pepper to taste. Serve.

Nutrition Info:
• 200 cal., 14g fat (2g sag. fat), 25mg chol, 300mg sod., 3g carb (1g sugars, 1g fiber), 15g pro.

Spinach, Apple & Pecan Salad

Servings:16 | Cooking Time: 15 Minutes

Ingredients:
• 2 packages (6 ounces each) fresh baby spinach
• 1 medium apple, chopped
• 1 cup (4 ounces) crumbled feta cheese
• 1 cup glazed pecans
• 1/2 cup chopped red onion
• 1/3 cup dried cranberries
• 5 bacon strips, cooked and crumbled, optional
• DRESSING
• 2 tablespoons cider vinegar
• 1 tablespoon sugar
• 1/2 teaspoon Dijon mustard
• 1/8 teaspoon pepper
• 1/4 cup canola oil

Directions:
1. In a large bowl, combine the first six ingredients; stir in bacon if desired.
2. For dressing, in a small bowl, whisk vinegar, sugar, mustard and pepper until blended. Gradually whisk in oil. Pour over salad; toss to coat.

Nutrition Info:
• 109 cal., 8g fat (1g sat. fat), 4mg chol., 116mg sod., 9g carb. (6g sugars, 1g fiber), 2g pro.

Thai Grilled-steak Salad

Servings:6 | Cooking Time:25 Minutes

Ingredients:
• 1 teaspoon paprika
• 1 teaspoon cayenne pepper
• 1 tablespoon white rice
• 3 tablespoons lime juice (2 limes)
• 2 tablespoons fish sauce
• 2 tablespoons water
• 1 (1½-pound) flank steak, trimmed of all visible fat
• ¼ teaspoon salt
• ¼ teaspoon white pepper
• 1½ cups fresh mint leaves, torn
• 1½ cups fresh cilantro leaves
• 4 shallots, sliced thin
• 1 Thai chile, stemmed and sliced into thin rounds
• 1 English cucumber, sliced ¼ inch thick on bias

Directions:
1. Heat paprika and cayenne in 8-inch skillet over medium heat and cook, shaking skillet, until fragrant, about 1 minute. Transfer to small bowl. Return now-empty skillet to medium-high heat, add rice, and toast, stirring frequently, until deep golden brown, about 5 minutes. Transfer to second small bowl and let cool for 5 minutes. Grind rice with spice grinder, mini food processor, or mortar and pestle until it resembles fine meal, 10 to 30 seconds (you should have about 1 tablespoon rice powder).
2. Whisk lime juice, fish sauce, water, and ¼ teaspoon toasted paprika mixture together in large bowl; set aside.
3. FOR A CHARCOAL GRILL Open bottom vent completely. Light large chimney starter filled with charcoal briquettes (6 quarts). When top coals are partially covered with ash, pour evenly over half of grill. Set cooking grate in place, cover, and open lid vent completely. Heat grill until hot, about 5 minutes.
4. FOR A GAS GRILL Turn all burners to high, cover, and heat grill until hot, about 15 minutes. Leave primary burner on high and turn off other burner(s).
5. Clean and oil cooking grate. Pat steak dry with paper towels, then sprinkle with salt and white pepper. Place steak over hotter part of grill and cook until beginning to char and beads of moisture appear on outer edges of meat, 5 to 6 minutes. Flip steak and continue to cook on second side until charred and meat registers 120 to 125 degrees (for medium-rare), about 5 minutes. Transfer steak to cutting board, tent with aluminum foil, and let rest for 5 to 10 minutes (or let cool completely, about 1 hour).
6. Slice steak about ¼ inch thick against grain on bias. Whisk lime juice mixture to recombine, then add steak, mint, cilantro, shallots, chile, and half of rice powder and gently toss to coat. Line serving platter with cucumber slices. Place steak mixture on top of cucumbers and serve, passing remaining toasted paprika mixture and remaining rice powder separately.

Nutrition Info:
• 220 cal., 8g fat (3g sag. fat), 80mg chol, 400mg sod., 11g carb (3g sugars, 3g fiber), 27g pro.

Cherry Tomato Salad

Servings:6 | Cooking Time: 15 Minutes

Ingredients:
• 1 quart cherry tomatoes, halved
• 1/4 cup canola oil
• 3 tablespoons white vinegar
• 1/2 teaspoon salt
• 1/2 teaspoon sugar
• 1/4 cup minced fresh parsley
• 1 to 2 teaspoons minced fresh basil
• 1 to 2 teaspoons minced fresh oregano

Directions:
1. Place tomatoes in a shallow bowl. In a small bowl, whisk oil, vinegar, salt and sugar until blended; stir in herbs. Pour over tomatoes; gently toss to coat. Refrigerate, covered, overnight.

Nutrition Info:

- 103 cal., 10g fat (1g sat. fat), 0 chol., 203mg sod., 4g carb. (3g sugars, 1g fiber), 1g pro.

Broccoli & Apple Salad

Servings:6 | Cooking Time: 15 Minutes

Ingredients:
- 3 cups small fresh broccoli florets
- 3 medium apples, chopped
- 1/2 cup chopped mixed dried fruit
- 1 tablespoon chopped red onion
- 1/2 cup reduced-fat plain yogurt
- 4 bacon strips, cooked and crumbled

Directions:
1. In a large bowl, combine broccoli, apples, dried fruit and onion. Add yogurt; toss to coat. Sprinkle with bacon. Refrigerate until serving.

Nutrition Info:
- 124 cal., 3g fat (1g sat. fat), 7mg chol., 134mg sod., 22g carb. (17g sugars, 3g fiber), 4g pro.

Toasted Pecan And Apple Salad

Servings: 4 | Cooking Time: 8 Minutes

Ingredients:
- 2 tablespoons pecan chips
- 2 cups chopped unpeeled red apples
- 1/4 cup dried raisin-cherry blend (or 1/4 cup dried cherries or golden raisins alone)
- 1 teaspoon honey (or 1 teaspoon packed dark brown sugar and 1 teaspoon water)

Directions:
1. Place a small skillet over medium-high heat until hot. Add the pecans and cook 1–2 minutes or until beginning to lightly brown, stirring constantly. Remove from the heat and set aside on paper towels to stop the cooking process and cool quickly.
2. Combine the apples and dried fruit in a medium bowl, drizzle honey over all, and toss gently.
3. Serve on a lettuce leaf (if desired) or a pretty salad plate. Sprinkle each serving evenly with the pecans.

Nutrition Info:
- 90 cal., 2g fat (0g sag. fat), 0mg chol, 0mg sod., 18g carb (14g sugars, 2g fiber), 1g pro.

Classic Vinaigrette

Servings:1 | Cooking Time:1 Week

Ingredients:
- This vinaigrette works well with all types of greens. To make an herb vinaigrette, whisk in 1 tablespoon minced fresh parsley or chives and ½ teaspoon minced fresh thyme, tarragon, marjoram, or oregano before serving.
- 1 tablespoon wine vinegar
- 1½ teaspoons minced shallot
- ½ teaspoon mayonnaise
- ½ teaspoon Dijon mustard
- ⅛ teaspoon salt
- Pinch pepper
- 3 tablespoons extra-virgin olive oil

Directions:
1. Whisk vinegar, shallot, mayonnaise, mustard, salt, and pepper together in bowl. While whisking constantly, drizzle in oil until completely emulsified. (Vinaigrette can be refrigerated for up to 1 week; whisk to recombine.)

Nutrition Info:
- 100 cal., 11g fat (1g sag. fat), 0mg chol, 90mg sod., 0g carb (0g sugars, 0g fiber), 0g pro.

Classic Wedge Salad

Servings:6 | Cooking Time:15minutes

Ingredients:
- 3 slices uncured bacon, cut into ¼-inch pieces
- ⅓ cup buttermilk
- 1 ounce strong blue cheese, such as Roquefort or Stilton, crumbled (¼ cup)
- ⅓ cup mayonnaise
- ⅓ cup low-fat sour cream
- 3 tablespoons water
- 1 tablespoon white wine vinegar
- ¼ teaspoon garlic powder
- ¼ teaspoon pepper
- 1 head iceberg lettuce (2 pounds), cored and cut into 6 wedges
- 3 tomatoes, cored and cut into ½-inch-thick wedges
- 2 tablespoons minced fresh chives

Directions:
1. Cook bacon in 12-inch nonstick skillet over medium-high heat until rendered and crisp, about 5 minutes. Using slotted spoon, transfer bacon to paper towel–lined plate.
2. Mash buttermilk and blue cheese together with fork in small bowl until mixture resembles cottage cheese with small curds. Stir in mayonnaise, sour cream, water, vinegar, garlic powder, and pepper until combined.
3. Divide lettuce and tomatoes among individual plates. Spoon dressing over top, then sprinkle with bacon and chives. Serve.

Nutrition Info:
- 170 cal., 13g fat (3g sag. fat), 15mg chol, 270mg sod., 7g carb (5g sugars, 2g fiber), 6g pro.

Beet Salad With Lemon Dressing

Servings:6 | Cooking Time: 1 1/4 Hours

Ingredients:
- 3 medium fresh beets (about 1 pound)
- 1 cup finely chopped English cucumber
- 6 green onions, thinly sliced
- 1/2 cup shredded carrot
- 1/2 cup chopped sweet yellow or red pepper
- 1/4 cup finely chopped red onion
- 1/4 cup finely chopped radish
- 3/4 cup minced fresh parsley
- DRESSING

- 3 tablespoons olive oil
- 2 teaspoons grated lemon peel
- 3 tablespoons lemon juice
- 1 garlic clove, minced
- 1/4 teaspoon salt
- 1/4 teaspoon pepper

Directions:

1. Preheat oven to 400°. Scrub beets and trim tops. Wrap beets in foil; place on a baking sheet. Bake until tender, 1 1/4-1 1/2 hours. Cool slightly. Peel beets and cut into cubes.
2. Place remaining vegetables and parsley in a large bowl. Whisk together the dressing ingredients; toss with cucumber mixture. Gently stir in beets.

Nutrition Info:

- 116 cal., 7g fat (1g sat. fat), 0 chol., 173mg sod., 13g carb. (8g sugars, 3g fiber), 2g pro.

Yogurt-mint Cucumber Salad

Servings:4 | Cooking Time:30 Minutes

Ingredients:

- 3 cucumbers, peeled, halved lengthwise, seeded, and sliced ¼ inch thick
- 1 small red onion, halved and sliced thin
- Salt and pepper
- 1 cup plain low-fat yogurt
- ¼ cup minced fresh mint
- 2 tablespoons extra-virgin olive oil
- 1 garlic clove, minced
- ½ teaspoon ground cumin

Directions:

1. Toss cucumbers and onion with 1 tablespoon salt in colander set over large bowl. Weight cucumber-onion mixture with 1 gallon-size zipper-lock bag filled with water; drain for 1 to 3 hours. Rinse and pat dry.
2. Whisk yogurt, mint, oil, garlic, and cumin together in large bowl. Add cucumber-onion mixture and gently toss to coat. Season with pepper to taste. Serve at room temperature or chilled.

Nutrition Info:

- 130 cal., 8g fat (1g sag. fat), 5mg chol, 340mg sod., 10g carb (7g sugars, 2g fiber), 5g pro.

Mixed Greens With Orange-ginger Vinaigrette

Servings:8 | Cooking Time: 20 Minutes

Ingredients:

- 1/4 cup orange juice
- 1/4 cup canola oil
- 2 tablespoons white vinegar
- 2 tablespoons honey
- 2 teaspoons grated fresh gingerroot
- 1/2 teaspoon salt
- 1/4 teaspoon cayenne pepper
- SALAD
- 12 cups torn mixed salad greens

- 2 medium navel oranges, peeled and sliced crosswise
- 1 cup thinly sliced red onion

Directions:

1. In a small bowl, whisk the first seven ingredients until blended. In a large bowl, toss the mixed greens with 1/4 cup vinaigrette; transfer to a serving dish. Top with oranges and onion. Serve immediately with remaining vinaigrette.

Nutrition Info:

- 119 cal., 7g fat (1g sat. fat), 0 chol., 202mg sod., 15g carb. (9g sugars, 3g fiber), 2g pro.

Zucchini Ribbon Salad With Shaved Parmesan

Servings:4 | Cooking Time:12 Minutes

Ingredients:

- 4 zucchini (6 ounces each), trimmed and sliced lengthwise into ribbons
- ¼ teaspoon pepper
- 3 tablespoons extra-virgin olive oil
- 2 tablespoons lemon juice
- 2 ounces Parmesan cheese, shaved
- 2 tablespoons minced fresh mint

Directions:

1. Gently toss zucchini with pepper, then arrange attractively on serving platter. Drizzle with oil and lemon juice, then sprinkle with Parmesan and mint. Serve immediately.

Nutrition Info:

- 190 cal., 15g fat (3g sag. fat), 10mg chol, 270mg sod., 7g carb (2g sugars, 2g fiber), 9g pro.

Bacon Onion Potato Salad

Servings: 4 | Cooking Time:4 Minutes

Ingredients:

- 12 ounces unpeeled red potatoes, diced (about 3 cups)
- 3 tablespoons reduced-fat ranch salad dressing
- 1/2 cup finely chopped green onion
- 2 tablespoons real bacon bits (not imitation)

Directions:

1. Bring water to boil in a medium saucepan over high heat. Add the potatoes and return to a boil. Reduce the heat, cover tightly, and cook 4 minutes or until just tender when pierced with a fork.
2. Drain the potatoes in a colander and run under cold water until cool, about 30 seconds. Drain well and place in a medium bowl with the remaining ingredients. Toss gently to blend well.
3. Serve immediately or cover with plastic wrap and refrigerate 2 hours for a more blended flavor. To serve, add salt, if desired and toss.

Nutrition Info:

- 110 cal., 3g fat (0g sag. fat), 5mg chol, 250mg sod., 16g carb (2g sugars, 2g fiber), 4g pro.

SPECIAL TREATS RECIPES

⬦ Special Treats Recipes ⬦

Pineapple Breeze Torte
Servings:12 | Cooking Time: 5 Minutes

Ingredients:
- 3 packages (3 ounces each) soft ladyfingers, split
- FILLING
- 1 package (8 ounces) fat-free cream cheese
- 3 ounces cream cheese, softened
- 1/3 cup sugar
- 2 teaspoons vanilla extract
- 1 carton (8 ounces) frozen reduced-fat whipped topping, thawed
- TOPPING
- 1/3 cup sugar
- 3 tablespoons cornstarch
- 1 can (20 ounces) unsweetened crushed pineapple, undrained

Directions:
1. Line bottom and sides of an ungreased 9-in. springform pan with ladyfinger halves; reserve remaining ladyfingers for layering.
2. Beat cream cheeses, sugar and vanilla until smooth; fold in whipped topping. Spread half of the mixture over bottom ladyfingers. Layer with the remaining ladyfingers, overlapping as needed. Spread with the remaining filling. Refrigerate, covered, while preparing topping.
3. In a small saucepan, mix sugar and cornstarch; stir in pineapple. Bring to a boil over medium heat, stirring constantly; cook and stir until thickened, 1-2 minutes. Cool the mixture completely.
4. Spread topping gently over torte. Refrigerate, covered, until set, at least 4 hours. Remove rim from pan.

Nutrition Info:
- 243 cal., 7g fat (5g sat. fat), 87mg chol., 156mg sod., 39g carb. (27g sugars, 1g fiber), 6g pro.

Frozen Chocolate Monkey Treats
Servings:1 | Cooking Time: 20 Minutes

Ingredients:
- 3 medium bananas
- 1 cup (6 ounces) dark chocolate chips
- 2 teaspoons shortening
- Toppings: chopped peanuts, toasted flaked coconut and/or colored jimmies

Directions:
1. Cut each banana into six pieces (about 1 in.). Insert a toothpick into each piece; transfer to a waxed paper-lined baking sheet. Freeze until completely firm, about 1 hour.
2. In a microwave, melt chocolate and shortening; stir until smooth. Dip banana pieces in chocolate mixture; allow excess to drip off. Dip in toppings as desired; return to baking sheet. Freeze 30 minutes before serving.

Nutrition Info:
- 72 cal., 4g fat (2g sat. fat), 0 chol., 0 sod., 10g carb. (7g sugars, 1g fiber), 1g pro.

Raspberry-banana Soft Serve
Servings:2 | Cooking Time: 10 Minutes

Ingredients:
- 4 medium ripe bananas
- 1/2 cup fat-free plain yogurt
- 1 to 2 tablespoons maple syrup
- 1/2 cup frozen unsweetened raspberries
- Fresh raspberries, optional

Directions:
1. Thinly slice bananas; transfer to a large resealable plastic freezer bag. Arrange slices in a single layer; freeze overnight.
2. Pulse bananas in a food processor until finely chopped. Add yogurt, maple syrup and raspberries. Process just until smooth, scraping sides as needed. Serve immediately, adding fresh berries if desired.

Nutrition Info:
- 104 cal., 0 fat (0 sat. fat), 1mg chol., 15mg sod., 26g carb. (15g sugars, 2g fiber), 2g pro.

Cream Cheese Swirl Brownies
Servings:1 | Cooking Time: 25 Minutes

Ingredients:
- 3 large eggs, divided
- 6 tablespoons reduced-fat butter, softened
- 1 cup sugar, divided
- 3 teaspoons vanilla extract
- 1/2 cup all-purpose flour
- 1/4 cup baking cocoa
- 1 package (8 ounces) reduced-fat cream cheese

Directions:
1. Preheat oven to 350°. Separate two eggs, putting each white in a separate bowl (discard yolks or save for another use); set aside. In a small bowl, beat butter and 3/4 cup sugar until crumbly. Beat in the whole egg, one egg white and vanilla until well combined. Combine flour and cocoa; gradually add to egg mixture until blended. Pour into a 9-in. square baking pan coated with cooking spray; set aside.
2. In a small bowl, beat cream cheese and remaining sugar until smooth. Beat in second egg white. Drop by rounded tablespoonfuls over the batter; cut through batter with a knife to swirl.
3. Bake 25-30 minutes or until set and edges pull away from sides of pan. Cool on a wire rack.

Nutrition Info:
- 172 cal., 8g fat (5g sat. fat), 36mg chol., 145mg sod., 23g carb. (18g sugars, 0 fiber), 4g pro.

Mini Chocolate Cupcakes With Creamy Chocolate Frosting

Servings:12 | Cooking Time: 20 Minutes

Ingredients:
- CAKE
- 1½ ounces bittersweet chocolate, chopped
- 3 tablespoons Dutch-processed cocoa powder
- ⅓ cup hot brewed coffee
- 6 tablespoons (2 ounces) bread flour
- ¼ cup (3½ ounces) granulated sugar
- ¼ teaspoon salt
- ¼ teaspoon baking soda
- ¼ teaspoon baking powder
- 3 tablespoons canola oil
- 1 large egg
- 1 teaspoon distilled white vinegar
- ½ teaspoon vanilla extract
- CHOCOLATE FROSTING
- 2 ounces bittersweet chocolate, chopped
- 6 tablespoons unsalted butter, softened
- ½ cup (2 ounces) confectioners' sugar
- ¼ cup (¾ ounce) Dutch-processed cocoa powder
- Pinch salt
- 1 teaspoon vanilla extract

Directions:
1. FOR THE CAKE Adjust oven rack to middle position and heat oven to 350 degrees. Line 12 cups of mini muffin tin with paper or foil liners.
2. Place chocolate and cocoa in medium bowl, add hot coffee, and whisk until melted and smooth. Refrigerate mixture until completely cool, about 20 minutes. In separate bowl, whisk flour, granulated sugar, salt, baking soda, and baking powder together.
3. Whisk oil, egg, vinegar, and vanilla into cooled chocolate mixture until smooth. Add flour mixture and whisk until smooth.
4. Portion batter evenly into prepared muffin tin, filling cups to rim. Bake cupcakes until toothpick inserted in center comes out with few crumbs attached, 14 to 16 minutes, rotating muffin tin halfway through baking.
5. Let cupcakes cool in muffin tin on wire rack for 10 minutes. Remove cupcakes from muffin tin and let cool completely on rack, about 1 hour. (Unfrosted cupcakes can be stored at room temperature for up to 2 days.)
6. FOR THE FROSTING Microwave chocolate in bowl at 50 percent power, stirring occasionally, until melted and smooth, 2 to 4 minutes. Let cool slightly. Process butter, confectioners' sugar, cocoa, and salt in food processor until smooth, about 20 seconds, scraping down sides of bowl as needed. Add vanilla and process until just combined, 5 to 10 seconds. Add melted chocolate and pulse until smooth and creamy, about 10 pulses, scraping down sides of bowl as needed. (Frosting can be kept at room temperature for up to 3 hours before using or refrigerated for up to 3 days. If refrigerated, let sit at room temperature for 1 hour before using.)
7. Spread frosting evenly over cupcakes and serve.

Nutrition Info:
- 210 cal., 13g fat (6g sag. fat), 30mg chol, 100mg sod., 22g carb (13g sugars, 2g fiber), 2g pro.

Holiday Cookies

Servings:2 | Cooking Time:20 Minutes

Ingredients:
- COOKIES
- 6 tablespoons (2⅔ ounces) granulated sugar
- 2½ cups (12½ ounces) all-purpose flour
- ⅛ teaspoon salt
- 16 tablespoons unsalted butter, cut into 16 pieces and softened
- 1 ounce cream cheese, softened
- 2 teaspoons vanilla extract
- GLAZE
- 1 ounce cream cheese
- 1–2 tablespoons 1 percent low-fat milk
- ⅛ teaspoon salt
- ¾ cup (3 ounces) confectioners' sugar

Directions:
1. FOR THE COOKIES Using stand mixer fitted with paddle, mix sugar, flour, and salt together on low speed until combined, about 1 minute. Add butter, 1 piece at a time, and mix until only pea-size pieces remain, about 1 minute. Add cream cheese and vanilla and mix until dough just begins to form large clumps, about 30 seconds.
2. Transfer dough to clean counter, knead until dough forms cohesive mass, then divide into 2 equal pieces. Shape each piece into 4-inch disk, then wrap in plastic wrap and refrigerate until firm, at least 30 minutes or up to 3 days.
3. Adjust oven rack to middle position and heat oven to 375 degrees. Working with 1 piece of dough at a time, roll ⅛ inch thick between 2 sheets of parchment paper. Slide dough, still between parchment, onto baking sheet and refrigerate until firm, about 20 minutes.
4. Line 2 baking sheets with parchment. Working with 1 sheet of dough at a time, remove top sheet of parchment and cut dough as desired using cookie cutters; space cookies ¾ inch apart on prepared sheets. (Dough scraps can be patted together, chilled, and rerolled once.)
5. Bake cookies, 1 sheet at a time, until lightly puffed but still underdone, about 5 minutes. Remove partially baked cookies from oven and, holding sheet firmly with both hands, rap pan flat against open oven door 3 to 5 times until puffed cookies flatten. Rotate pan, return cookies to oven, and continue to bake until light golden brown around edges, 4 to 6 minutes. Let cookies cool completely on sheet.
6. FOR THE GLAZE Whisk cream cheese, 1 tablespoon milk, and salt together in medium bowl until smooth. Whisk in confectioners' sugar until smooth, adding remaining 1 tablespoon milk as needed until glaze is thin enough to drizzle. Drizzle or decorate each cookie with glaze as desired. Let glaze set for at least 6 hours before serving.

Nutrition Info:

- 90 cal., 5g fat (3g sag. fat), 15mg chol, 20mg sod., 11g carb (4g sugars, 0g fiber), 1g pro.

No-fuss Banana Ice Cream

Servings:1 | Cooking Time: 15 Minutes

Ingredients:
- 6 very ripe bananas
- ½ cup heavy cream
- 1 tablespoon vanilla extract
- 1 teaspoon lemon juice
- ¼ teaspoon salt
- ¼ teaspoon ground cinnamon

Directions:
1. Peel bananas, place in large zipper-lock bag, and press out excess air. Freeze bananas until solid, at least 8 hours.
2. Let bananas sit at room temperature to soften slightly, about 15 minutes. Slice into ½-inch-thick rounds and place in food processor. Add cream, vanilla, lemon juice, salt, and cinnamon and process until smooth, about 5 minutes, scraping down sides of bowl as needed.
3. Transfer mixture to airtight container and freeze until firm, at least 2 hours or up to 5 days. Serve.

Nutrition Info:
- 160 cal., 6g fat (3g sag. fat), 15mg chol, 75mg sod., 28g carb (18g sugars, 3g fiber), 1g pro.

Carrot Snack Cake

Servings:12 | Cooking Time: 2 Hours

Ingredients:
- 12 ounces carrots, peeled
- ⅔ cup (4⅔ ounces) sugar
- ¼ cup canola oil
- ¼ cup 1 percent low-fat milk
- 2 large eggs
- 2 teaspoons vanilla extract
- 1 teaspoon baking powder
- ¾ teaspoon ground cinnamon
- ½ teaspoon baking soda
- ¼ teaspoon ground nutmeg
- ¼ teaspoon salt
- 1⅓ cups (7⅓ ounces) whole-wheat flour

Directions:
1. Adjust oven rack to middle position and heat oven to 350 degrees. Make foil sling for 8-inch square baking pan by folding 2 long sheets of aluminum foil so each is 8 inches wide. Lay sheets of foil in pan perpendicular to each other, with extra foil hanging over edges of pan. Push foil into corners and up sides of pan, smoothing foil flush to pan. Grease foil. Working in batches, use food processor fitted with shredding disk to shred carrots; transfer carrots to bowl.
2. Fit now-empty processor with chopping blade. Process sugar, oil, milk, eggs, vanilla, baking powder, cinnamon, baking soda, nutmeg, and salt until sugar is mostly dissolved and mixture is emulsified, 10 to 12 seconds, scraping down sides of bowl as needed. Add shredded carrots and

pulse until combined, about 3 pulses. Add flour and pulse until just incorporated, about 5 pulses; do not overmix.
3. Scrape batter into prepared pan and smooth top. Bake until cake is light golden and toothpick inserted in center comes out clean, 26 to 30 minutes, rotating pan halfway through baking.
4. Let cake cool in pan on wire rack for 10 minutes. Using foil overhang, remove cake from pan and return to wire rack. Discard foil and let cake cool completely on rack, about 2 hours. Cut cake into 12 pieces and serve.

Nutrition Info:
- 170 cal., 6g fat (0g sag. fat), 30mg chol, 170mg sod., 27g carb (13g sugars, 3g fiber), 4g pro.

Buttermilk Peach Ice Cream

Servings:2 | Cooking Time: 15 Minutes

Ingredients:
- 2 pounds ripe peaches (about 7 medium), peeled and quartered
- 1/2 cup sugar
- 1/2 cup packed brown sugar
- 1 tablespoon lemon juice
- 1 teaspoon vanilla extract
- Pinch salt
- 2 cups buttermilk
- 1 cup heavy whipping cream

Directions:
1. Place peaches in a food processor; process until smooth. Add sugars, lemon juice, vanilla and salt; process until blended.
2. In a bowl, mix buttermilk and cream. Stir in the peach mixture. Refrigerate, covered, 1 hour or until cold.
3. Fill cylinder of ice cream maker no more than two-thirds full. Freeze according to manufacturer's directions, refrigerating any remaining mixture to process later. Transfer ice cream to freezer containers, allowing headspace for expansion. Freeze 2-4 hours or until firm. Let ice cream stand at room temperature 10 minutes before serving.

Nutrition Info:
- 137 cal., 6g fat (4g sat. fat), 22mg chol., 75mg sod., 20g carb. (19g sugars, 1g fiber), 2g pro.

Apple Cinnamon Rollups

Servings:6 | Cooking Time:26 Minutes

Ingredients:
- 2 apples (6 ounces each), cored, halved, and sliced thin
- 1 tablespoon unsalted butter, melted and cooled
- 2 teaspoons lemon juice
- 1 teaspoon ground cinnamon
- ½ teaspoon ground ginger
- ¼ teaspoon salt
- 2 tablespoons sugar
- 1 (9½ by 9-inch) sheet puff pastry, thawed
- 2 tablespoons apricot preserves

Directions:

1. Adjust oven rack to middle position and heat oven to 375 degrees. Toss apples with melted butter, lemon juice, ½ teaspoon cinnamon, ginger, and salt in bowl. Spread apples in single layer on parchment paper–lined rimmed baking sheet and bake until softened, about 10 minutes. Set aside until cool enough to handle, about 10 minutes.

2. Line clean baking sheet with parchment and lightly spray with canola oil spray. Combine sugar and remaining ½ teaspoon cinnamon in bowl.

3. Roll pastry into 12 by 10-inch rectangle on lightly floured counter, with long side parallel to counter edge. Brush preserves evenly over top and sprinkle with cinnamon sugar. Using sharp knife or pizza wheel, cut pastry lengthwise into six 10 by 2-inch strips.

4. Working with 1 strip of dough at a time, shingle 12 apple slices, peel side out, along length of dough, leaving 1-inch border of dough on one side. Fold bare inch of dough over bottom of apple slices, leaving top of apple slices exposed. Roll up dough and apples into tight pinwheel and place, apple side up, on prepared sheet.

5. Bake until golden brown and crisp, 22 to 26 minutes, rotating sheet halfway through baking. Let Danish cool on sheet for 15 minutes before serving.

Nutrition Info:
• 240 cal., 12g fat (6g sag. fat), 5mg chol, 240mg sod., 36g carb (13g sugars, 2g fiber), 3g pro.

Strawberry Pot Stickers
Servings:32 | Cooking Time: 10 Minutes

Ingredients:
• 3 ounces milk chocolate, chopped
• 1/4 cup half-and-half cream
• 1 teaspoon butter
• 1 teaspoon vanilla extract
• 1/4 teaspoon ground cinnamon
• POT STICKERS
• 2 cups chopped fresh strawberries
• 3 ounces milk chocolate, chopped
• 1 tablespoon brown sugar
• 1/4 teaspoon ground cinnamon
• 32 pot sticker or gyoza wrappers
• 1 large egg, lightly beaten
• 2 tablespoons canola oil, divided
• 1/2 cup water, divided

Directions:
1. Place chocolate in a small bowl. In a small saucepan, bring cream and butter just to a boil. Pour over chocolate; whisk until smooth. Stir in vanilla and cinnamon. Cool to room temperature, stirring occasionally.

2. For pot stickers, in a small bowl, toss strawberries and chopped chocolate with brown sugar and cinnamon. Place 1 tablespoon mixture in center of 1 gyoza wrapper. (Cover remaining wrappers with a damp paper towel until ready to use.)

3. Moisten wrapper edge with egg. Fold wrapper over filling; seal edges, pleating the front side several times to form a pleated pouch. Repeat with remaining wrappers and filling. Stand pot stickers on a work surface to flatten bottoms; curve slightly to form crescent shapes, if desired.

4. In a large skillet, heat 1 tablespoon oil over medium-high heat. Arrange half of the pot stickers, flat side down, in concentric circles in pan; cook 1-2 minutes or until bottoms are golden brown. Add 1/4 cup water; bring to a simmer. Cook, covered, 3-5 minutes or until water is almost absorbed and wrappers are tender.

5. Cook, uncovered, 1 minute or until bottoms are crisp and the water is completely evaporated. Repeat with remaining pot stickers. Serve the pot stickers with chocolate sauce.

Nutrition Info:
• 58 cal., 3g fat (1g sat. fat), 6mg chol., 18mg sod., 8g carb. (4g sugars, 0 fiber), 1g pro.

Nectarines And Berries In Prosecco
Servings:8 | Cooking Time:15 Minutes

Ingredients:
• 10 ounces (2 cups) blackberries or raspberries
• 10 ounces strawberries, hulled and quartered (2 cups)
• 1 pound nectarines, pitted and cut into ¼-inch wedges
• 1 tablespoon sugar
• 1 tablespoon orange liqueur, such as Grand Marnier or triple sec
• 2 tablespoons chopped fresh mint
• ¼ teaspoon grated lemon zest
• ¾ cup chilled prosecco

Directions:
1. Gently toss blackberries, strawberries, nectarines, sugar, orange liqueur, mint, and lemon zest together in large bowl. Let sit at room temperature, stirring occasionally, until fruit begins to release its juices, about 15 minutes. Just before serving, pour prosecco over fruit.

Nutrition Info:
• 80 cal., 0g fat (0g sag. fat), 0mg chol, 0mg sod., 14g carb (10g sugars, 3g fiber), 1g pro.

Two-berry Pavlova
Servings:12 | Cooking Time: 45 Minutes

Ingredients:
• 4 large egg whites
• 1/2 teaspoon cream of tartar
• 1 cup sugar
• 1 tablespoon cornstarch
• 1 teaspoon lemon juice
• TOPPINGS
• 2 cups fresh blackberries
• 2 cups sliced fresh strawberries
• 1/4 cup plus 3 tablespoons sugar, divided
• 1 1/4 cups heavy whipping cream

Directions:
1. Place egg whites in a large bowl; let stand at room temperature 30 minutes. Meanwhile, line a baking sheet with parchment paper; draw a 10-in. circle on paper. Invert pa-

per.

2. Preheat oven to 300°. Add cream of tartar to egg whites; beat on medium speed until soft peaks form. Gradually add sugar, 1 tablespoon at a time, beating on high after each addition until sugar is dissolved. Continue beating until stiff glossy peaks form. Fold in cornstarch and lemon juice.

3. Spoon meringue onto prepared pan; with the back of a spoon, shape into a 10-in. circle, forming a shallow well in the center. Bake 45-55 minutes or until meringue is set and dry. Turn off oven (do not open oven door); leave meringue in oven 1 hour. Remove from oven; cool completely on baking sheet.

4. To serve, toss berries with 1/4 cup sugar in a small bowl; let stand about 10 minutes. Meanwhile, in a large bowl, beat cream until it begins to thicken. Add remaining sugar; beat until soft peaks form.

5. Remove meringue from parchment paper; place on a serving plate. Spoon the whipped cream over top, forming a slight well in the center. Top with the berries.

Nutrition Info:
• 208 cal., 9g fat (6g sat. fat), 34mg chol., 29mg sod., 30g carb. (27g sugars, 2g fiber), 2g pro.

Citrus Gingerbread Cookies
Servings:6 | Cooking Time: 10 Minutes

Ingredients:
• 3/4 cup sugar
• 1/2 cup honey
• 1/2 cup molasses
• 1/2 cup unsalted butter, cubed
• 1 large egg
• 3 1/2 cups all-purpose flour
• 1/4 cup ground almonds
• 2 teaspoons baking powder
• 2 teaspoons grated lemon peel
• 2 teaspoons grated orange peel
• 1 teaspoon each ground cardamom, ginger, nutmeg, cinnamon and cloves
• GLAZE
• 1/2 cup honey
• 2 tablespoons water

Directions:
1. In a large saucepan, combine sugar, honey and molasses. Bring to a boil; remove from heat. Let stand about 20 minutes. Stir in butter; let stand 20 minutes longer.

2. Beat in egg. In another bowl, whisk flour, almonds, baking powder, lemon peel, orange peel and spices; gradually beat into sugar mixture. Refrigerate, covered, 8 hours or overnight.

3. Preheat oven to 375°. On a lightly floured surface, divide dough into three portions. Roll each portion to 1/4-in. thickness. Cut with a floured 2-in. tree-shaped cookie cutter. Place 2 in. apart on baking sheets coated with cooking spray.

4. Bake 7-8 minutes or until lightly browned. Cool on pans 1 minute. Remove cookies to wire racks to cool completely.

In a small bowl, mix glaze ingredients; brush over cookies. Let stand until set.

Nutrition Info:
• 66 cal., 2g fat (1g sat. fat), 6mg chol., 13mg sod., 12g carb. (7g sugars, 0 fiber), 1g pro.

Oatmeal Cookies With Chocolate And Goji Berries
Servings:24 | Cooking Time:10 Minutes

Ingredients:
• 1 cup (5 ounces) all-purpose flour
• ¾ teaspoon salt
• ½ teaspoon baking soda
• 1 cup packed (7 ounces) dark brown sugar
• ⅔ cup canola oil
• 1 tablespoon water
• 1 teaspoon vanilla extract
• 1 large egg plus 1 large yolk
• 3 cups (9 ounces) old-fashioned rolled oats
• 1 cup dried goji berries
• 3½ ounces 70 percent dark chocolate, chopped into ¼-inch pieces

Directions:
1. Adjust oven rack to middle position and heat oven to 375 degrees. Line 2 rimmed baking sheets with parchment paper. Whisk flour, salt, and baking soda together in bowl; set aside.

2. Whisk sugar, oil, water, and vanilla together in large bowl until well combined. Add egg and yolk and whisk until smooth. Using rubber spatula, stir in flour mixture until fully combined. Add oats, goji berries, and chocolate and stir until evenly distributed (mixture will be stiff).

3. Divide dough into 24 portions, each about heaping 2 tablespoons. Using damp hands, tightly roll into balls and space 2 inches apart on prepared sheets, 12 balls per sheet. Press balls to ¾-inch thickness.

4. Bake, 1 sheet at a time, until edges are set and centers are soft but not wet, 8 to 10 minutes, rotating sheet halfway through baking. Let cookies cool on sheets for 5 minutes, then transfer to wire rack. Let cookies cool completely before serving.

Nutrition Info:
• 190 cal., 9g fat (2g sag. fat), 15mg chol, 100mg sod., 24g carb (11g sugars, 2g fiber), 3g pro.

Fig Bars
Servings:16 | Cooking Time:45 Minutes

Ingredients:
• 1 cup (5 ounces) all-purpose flour
• 2 teaspoons ground allspice
• ½ teaspoon salt
• ¼ teaspoon baking powder
• 8 tablespoons unsalted butter, cut into ½-inch pieces and chilled
• ½ cup plus 3 tablespoons no-sugar-added apple juice

- 1 cup dried Turkish or Calimyrna figs, stemmed and quartered
- ¼ cup sliced almonds, toasted
- ¼ cup shelled pistachios, toasted and chopped

Directions:

1. Adjust oven rack to middle position and heat oven to 375 degrees. Make foil sling for 8-inch square baking pan by folding 2 long sheets of aluminum foil so each is 8 inches wide. Lay sheets of foil in pan perpendicular to each other, with extra foil hanging over edges of pan. Push foil into corners and up sides of pan, smoothing foil flush to pan. Grease foil.

2. Pulse flour, allspice, salt, and baking powder in food processor until combined, about 3 pulses. Scatter chilled butter over top and pulse until mixture resembles wet sand, about 10 pulses. Add 3 tablespoons apple juice and pulse until dough comes together, about 8 pulses.

3. Transfer mixture to prepared pan and press into even layer with bottom of dry measuring cup. Bake crust until golden brown, 35 to 40 minutes, rotating pan halfway through baking. Let crust cool completely in pan, about 45 minutes.

4. Microwave figs and remaining ½ cup apple juice in covered bowl until slightly softened, about 2 minutes. Puree fig mixture in now-empty food processor until smooth, about 15 seconds. Spread fig mixture evenly over cooled crust, then sprinkle with almonds and pistachios, pressing to adhere. Using foil overhang, lift bars from pan and transfer to cutting board. Cut into 16 squares and serve.

Nutrition Info:
- 130 cal., 7g fat (3g sag. fat), 15mg chol, 80mg sod., 15g carb (6g sugars, 2g fiber), 2g pro.

Dark Chocolate Bark With Pepitas And Goji Berries

Servings:16 | Cooking Time: 30 Minutes

Ingredients:
- 1 pound 70 percent dark chocolate, 12 ounces chopped fine, 4 ounces grated
- 2 teaspoons ground cinnamon
- 1 teaspoon chipotle chile powder
- 2 cups roasted pepitas, 1¾ cups left whole, ¼ cup chopped
- 1 cup dried goji berries, chopped
- 1 teaspoon coarse sea salt

Directions:

1. Make parchment paper sling for 13 by 9-inch baking pan by folding 2 long sheets of parchment; first sheet should be 13 inches wide and second sheet should be 9 inches wide. Lay sheets in pan perpendicular to each other, with extra parchment hanging over edges of pan. Push parchment into corners and up sides of pan, smoothing parchment flush to pan.

2. Microwave 12 ounces finely chopped chocolate in large bowl at 50 percent power, stirring every 15 seconds, until melted but not much hotter than body temperature (check by holding in the palm of your hand), 2 to 3 minutes. Stir in 4 ounces grated chocolate, cinnamon, and chile powder until smooth and chocolate is completely melted (returning to microwave for no more than 5 seconds at a time to finish melting if necessary).

3. Stir 1¾ cups whole pepitas and ¾ cup goji berries into chocolate mixture. Working quickly, use rubber spatula to spread chocolate mixture evenly into prepared pan. Sprinkle with remaining ¼ cup chopped pepitas and remaining ¼ cup goji berries and gently press topping into chocolate. Sprinkle evenly with salt and refrigerate until chocolate is set, about 30 minutes.

4. Using parchment overhang, lift chocolate out of pan and transfer to cutting board; discard parchment. Using serrated knife and gentle sawing motion, cut chocolate into 16 even pieces. Serve.

Nutrition Info:
- 260 cal., 21g fat (9g sag. fat), 0mg chol, 140mg sod., 20g carb (10g sugars, 4g fiber), 8g pro.

Lemon Cupcakes With Strawberry Frosting

Servings:2 | Cooking Time: 25 Minutes

Ingredients:
- 1 package white cake mix (regular size)
- 1/4 cup lemon curd
- 3 tablespoons lemon juice
- 3 teaspoons grated lemon peel
- 1/2 cup butter, softened
- 3 1/2 cups confectioners' sugar
- 1/4 cup seedless strawberry jam
- 2 tablespoons 2% milk
- 1 cup sliced fresh strawberries

Directions:

1. Line 24 muffin cups with paper liners. Prepare cake mix batter according to package directions, decreasing water by 1 tablespoon and adding lemon curd, lemon juice and lemon peel before mixing batter. Fill the prepared cups about two-thirds full. Bake and cool cupcakes as the package directs.

2. In a large bowl, beat the butter, confectioners' sugar, jam and milk until smooth. Frost cooled cupcakes; top with strawberries. Refrigerate leftovers.

Nutrition Info:
- 219 cal., 7g fat (3g sat. fat), 13mg chol., 171mg sod., 23g carb. (29g sugars, 0 fiber), 1g pro.

Fresh Fruit Sauce

Servings:2 | Cooking Time: 10 Minutes

Ingredients:
- 1 tablespoon cornstarch
- 1 cup orange juice
- 1/3 cup honey
- 1 cup sliced fresh peaches
- 1 cup sliced fresh plums
- Vanilla ice cream

Directions:

1. In a small saucepan, mix cornstarch and orange juice until smooth; stir in honey. Bring to a boil over medium heat; cook and stir until thickened, about 1 minute.
2. Remove from heat; stir in fruit. Serve warm over ice cream.

Nutrition Info:

• 71 cal., 0 fat (0 sat. fat), 0 chol., 1mg sod., 18g carb. (16g sugars, 1g fiber), 0 pro.

Saucy Spiced Pears

Servings:4 | Cooking Time: 20 Minutes

Ingredients:

• 1/2 cup orange juice
• 2 tablespoons butter
• 2 tablespoons sugar
• 2 teaspoons lemon juice
• 1 teaspoon vanilla extract
• 1 teaspoon ground ginger
• 1/4 teaspoon ground cinnamon
• 1/8 teaspoon salt
• 1/8 teaspoon ground allspice
• 1/8 teaspoon cayenne pepper, optional
• 3 large Bosc pears (about 1 3/4 pounds), cored, peeled and sliced
• Thinly sliced fresh mint leaves, optional

Directions:

1. In a large skillet, combine the first nine ingredients and, if desired, cayenne. Cook over medium-high heat 1-2 minutes or until butter is melted, stirring occasionally.
2. Add pears; bring to a boil. Reduce heat to medium; cook, uncovered, 3-4 minutes or until sauce is slightly thickened and pears are crisp-tender, stirring occasionally. Cool slightly. If desired, top with mint.

Nutrition Info:

• 192 cal., 6g fat (4g sat. fat), 15mg chol., 130mg sod., 36g carb. (26g sugars, 5g fiber), 1g pro.

Super Spud Brownies

Servings:16 | Cooking Time: 25 Minutes

Ingredients:

• 3/4 cup mashed potatoes
• 1/2 cup sugar
• 1/2 cup packed brown sugar
• 1/2 cup canola oil
• 2 large eggs, lightly beaten
• 1 teaspoon vanilla extract
• 1/2 cup all-purpose flour
• 1/3 cup cocoa powder
• 1/2 teaspoon baking powder
• 1/8 teaspoon salt
• 1/2 cup chopped pecans, optional
• Confectioners' sugar

Directions:

1. In a large bowl, combine the mashed potatoes, sugars, oil, eggs and vanilla. Combine the flour, cocoa, baking powder and salt; gradually add to potato mixture. Fold in pecans if desired. Transfer to a greased 9-in. square baking pan.
2. Bake at 350° for 23-27 minutes or until toothpick inserted near the center comes out clean. Cool on a wire rack. Dust with confectioners' sugar.

Nutrition Info:

• 150 cal., 8g fat (1g sat. fat), 27mg chol., 68mg sod., 19g carb. (13g sugars, 0 fiber), 2g pro.

Dark Chocolate–avocado Pudding

Servings:8 | Cooking Time: 2 Hours

Ingredients:

• 1 cup water
• ¼ cup (1¾ ounces) sugar
• ¼ cup (¾ ounce) unsweetened cocoa powder
• 1 tablespoon vanilla extract
• 1 teaspoon instant espresso powder (optional)
• ¼ teaspoon salt
• 2 large ripe avocados (8 ounces each), halved and pitted
• 3½ ounces 70 percent dark chocolate, chopped

Directions:

1. Combine water, sugar, cocoa, vanilla, espresso powder (if using), and salt in small saucepan. Bring to simmer over medium heat and cook, stirring occasionally, until sugar and cocoa dissolve, about 2 minutes. Remove saucepan from heat and cover to keep warm.
2. Scoop flesh of avocados into food processor bowl and process until smooth, about 2 minutes, scraping down sides of bowl as needed. With processor running, slowly add warm cocoa mixture in steady stream until completely incorporated and mixture is smooth and glossy, about 2 minutes.
3. Microwave chocolate in bowl at 50 percent power, stirring occasionally, until melted, 2 to 4 minutes. Add to avocado mixture and process until well incorporated, about 1 minute. Transfer pudding to bowl, cover, and refrigerate until chilled and set, at least 2 hours or up to 24 hours. Serve.

Nutrition Info:

• 170 cal., 12g fat (4g sag. fat), 0mg chol, 75mg sod., 17g carb (10g sugars, 5g fiber), 2g pro.

Peaches, Blackberries, And Strawberries With Basil And Pepper

Servings:6 | Cooking Time:15 Minutes

Ingredients:

• Nectarines can be substituted for the peaches.
• 2 teaspoons sugar
• 2 tablespoons chopped fresh basil
• ½ teaspoon pepper
• 3 peaches, halved, pitted, and cut into ½-inch pieces
• 10 ounces (2 cups) blackberries
• 10 ounces strawberries, hulled and quartered (2 cups)
• 1 tablespoon lime juice, plus extra for seasoning

Directions:

1. Combine sugar, basil, and pepper in large bowl. Using rubber spatula, press mixture into side of bowl until sugar becomes damp, about 30 seconds. Add peaches, blackberries, and strawberries and gently toss to combine. Let sit at room temperature, stirring occasionally, until fruit releases its juices, 15 to 30 minutes. Stir in lime juice and season with extra lime juice to taste. Serve.

Nutrition Info:

• 70 cal., 0g fat (0g sag. fat), 0mg chol, 0mg sod., 18g carb (13g sugars, 5g fiber), 2g pro.

Raspberry-chocolate Meringue Squares

Servings:9 | Cooking Time: 20 Minutes

Ingredients:

• 3 large egg whites, divided
• 1/4 cup butter, softened
• 1/4 cup confectioners' sugar
• 1 cup all-purpose flour
• 1/4 cup sugar
• 1/2 cup seedless raspberry jam
• 3 tablespoons miniature semisweet chocolate chips

Directions:

1. Preheat oven to 350°. Place two egg whites in a small bowl; let stand at room temperature 30 minutes. Meanwhile, in a large bowl, cream the butter and confectioners' sugar until light and fluffy. Beat in remaining egg white; gradually add flour to creamed mixture, mixing well.

2. Press into a greased 8-in. square baking pan. Bake 9-11 minutes or until lightly browned. Increase oven setting to 400°.

3. With clean beaters, beat reserved egg whites on medium speed until foamy. Gradually add the sugar, 1 tablespoon at a time, beating on high after each addition until sugar is dissolved. Continue beating until stiff glossy peaks form. Spread jam over crust; sprinkle with chocolate chips. Spread meringue over top.

4. Bake 8-10 minutes or until meringue is lightly browned. Cool completely in pan on a wire rack.

Nutrition Info:

• 198 cal., 6g fat (4g sat. fat), 14mg chol., 60mg sod., 33g carb. (22g sugars, 1g fiber), 3g pro.

Maple-caramel Apples

Servings:8 | Cooking Time:10 Minutes

Ingredients:

• 2 tablespoons unsalted butter
• 4 crisp apples (6½ ounces each), peeled, cored, and halved
• 6 tablespoons maple syrup
• ¼ cup heavy cream
• 1 tablespoon Calvados or apple brandy
• ¼ teaspoon salt
• ½ cup sliced almonds, toasted

Directions:

1. Melt butter in 12-inch nonstick skillet over medium heat. Place apples cut side down in skillet and cook until beginning to brown, 8 to 10 minutes. Flip apples cut side up, add 2 tablespoons maple syrup to skillet, and cook until apples are just tender and tip of paring knife easily pierces fruit, 4 to 6 minutes, adjusting heat as needed to prevent syrup from getting too dark. Off heat, turn apples to coat with caramel, then transfer, cut side up, to platter.

2. Add remaining ¼ cup maple syrup to now-empty skillet and bring to boil over medium heat. Reduce heat to medium-low and cook until mixture thickens slightly and registers 260 degrees, 3 to 4 minutes. Off heat, carefully whisk in cream, Calvados, and salt. Return skillet to medium-low heat and simmer until alcohol has evaporated and mixture thickens again, about 1 minute.

3. Drizzle caramel evenly over apples and sprinkle with almonds. Serve.

Nutrition Info:

• 170 cal., 8g fat (3g sag. fat), 15mg chol, 75mg sod., 23g carb (18g sugars, 3g fiber), 2g pro.

Recipe

....

From the kicthen of ....

Serves .... Prep time .... Cook time ....

☐ Difficulty   ☐ Easy   ☐ Medium   ☐ Hard

Yummy!

Ingredient

....

....

....

....

....

....

Directions ....

....

....

....

....

....

....

Date: _____

MY SHOPPING LIST

◇ Appendix A: Measurement Conversions ◇

BASIC KITCHEN CONVERSIONS & EQUIVALENTS

DRY MEASUREMENTS CONVERSION CHART

3 TEASPOONS = 1 TABLESPOON = 1/16 CUP

6 TEASPOONS = 2 TABLESPOONS = 1/8 CUP

12 TEASPOONS = 4 TABLESPOONS = 1/4 CUP

24 TEASPOONS = 8 TABLESPOONS = 1/2 CUP

36 TEASPOONS = 12 TABLESPOONS = 3/4 CUP

48 TEASPOONS = 16 TABLESPOONS = 1 CUP

METRIC TO US COOKING CONVERSIONS

OVEN TEMPERATURES

120 °C = 250 °F

160 °C = 320 °F

180° C = 350 °F

205 °C = 400 °F

220 °C = 425 °F

LIQUID MEASUREMENTS CONVERSION CHART

8 FLUID OUNCES = 1 CUP = 1/2 PINT = 1/4 QUART

16 FLUID OUNCES = 2 CUPS = 1 PINT = 1/2 QUART

32 FLUID OUNCES = 4 CUPS = 2 PINTS = 1 QUART

 = 1/4 GALLON

128 FLUID OUNCES = 16 CUPS = 8 PINTS = 4 QUARTS = 1 GALLON

BAKING IN GRAMS

1 CUP FLOUR = 140 GRAMS

1 CUP SUGAR = 150 GRAMS

1 CUP POWDERED SUGAR = 160 GRAMS

1 CUP HEAVY CREAM = 235 GRAMS

VOLUME

1 MILLILITER = 1/5 TEASPOON

5 ML = 1 TEASPOON

15 ML = 1 TABLESPOON

240 ML = 1 CUP OR 8 FLUID OUNCES

1 LITER = 34 FL. OUNCES

WEIGHT

1 GRAM = .035 OUNCES

100 GRAMS = 3.5 OUNCES

500 GRAMS = 1.1 POUNDS

1 KILOGRAM = 35 OUNCES

US TO METRIC COOKING CONVERSIONS

1/5 TSP = 1 ML

1 TSP = 5 ML

1 TBSP = 15 ML

1 FL OUNCE = 30 ML

1 CUP = 237 ML

1 PINT (2 CUPS) = 473 ML

1 QUART (4 CUPS) = .95 LITER

1 GALLON (16 CUPS) = 3.8 LITERS

1 OZ = 28 GRAMS

1 POUND = 454 GRAMS

BUTTER

1 CUP BUTTER = 2 STICKS = 8 OUNCES = 230 GRAMS = 8 TABLESPOONS

WHAT DOES 1 CUP EQUAL

1 CUP = 8 FLUID OUNCES

1 CUP = 16 TABLESPOONS

1 CUP = 48 TEASPOONS

1 CUP = 1/2 PINT

1 CUP = 1/4 QUART

1 CUP = 1/16 GALLON

1 CUP = 240 ML

BAKING PAN CONVERSIONS

1 CUP ALL-PURPOSE FLOUR = 4.5 OZ

1 CUP ROLLED OATS = 3 OZ 1 LARGE EGG = 1.7 OZ

1 CUP BUTTER = 8 OZ 1 CUP MILK = 8 OZ

1 CUP HEAVY CREAM = 8.4 OZ

1 CUP GRANULATED SUGAR = 7.1 OZ

1 CUP PACKED BROWN SUGAR = 7.75 OZ

1 CUP VEGETABLE OIL = 7.7 OZ

1 CUP UNSIFTED POWDERED SUGAR = 4.4 OZ

BAKING PAN CONVERSIONS

9-INCH ROUND CAKE PAN = 12 CUPS

10-INCH TUBE PAN =16 CUPS

11-INCH BUNDT PAN = 12 CUPS

9-INCH SPRINGFORM PAN = 10 CUPS

9 X 5 INCH LOAF PAN = 8 CUPS

9-INCH SQUARE PAN = 8 CUPS

Appendix B: Recipes Index

Made in the USA
Monee, IL
31 December 2023

50854478R00066